INTERPRETING BLAKE

'The Man Sweeping the Interpreter's Parlour'

INTERPRETING BLAKE

ESSAYS SELECTED AND EDITED BY
MICHAEL PHILLIPS

CAMBRIDGE UNIVERSITY PRESS

CAMBRIDGE

LONDON · NEW YORK · MELBOURNE

Published by the Syndics of the Cambridge University Press
The Pitt Building, Trumpington Street, Cambridge CB2 1RP
Bentley House, 200 Euston Road, London NW1 2DB
32 East 57th Street, New York, NY 10022, USA
296 Beaconsfield Parade, Middle Park, Melbourne 3206, Australia

© Cambridge University Press 1978

First published 1978

Printed litho in Great Britain by
W & J Mackay Ltd, Chatham

Library of Congress Cataloguing in Publication Data
Main entry under title:
Interpreting Blake.
Except for two essays, revised papers previously presented at a May 1974 symposium on
William Blake, held at the Institute for Advanced Studies in the Humanities of the
University of Edinburgh.
Includes index.
1. Blake, William, 1757–1827 – Criticism and interpretation – Addresses, essays, lectures.
I. Phillips, Michael Curtis. II. Edinburgh, University.
Institute for Advanced Studies in the Humanities.
PR4147.I5   821'.7   78-8322
ISBN 0 521 22176 5

CONTENTS

List of illustrations   *page* vii

Preface   ix

1 Introduction   1
MICHAEL PHILLIPS

2 'London'   5
E. P. THOMPSON

3 Blake's Criticism of Moral Thinking in *Songs of Innocence and of Experience*   32
HEATHER GLEN

4 Emblems of Melancholy: *For Children: The Gates of Paradise*   70
FRANK M. PARISI

5 *The Book of Urizen* and *An Essay Concerning Human Understanding*   111
HARALD A. KITTEL

6 *Milton*: The Final Plates   145
PETER BUTTER

7 Prefaces to *Jerusalem*   164
JAMES FERGUSON

8 Influence and Independence in Blake   196
JOHN BEER

Index   263

v

ILLUSTRATIONS

Frontispiece: 'The Man Sweeping the Interpreter's Parlour' *page* ii
Repr. by courtesy of Sir Geoffrey Keynes

1 T. Bewick: engraving for J. H. Wynne, *Tales for Youth*, 'Tale of the Earth Worm' (1790) 75
National Library of Scotland

2 Design for Young's *Night Thoughts*, no. 257 (unpublished, 1795–7). Watercolour 78
British Museum

3 J. Sturt: engraving for R. Ware's Bible, frontispiece (Oxford, 1722) 85
New College Library, University of Edinburgh

4 T. Bewick: engraving for J. H. Wynne, *Tales for Youth*, 'The Benighted Traveller' (1790) 98
National Library of Scotland

5 T. Bewick: engraving for *Emblems of Mortality*, 'The Old Man' (1789) 101
National Library of Scotland

6 O. van Veen: engraving for Q. *Horati Flacci Emblemata*, no. 100 (Antwerp, 1607) 102
National Library of Scotland

7 *Jerusalem*, Plate 51 181
British Museum

8 Original pencil drawing for *Jerusalem*, Plate 51 182
Kunsthalle, Hamburg

9 *The Gates of Paradise*, Plate 12, 'Does thy God O Priest' 204
British Museum

10 Pencil sketch for illustration to Dante's *Inferno* XXXIII, 'Count Ugolino and his sons' 205
British Museum

11 Tempera painting, 'Ugolino and his sons in prison' (1827) 205
Fitzwilliam Museum

vii

12 John Dixon: mezzotint after Reynolds, 'Count Ugolino and his sons' (1774)
    Fitzwilliam Museum   208

13 F. Bartolozzi: stipple engraving after Cipriani, 'Perseus having rescued
    Andromeda . . .'   212
    Fitzwilliam Museum

14 *Visions of the Daughters of Albion*, frontispiece. Colour print   213
    Fitzwilliam Museum

15 Detail from 'The Game of Life' (1790)   232

16 *The Gates of Paradise*, Plate 13, 'Fear & Hope are – Vision'   233
    British Museum

17 *The Gates of Paradise*, Plate 14, 'The Traveller hasteth in the Evening' 233
    British Museum

18 *America*, Plate 6, copy P. Relief etching   255
    Fitzwilliam Museum

19 Emblem from Michael Maier, *Tripus Aureus* (1618), p. 67   256
    Cambridge University Library

20 Blake's 'signature': detail from pencil sketch for *The Book of Job*, 'When
    the morning stars sang together'   259
    Fitzwilliam Museum

PREFACE

In May 1974 a symposium on William Blake was held at the Institute for
Advanced Studies in the Humanities of the University of Edinburgh. The
programme was modest, though greatly enhanced by the presence of
scholars and critics from North America, Australia and Great Britain. I
wish to thank all of those who attended and in particular those who
presented papers. The majority of the papers which were presented are
included in this volume in revised form. The essays by Harald Kittel and
E. P. Thompson have been added. For the occasion of the symposium
E. P. Thompson delivered a lecture to the University entitled 'Blake in
the 1790s'. The subject matter of his lecture is reflected in the essay which
he subsequently composed for this volume. I am also particularly grateful
to Professor Janet Warner for providing her video production of *The
Visions of the Daughters of Albion*; to the Curator of Pollack House, Glasgow,
for arranging a private showing of the museum's collection of Blake
paintings; and to the staff of the University Library, Glasgow, for arranging a private display of the library's holdings of Blake's original illuminated
books and related contemporary materials. My special thanks are due to
Dr Roger Savage and to Professor William Beattie. Roger Savage's
'Conversations at Mr Quid's', a dramatization of Blake's *An Island in the
Moon* and *The Book of Thel*, delighted everyone who attended, and also
taught us all a great deal about Blake. William Beattie, the Director of the
Institute for Advanced Studies, welcomed the idea of holding a symposium
on Blake. His encouragement and support were constant, and to him this
volume is dedicated with affection.

References to Blake's works are given by page number to D. V.
Erdman (ed.), *The Poetry and Prose of William Blake* (N.Y., 1965) (cited as
E) and to G. L. Keynes (ed.), *The Complete Writings of William Blake*
(Oxford, 1966) (cited as K).

Michael Phillips

To
WILLIAM BEATTIE
Director of the Institute for Advanced Studies
University of Edinburgh

CHAPTER I

INTRODUCTION

―――――――――

MICHAEL PHILLIPS

Interpreting Blake provides a series of close analyses of specific texts which offer respectively a distinctive critical or interpretative approach to their subject. The following factors particularly influenced the selection and organization of the essays. Where interpretation is concerned, an essential principle has been observed that it should not be imposed; on the contrary, it is those features which help us to define and place the text – subject matter and style, point of view and tone, tradition and genre, biographical and historical context – that also disclose how we should read and objectively explain its meaning. With this principle in mind, I wished to concentrate upon Blake's poetry, though not exclusively; and also to provide the reader with discussions representing his principal types of poem in the order of their creation: the lyric of the *Songs of Innocence and of Experience*, the short but intense prophetic work of the Lambeth period, and the sustained prophecies which were Blake's final and perhaps his finest poetical accomplishment. At the same time it was important to represent the problems which we are becoming increasingly aware of in our attempts to comprehend and articulate objectively the nature of Blake's artistry in its predominantly visual medium, especially in terms of his position with regard to, and his uses of, tradition.

E. P. Thompson's essay on 'London', the first in the volume, challenges us by its concentration upon the text, a concentration which evolves an interpretation and a perspective with implications for the whole of Blake. Our attention on the *Songs* is maintained by Heather Glen who selects poems from both *Innocence* and *Experience*. She addresses herself to a central issue in Blake, his moral stance, with its disturbing immediacy and continuing relevance. Here we see, most forcefully by its subtlety, how Blake imposes interpretation from *within* the poem. The more we attempt to discern the nature and moral implications of social concern, mercy, pity and love, the more we find that these questions are being addressed to

I

ourselves – in a manner not unlike Swift's – and embarrassing us by making us aware of our equivocations. For Blake's contemporary reader the acceptance of the moral challenge that his poems impose may be seen as the necessary catalyst in initiating those same changes which E. P. Thompson's essay suggests were a motivating force of Blake's vision. The vision of 'London' that is revealed by Thompson through the poem may also be seen to be logically extended in the prophecies of the Lambeth period, subsequently finding its spiritual harbinger in *Milton* and its realization in *Jerusalem*. Throughout the sequence the inherent moral disposition and challenge remain unwavering.

With Frank Parisi's essay on *For Children: The Gates of Paradise*, our awareness of the extent and complexity of Blake's dependence upon and use of tradition is sharpened. Interpretation is here informed and guided by seeing Blake's series of emblems in the light of the historical development of the tradition of emblem literature during the sixteenth, seventeenth and eighteenth centuries. Thus we are better able to appreciate the subtle variation upon received images and the implications of their rich association of ideas, which together urge a reconsideration of the meaning of *The Gates of Paradise*. In exploring the literary and art history of the emblem tradition as it relates directly to Blake's series, Parisi's essay exemplifies an essential and still urgently required approach. After Sir Geoffrey Keynes, who has provided us with Blake's text and his own documentation of his life and works, it is perhaps mostly the historians of Blake's cultural awareness, and those who have led the way in relating that awareness to a greater understanding of the works themselves, who have shown Blake's significance in transforming the inheritance of the Renaissance to the purpose and bearing of the twentieth century.

In Harald Kittel's essay on *The Book of Urizen* and Locke's *Essay Concerning Human Understanding*, we engage in a form of interpretation that is again invoked by Blake himself. It is most evident in Blake's marginalia and his underlining of books that he owned and borrowed: the highly articulate contrary response.

What Bacon calls Lies is Truth itself (E610/K397)

This idea of the perfect state of nature, which the Artist calls the Ideal Beauty, is the great leading principle by which works of genius are conducted. [Reynolds]

2

Knowledge of Ideal Beauty is Not to be Acquired. It is born with us. Innate Ideas are in Every Man, Born with him; they are truly Himself. The Man who says that we have No Innate Ideas must be a Fool and Knave, Having No Con-Science or Innate Science. (E637/K459)

'Without contraries is no progression': that epitomizes much of Blake's thinking and organizing of his artistic response. In Kittel's essay we may see how Blake discerned and then turned in upon itself Locke's perception of the nature of mind. The approach is transferable. It is a significant aid to an appreciation of the organization of *The Marriage of Heaven and Hell* in relation to the works of Swedenborg; or *Europe a Prophecy* in relation to Milton's 'Ode on the Morning of Christ's Nativity'; or *Vala* in its response to Young – and ultimately to Pope, Milton, Chaucer and Langland and the tradition of the 'dream vision' poem; or *Milton* in terms of the received idea of Milton's sense of vocation and poetical achievement; or *Jerusalem* in its contrary response to Gibbon's *The Decline and Fall of the Roman Empire*.

In his discussion of the final plates of *Milton*, Peter Butter poses a fundamental critical question: is poetic quality consistently present and, if it is, is it always immediately recognized? This is a question that students of Blake, when faced with the prophetic works, frequently neglect or hesitate to ask. Peter Butter asks it clearly, and knowing that in doing so there is a risk of exposing his own misunderstanding. But in defining what it is that we feel uncertain about – what appears poetically inadequate or obscure – we alert others to a specific need for clarification that will adjust our own way of reading, and consequently our valuation. We may be reminded how much progress we have made in our estimation of Blake by recalling the remarks which open Swinburne's discussion of *Jerusalem* in *A Critical Essay* (1866).

Of that terrible 'emanation', hitherto the main cornerstone of offence to all students of Blake, what can be said within any decent limit? or where shall any traveller find a rest for feet or eyes in that noisy and misty land? It were a mere frenzy of discipleship that would undertake by force of words to make straight these crooked ways or compel things incoherent to cohere.

We now share a recognition that *Jerusalem* may be Blake's supreme achievement. My qualification is significant. For many of us this recognition is still made from afar or as a result of having travelled with difficulty this 'misty' though sublime land. The structure of the poem is not easy to comprehend nor is the quality of the poetry always apparent. James Ferguson, confronting both problems, finds in the prefaces to *Jerusalem* means of direction through the chapters themselves. The poem's structure then provides insight into how we should appreciate the poetry. Part of the enjoyment of this poem has to do with a belief that our generation is the first to begin to understand it clearly.

The final essay in the volume, by John Beer, is different in kind. Beer takes up the general question anticipated by a number of the previous essays in the volume: he discusses the nature of Blake's originality in terms of the relationship between works which served to influence his writing and design and asks, from the advantage of this perspective, what constituted their creative transformation. Beer considers various kinds of 'influence' that condition both the creation of a work of art and the nature of its 'independence' – for example, the way in which the association of ideas and images in a poem's language evokes its relationship to tradition and genre and to the work of other authors and artists. His chosen examples include some that previous essays in the volume have discussed, and his analyses sharpen our awareness of the character of Blake's originality.

We may now enter the interpreter's parlour. It remains for the reader to assess whether more dust has been raised than cleared.

CHAPTER 2

'LONDON'

E. P. THOMPSON

'London' is among the most lucid and instantly available of the *Songs of Experience*. 'The poem', John Beer writes, 'is perhaps the least controversial of all Blake's works', and 'no knowledge of his personal vision is necessary to assist the understanding'.[1] I agree with this: the poem does not require an interpreter since the images are both concrete and self-sufficient within the terms of the poem's own development. Every reader can, without the help of a critic, see London simultaneously as Blake's own city, as an image of the state of English society and as an image of the human condition. So far from requiring a knowledge of Blake's personal vision, it is one of those foundation poems upon which our knowledge of that vision can be built. A close reading may confirm, but is likely to add very little to, what a responsive reader had already experienced.

But since the poem is found in draft in Blake's notebook we are unusually well placed to examine it not only as product but in its process of creation. Here is the finished poem:

> I wander thro' each charter'd street,
> Near where the charter'd Thames does flow.
> And mark in every face I meet
> Marks of weakness, marks of woe.
>
> In every cry of every Man,
> In every Infants cry of fear,
> In every voice: in every ban,
> The mind-forg'd manacles I hear
>
> How the Chimney-sweepers cry
> Every blackning Church appalls,
> And the hapless Soldiers sigh
> Runs in blood down Palace walls

[1] John Beer, *Blake's Humanism* (Manchester, 1968), p. 75.

> But most thro' midnight streets I hear
> How the youthful Harlots curse
> Blasts the new-born Infants tear
> And blights with plagues the Marriage hearse (E26–7/K216)

In Blake's draft the first verse was originally thus:

> I wander thro each dirty street
> Near where the dirty Thames does flow
> And see in every face I meet
> Marks of weakness marks of woe[2]

The first important change is from 'dirty' to 'charter'd'. Another fragment in the notebook helps to define this alteration:

> Why should I care for the men of thames
> Or the cheating waves of charter'd streams
> Or shrink at the little blasts of fear
> That the hireling blows into my ear
>
> Tho born on the cheating banks of Thames
> Tho his waters bathed my infant limbs
> I spurnd his waters away from me ·
> I was born a slave but I long to be free[3]

Thus 'charter'd' arose in Blake's mind in association with 'cheating' and with the 'little blasts of fear' of the 'hireling'. The second association is an obvious political allusion. To reformers the corrupt political system was a refuge for hirelings: indeed, Dr Johnson had defined in his dictionary a 'pension' as 'In England it is generally understood to mean pay given to a state hireling for treason to his country.' David Erdman is undoubtedly right that the 'little blasts of fear' suggest the proclamations, the Paine-burnings, and the political repressions of the State and of Reeves's Association for Preserving Liberty and Property against Republicans and Levellers

---

[2] *The Notebook of William Blake*, ed. David V. Erdman (Oxford, 1973), p. 109; hereafter cited as N. See also V. Doyne, 'Blake's Revision of "London"', *Essays on Criticism*, XXII: 1 (January 1972), 58–60, which, however, seems to me more helpful on technical points than on matters of substantial interpretation.

[3] N 113. The obliterated title of this fragment has been recovered by David Erdman as 'Thames'. Blake altered the final two lines to:

> The Ohio shall wash his stains from me
> I was born a slave but I go to be free

which dominated the year in which these poems were written.[4] In the revised version of 'Thames' Blake introduces the paradox which was continually to be in the mouths of radicals and factory reformers in the next fifty years: the slavery of the English poor. And he points also ('I was born a slave but I go to be free') to the first wave of emigration of reformers from the attention of Church-and-King mobs or hirelings.

But 'charter'd' is more particularly associated with 'cheating'. It is clearly a word to be associated with commerce: one might think of the Chartered Companies which, increasingly drained of function, were bastions of privilege within the government of the city. Or, again, one might think of the monopolistic privileges of the East India Company, whose ships were so prominent in the commerce of the Thames, which applied in 1793 for twenty-years' renewal of its charter, and which was under bitter attack in the reformers' press.[5]

But 'charter'd' is, for Blake, a stronger and more complex word than that, which he endows with more generalized symbolic power. It has the feel of a word which Blake has recently discovered, as, years later, he was to 'discover' the word 'golden' (which, nevertheless, he had been using for years). He is savouring it, weighing its poetic possibilities in his hand.

[4] See David Erdman, *Blake: Prophet against Empire*, revised edn (New York, 1969) which fully argues these points on pp. 272–9. These poems were 'forged in the heat of the Year One of Equality (September 1792 to 1793) and tempered in the "grey-brow'd snows" of Antijacobin alarms and proclamations'. See also A. Mitchell. 'The Association Movement of 1792–3', *Historical Journal*, IV: 1 (1961), 56–77; E. P. Thompson, *The Making of the English Working Class* (Harmondsworth, 1968), pp. 115–26; D. E. Ginter, 'The Loyalist Association Movement, 1792–3', *Historical Journal*, IV: 2 (1966), 179–90.

[5] 'The cheating waves of charter'd streams' and 'the cheating banks of Thames' should prompt one to think carefully of this as the source which first gave to Blake this use of 'charter'd'. The fullest attack from a Painite source on the East India Company did not appear until 1794: see the editorial articles in four successive numbers of Daniel Isaac Eaton's *Politics for the People*, II: 8–11: 'The East India Charter Considered'. These constituted a full-blooded attack on the Company's commercial and military imperialism ('If it be deemed expedient to *murder* half the inhabitants of India, and *rob* the remainder, surely it is not requisite to call it *governing* them?') which carried to their furthest point criticisms of the Company to be found in the reforming and Foxite press of 1792–3. No social historian can be surprised to find the banks of the Thames described as 'cheating' in the eighteenth century: every kind of fraud and racket, big, small and indifferent, flourished around the docks. The association of the banks of Thames with commerce was already traditional when Samuel Johnson renewed it in his 'London' (1738), esp. lines 20–30. Johnson's attitude is already ambiguous: 'Britannia's glories' ('The guard of commerce, and the dread of Spain') are invoked retrospectively, in conventional terms: but on Thames-side already 'all are slaves to gold, /Where looks are merchandise, and smiles are sold'. Erdman argues that the 'golden London' and 'silver Thames' of Blake's 'King Edward the Third' have already assimilated this conventional contrast in the form of irony: see Erdman, *Prophet against Empire*, pp. 80–1.

It is in no sense a 'new' word, but he has found a way to use it with a new ironic inversion. For the word is standing at an intellectual and political cross-roads. On the one hand it was a stale counter of the customary libertarian rhetoric of the polite culture. Blake himself had used it in much this way in his early 'King Edward the Third':

> Let Liberty, the charter'd right of Englishmen,
> Won by our fathers in many a glorious field,
> Enerve my soldiers; let Liberty
> Blaze in each countenance, and fire the battle.
> The enemy fight in chains, invisible chains, but heavy;
> Their minds are fetter'd; then how can they be free?[6]

It would be only boring to accumulate endless examples from eighteenth-century constitutional rhetoric or poetry of the use of chartered rights, chartered liberties, magna carta: the word is at the centre of Whig ideology.

There is, however, an obvious point to be made about this tedious usage of 'charter'. A charter of liberty is, simultaneously, a denial of these liberties to others. A charter is something given or ceded; it is bestowed upon some group by some authority; it is not claimed as of right. And the liberties (or privileges) granted to this guild, company, corporation or even nation *exclude* others from the enjoyment of these liberties. A charter is, in its nature, exclusive.

We are at a cross-roads because it is exactly this exclusive and granted quality of liberties which was under challenge; and it was under challenge from the claim to universal rights. The point becomes clear when we contrast Burke's *Reflections* and Paine's *Rights of Man*. Although Burke was every inch a rhetorician he had no taste for stale rhetoric, and he used the word 'charter' lightly in the *Reflections*. 'Our oldest reformation', he wrote, 'is that of Magna Charta':

From Magna Charta to the Declaration of Right it has been the uniform policy of our constitution to claim and assert our liberties as an *entailed inheritance* derived to us from our forefathers, and to be transmitted to our posterity . . . We have an inheritable crown, an inheritable peerage, and a House of Commons

---

[6] E415/K18: If we take the intention of this fragment to be ironic, then Blake was already regarding the word as suspect rhetoric.

and a people inheriting privileges, franchises, and liberties from a long line of ancestors.

Burke was concerned explicitly to define this chartered, heritable set of liberties and privileges (exclusive in the sense that it is 'an estate specially belonging to the people of this kingdom') as against any general uncircumscribed notion of 'the rights of man'. It is in vain, he wrote, to talk to these democratists:

of the practice of their ancestors, the fundamental laws of their country . . . They have wrought underground a mine that will blow up, at one grand explosion, all examples of antiquity, all precedents, charters, and acts of parliament. They have 'the rights of men'. Against these there can be no prescription . . .

Liberty, for Burke, must have its 'gallery of portraits, its monumental inscriptions, its records, evidences, and titles'. The imagery, as so often, is that of the great house of the landed gentry, with its walks and statuary, its galleries and muniments' room.

For Burke, then, 'charter' and 'charter'd', while not over-laboured, remain among the best of good words. But not for Paine: 'I am contending for the rights of the *living*, and against their being willed away, and controuled and contracted for, by the manuscript assumed authority of the dead.' A charter implied not a freedom but monopoly: 'Every chartered town is an aristocratical monopoly in itself, and the qualification of electors proceeds out of those chartered monopolies. Is this freedom? Is this what Mr. Burke means by a constitution?' It was in the incorporated towns, with their charters, that the Test and Corporation Acts against Dissenters operated with most effect. Hence (Paine argued – and economic historians have often agreed with him) the vitality of the commerce of un-incorporated towns like Manchester, Birmingham, and Sheffield. The Dissenters (he wrote), 'withdrew from the persecution of the chartered towns, where test laws more particularly operate, and established a sort of asylum for themselves in those places . . . But the case is now changing. France and America bid all comers welcome, and initiate them into all the rights of citizenship.'

This is (for Paine) the first offence of 'chartered': it implies exclusion and limitation. Its second offence was in its imputation that anyone had the right to *grant* freedoms or privileges to other men: 'If we begin with

9

William of Normandy, we find that the government of England was originally a tyranny, founded on an invasion and conquest of the country . . . Magna Charta . . . was no more than compelling the government to renounce a part of its assumptions.' Both these offences were criticized in a central passage which I argue lay somewhere in Blake's mind when he selected the word:

It is a perversion of terms to say that a charter gives rights. It operates by a contrary effect – that of taking rights away. Rights are inherently in all the inhabitants; but charters, by annulling those rights in the majority, leave the right, by exclusion, in the hands of a few . . . The only persons on whom they operate are the persons whom they exclude . . . Therefore, all charters have no other than an indirect negative operation.

Charters, he continued, 'are sources of endless contentions in the places where they exist, and they lessen the common rights of national society'. The charters of corporate towns might, he suggested, have arisen because of garrison service: 'Their refusing or granting admission to strangers, which has produced the custom of *giving, selling, and buying freedom*, has more of the nature of garrison authority than civil government' (my italics).

Blake shared much of Paine's political outlook, although he did not share his faith in the beneficence of commerce. He thus chose 'charter'd' out of the biggest political argument that was agitating Britain in 1791–3, and he chose it with that irony which inverted the rhetoric of Burke and asserted the definitions of 'exclusion', the annulling of rights, 'negative operation' and 'giving, selling, and buying freedom'. The adjectival form – charter'd – enforces the direct commercial allusion: 'the organisation of a city in terms of trade'.[7]

The other emendation to the first verse is trivial: in the third line 'And *see* in every face I meet' is altered to 'And mark . . .'. And yet, is it as trivial as it seems? For we already have, in the fourth line, 'Marks of weakness marks of woe'. Thus Blake has chosen, with deliberation, the triple beat of 'mark'. And we respond to this, whether we are conscious of the nature of the response or whether the words beat upon us in subliminal ways: even in these biblically illiterate days we have all heard

[7] Raymond Williams, *The Country and the City* (London, 1973), p. 148.

of 'the mark of the beast'. Some of Blake's central images – his trees, and clouds, and caves, and serpents, and roots – have such a universal presence in mythology and literature that one may spend half a lifetime in the game of hunt-the-source. And sometimes the hunting is fruitful, provided that we remember always that the source (or its echo in Blake's mind) is not the same thing as what he makes of it in his own art. Miss Kathleen Raine, a Diana among huntsmen, has found this:

The opening lines of *London* suggest very strongly Vergil's account of the damned in Hades:

> Nor Death itself can wholly wash their Stains;
> But long-contracted Filth ev'n in the Soul remains.
> The Reliques of inveterate Vice they wear;
> And spots of Sin obscene in ev'ry Face appear.[8]

The suggestion need not be excluded; this echo, with others, could have been in Blake's mind. But if so, *what does Blake do with it?* For Blake's poem evokes pity and forgiveness – the cries, the 'hapless Soldiers sigh', 'weakness' and 'woe' – and not the self-righteous eviction to Hades of 'long-contracted Filth', 'inveterate Vice' and 'spots of Sin obscene'. Moreover, in the amendment from 'And see' to 'And mark', Blake (or the speaker of his poem) closes the gap between the censorious observer and the faces which are observed, assimilating both within a common predicament: the marker himself appears to be marked or even to be mark*ing*.[9]

But 'mark' undoubtedly came through to the reader with a much stronger, biblical resonance. The immediate allusion called to mind will most probably have been 'the mark of the beast', as in Revelation xiii. 16–17:

And he causeth all, both small and great, rich and poor, free and bond, to receive a mark in their right hand, or in their foreheads:

---

[8] Kathleen Raine, *Blake and Tradition* (2 vols., Princeton, 1968), vol. 1, pp. 24–5 (citing Dryden's *Aeneid* VI. 998–1001).

[9] Heather Glen has noted that 'the sense of an inevitable and imprisoning relationship between the "facts" he sees and the way in which he sees is reinforced by the use of "mark" as both verb and object'. I can assent to this, although I cannot assent to her reading of the first two verses, in which the voice of the poem's 'speaker' is 'deliberately dramatized as thin and obsessive', 'isolated and at a remove from real human warmth and reciprocity, yet imprinting its own damning stamp on everything'. See Heather Glen, 'The Poet in Society: Blake and Wordsworth on London', *Literature and History* 3 (March 1976).

And that no man might buy or sell, save he that had the mark, or the name of the beast, or the number of his name.

The mark of the beast would seem, like 'charter'd', to have something to do with the buying and selling of human values.

This question is incapable of any final proof. The suggestion has been made[10] that Blake's allusion is not to Revelation but to Ezekiel ix.4: 'And the Lord said unto him, Go through the midst of the city, through the midst of Jerusalem, and set a mark upon the foreheads of the men that sigh and that cry for all the abominations that be done in the midst thereof.' The man who is ordered to go through the city has 'a writer's inkhorn by his side'. This seems at first to fit the poem closely: in 'London' a writer goes through the city of abominations and listens to 'sighs' and 'cries'. But even a literal reading does not fit the poem's meaning. For Blake – or the 'I' of his poem – is not setting marks on foreheads, he is observing them; and the marks are those of weakness and of woe, not of lamentations over abominations. Moreover, in Ezekiel's vision the Lord then orders armed men to go through the city and to 'slay utterly old and young, both maids and little children, and women: but come not near any man upon whom is the mark. . . '. Thus those who are marked are set apart and saved. Neither the intention nor the tone of Blake's poem coincides with Ezekiel's unedifying vision. Nor are we entitled to conflate the allusions to Revelation and to Ezekiel with some gesture towards an ulterior 'ambivalence' in which Blake has assimilated the damned to the elect. For if one point is incontestable about this poem it is that *every* man is marked: *all* share this human condition: whereas with Ezekiel it is the great *un*marked majority who are to be put to the sword. Such a conflation offers temptations to a critic but it would destroy the poem by introducing into its heart a direct contradiction of intention and of feeling. Ambiguities of this dimension are not fruitful multipliers of meaning.

There is, further, the question of what response the word 'mark' is most likely to have called up among Blake's contemporaries. I must assert that the allusions called first to mind will have been either to the 'mark of Cain' (Genesis iv.15)[11] or to the 'mark of the beast' in Revelation. And the

10 Among others, by Harold Bloom and David Erdman, and, with a different emphasis, by Heather Glen.
11 This suggestion has been pressed by Stan Smith, 'Some Responses to Heather Glen's "The Poet

more radical the audience, the more preoccupied it will have been with the second. For generations radical Dissent had sermonized and pamphleteered against the beast (Antichrist) who had his servitors 'which worshipped his image' (Revelation xvi.2): social radicalism equated these with usurers, with the rich, with those successful in buying and selling. And interpreters of Revelation always fastened with fascination upon the enigmatic verse (xiii.18): 'Let him that hath understanding count the number of the beast: for it is the number of a man.' Such interest in millennial interpretation became rife once more in the 1790s;[12] it turned above all on these chapters of Revelation with their recurrent images of the beast and of the destruction of Babylon, and the humble were able to turn to their own account the imprecations against kings, false prophets, and the rich with which these chapters are rife. We hardly need to argue that Blake, like most radical Dissenters of his time, had saturated his imagination with the imagery of Revelation: chapter xiv (the Son of Man with the sickle, and the Last Vintage) is implanted in the structure of *The Four Zoas* and of *Jerusalem*.

These considerations, which are ones of cultural context rather than of

in Society" ', *Literature and History* 4 (Autumn 1976). The 'mark of Cain' in Genesis was sometimes assimilated in theological exegesis to the mark of the beast. The Lord curses Cain and condemns him to be a fugitive and a vagabond. Cain complains that he will be killed as an outlaw, and the Lord replies: 'Whosoever slayeth Cain, vengeance shall be taken on him sevenfold. And the Lord set a mark upon Cain, lest any finding him should kill him.' Whether the Lord did this as an act of forgiveness or as a protraction of the punishment of ostracism and outlawry (as anthropologists would argue) is a matter of interpretation. Stan Smith certainly carries the Lord's intentions very much too far when he takes the mark as a sign of 'election'. But he is surely right to argue that the poem can carry *this* ambivalence (men are 'both agents and patients, culprits and victims'), since in Blake's Christian dialectic the mark of Cain could stand simultaneously as a sign of sin and as a sign of its forgiveness. See Blake's chapter title to the 'Genesis' fragment: 'Chapter IV How Generation & Death took possession of the Natural Man & of the Forgiveness of Sins written upon the Murderers Forehead' (E667).

[12] See e. g. Thompson, pp. 127–9, 420–6, and sources cited there; and Morton D. Paley, 'William Blake, the Prince of the Hebrews, and the Woman Clothed with the Sun', in Morton D. Paley and Michael Phillips (eds.), *William Blake: Essays in Honour of Sir Geoffrey Keynes* (Oxford, 1973). Swedenborgians were much concerned with interpretation of Revelation; and the verses which I have cited ('no man might buy or sell, save he that had the mark . . . of the beast') were discussed in the *New Magazine of Knowledge Concerning Heaven and Hell*, 1 (July 1790), 209–11, a journal which Blake is likely to have read. When Blake's acquaintance Stedman heard the news, on 6 April 1792, that Gustavus III, the King of Sweden, had been assassinated, his mind turned in the same direction: 'despotism dies away. Witness France, whose King may be compared to the beast in Revelation, whose number is 666, and LUDOVICUS added together makes the same. One, Sutherland, lately shot himself before King George . . . Such are the times': *The Journal of John Gabriel Stedman 1744–1797*, ed. Stanbury Thompson (London, 1962), pp. 340–1; I am indebted to Michael Phillips for this reference.

superficial verbal similarities, lead me to reject the suggested allusion to Ezekiel. What Blake's contemporaries were arguing about in the 1790s was the rule of Antichrist and the hope of the millennium: the mark seen in 'every face' is the mark of the beast, a mark explicitly associated with commercialism. And if we require conclusive evidence that Blake was thinking, in 'London', of Revelation, he has given us this evidence himself, with unusual explicitness. For the illumination to the poem[13] appears to be an independent, but complementary, conception; and for this reason I feel entitled to discuss the poem also as an independent conception and within its own terms. The illumination (if I am pressed to confess my own view) adds nothing essential to the poem, but comments upon the same theme in different terms. Nor are we even certain how the poem and the illumination are united, nor why they complement each other, until we turn to *Jerusalem*, Plate 84 (E241/K729):

> I see London blind & age-bent begging thro the Streets
> Of Babylon, led by a child. his tears run down his beard

In both the poem and the illumination, London's streets appear as those of Babylon of Revelation; but in the illumination it is London himself who is wandering through them.[14]

In the second verse the important change is from 'german forg'd links' to 'mind-forg'd manacles'. The reference was of course to the Hanoverian monarchy, and perhaps to the expectation that Hanoverian troops would

---

[13] Repr. in D. V. Erdman (ed.), *The Illuminated Blake* (London, 1975), plate 46 g, p. 88.

[14] One further suggestion may be offered about the mark of the beast. In a forthcoming study of Blake and the antinomian tradition (Cambridge, 1979) I shall present evidence which suggests that Blake – and, perhaps, other early Swedenborgians in London – had been influenced by the Muggletonians. This affords yet one more possible resonance of 'mark'. In Swedenborgian exegesis the 'mark of the beast' was sometimes taken to signify the solifidian doctrine of justification by faith without works. But Blake can scarcely have been using 'mark' in this way, since this was precisely his own, antinomian, 'heresy'. The Muggletonians, however, offer a very different interpretation. In their meetings prayer was rejected, as a 'mark of weakness', and Muggleton wrote:

'The mark of the beast is this, when a head magistrate or chief council in a nation or kingdom, shall set up . . . a set form of worship, he or they having no commission from God so to do, and shall cause the people by their power and authority . . . to worship after this manner of worship that is set up by authority, as this beast did . . .'

Hence to receive the mark of the beast signifies 'to worship the image set up' by established authority. L. Muggleton, *A True Interpretation of . . . the Whole Book of the Revelation of St. John* (London, 1808), pp. 174–5. This appears to take us very much closer to the universe of Blakean symbolism than do the Sweden-borgian glosses.

14

be used against British reformers.[15] The change to 'mind-forg'd' both generalizes and also places us again in that universe of Blakean symbolism in which we must turn from one poem to another for cumulative elucidation. In this case we have already noted that the image of the mind as 'fettered' by the invisible chains of its own unfreedom had appealed to Blake in his youthful 'King Edward the Third'. The development of the image is shown in another fragment in the notebook, 'How to know Love from Deceit':

> Love to faults is always blind
> Always is to joy inclind
> Lawless wingd & unconfind
> And breaks all chains from every mind
>
> Deceit to secresy confind
> Lawful cautious & refind
> To every thing but interest blind
> And forges fetters for the mind

The 'mind-forg'd manacles', then, are those of deceit, self-interest, absence of love, of law, repression, and hypocrisy.[16] They are stronger and harder to break than the manacles of the German king and his mercenaries, since they bind the minds not only of the oppressors but also of the oppressed; moreover, they are self-forged. How then are we to read 'ban'? Mr F. W. Bateson, who is a confident critic, tells us 'in every execration or curse (*not* in every prohibition)'.[17] I can't share his confidence: one must be prepared for seventeen types of ambiguity in Blake, and, in any case, the distinction between a curse and a prohibition is not a large one. The 'bans' may be execrations, but the mind may be encouraged to move through further associations, from the banns before marriage, the prohibitive and possessive ethic constraining 'lawless' love ('"Thou Shalt Not" writ over the door'), to the bans of Church and State against the publica-

---

15 See Erdman, *Prophet against Empire*, pp. 277–8.
16 Blake was also thinking of priestcraft, as we know from 'The Human Abstract'. Nancy Bogen suggests (*Notes and Queries*, new series, xv: 1 (January 1968)) that he may have been reading Gilbert Imlay's *Topographical Description* (London, 1792): on the Ohio (where the Thames-born slave will go to be free) Imlay found freedom from priestcraft which elsewhere 'seems to have forged fetters for the human mind'. But the poem itself carries this suggestion only insofar as the manacles immediately precede the 'blackning Church'. Fetters and manacles were anyway part of a very general currency of imagery: see e.g. Erdman, *Prophet against Empire*, p. 129, n. 35.
17 F. W. Bateson, *Selected Poems of William Blake* (London, 1957), p. 126.

tions and activities of the followers of Tom Paine.[18] All these associations are gathered into the central one of a code of morality which constricts, denies, prohibits and punishes.

The third verse commenced in the notebook as:

> But most the chimney sweepers cry
> Blackens oer the churches walls

This second line was then changed to:

> Every blackning church appalls

The effect is one of concentration. Pertinacious critics have been able to invert most of Blake's meanings, and readers have even been found to suppose that these two lines (in their final form) are a comment upon the awakening social conscience of the churches under the influence of the evangelical revival: the churches are appalled by the plight of the chimney-sweeping boys.[19] The meaning, of course, is the opposite; and on this point the notebook entitles us to have confidence. In the first version the churches are clearly shown as passive, while the cry of the chimney-sweepers attaches itself, with the smoke of commerce, to their walls. By revising the line Blake has simply tightened up the strings of his indignation by another notch. He has packed the meaning of 'The Chimney Sweeper' of the *Songs of Experience* (whose father and mother 'are both gone up to the church' to 'praise God & his Priest & King, / Who make up a heaven of our misery') into a single line, the adjective 'blackning' visually attaching to the Church complicity in the brutal exploitation of young childhood along with the wider consequences of the smoke of expanding commerce. 'Appalls' is used in a transitive sense familiar in Blake's time – not as 'is appalled by' but as puts to shame, puts in fear, challenges, indicts, in the same way as the dying sigh of the soldier indicts (and also threatens, with an apocalyptic image)[20] the Palace.[21] 'An ancient

18 See E. D. Hirsch, *Innocence and Experience* (New Haven, 1964), p. 264.

19 For a recent example of this confusion, see D. G. Gillham, *Blake's Contrary States* (Cambridge, 1966), p. 12: 'the Church is horrified at the evil of the sweeper's condition, but it is helpless to do much about it . . .'.

20 On this point see Erdman, *Prophet against Empire*, pp. 278–9. The British reformers of the 1790s were of course at pains to stress the identity of interests of the soldiers and the people: and also to expose military injustices, flogging, forcible recruitment ('crimping') etc.

21 Many examples could be given of this transitive use of 'appal': see also the O.E.D. and the last line of 'Holy Thursday' in *Experience*. Thus William Frend, who shared something of Blake's ultra-radical Christian values, wrote: 'Oh! that I had the warning voice of an ancient prophet,

Proverb' in the notebook gives the three elements of a curse upon England:

> Remove away that blackning church
> Remove away that marriage hearse
> Remove away that [place: *del.*] man of blood
> You'll quite remove the ancient curse.[22]

Church, marriage, and monarchy: but if he had left it at 'place', then it could have been Tyburn (or Newgate), the place of public execution – the altar of the 'Moral & Self-Righteous Law' of Babylon and Cruel Og, in the centre of London, whose public rituals Blake may have witnessed.

The poem, in its first version, was to end at this point, at 'Runs in blood down Palace walls'. But Blake was not yet satisfied: he returned, and worked through three versions of a fourth, concluding verse, squeezing it in between other drafts already on the page. One attempt reads:

> But most thro wintry streets I hear
> How the midnight harlots curse
> Blasts the new born infants tear
> And smites with plagues the marriage hearse.

Mr Bateson tells us that 'the images are sometimes interpreted as a reference to venereal disease. But this is to read Blake too literally. The diseases that descend upon the infant and the newly married couple are apocalyptic horrors similar to the blood that runs down the palace walls.'[23]

that I might penetrate into the innermost recesses of palaces, and appal the haranguers of senates!' Frend's 'appal' means 'throw into consternation', 'warn', 'shock'. The phrase was used in the appendix to William Frend, *Peace and Union Recommended* (St Ives, 1792): this pamphlet occasioned the celebrated case of Frend's trial before the Vice-Chancellor and his expulsion from Cambridge: see Frida Knight, *University Rebel* (London, 1971), esp. chapter 8. The pamphlet was on sale by mid-February 1793 (William Frend, *Account of the Proceedings . . .* (Cambridge, 1793), p. 72), and the appendix caused especial outrage among loyalists, and by the first week in May the University had opened its proceedings against Frend. From the juxtaposition of ancient prophet, palaces, and appal, and from the fact that Blake and Frend shared friends and sympathies (see Erdman, *Prophet against Empire*, pp. 158–9), one could argue that Blake's line could carry an echo of this celebrated case. But this is highly unlikely: Erdman gives a terminal date for inscribing the *Experience* drafts in the notebook as October 1792 (*N* 7) – although 'appalls' was introduced as a revision, perhaps subsequently. But it is unnecessary to argue for such direct influence. What we are really finding is a vocabulary and stock of images common to a particular group or a particular intellectual tradition, in this case that of radical Dissent. It is helpful to identify these groups and traditions, since they both place Blake and help us to unlock his meanings: but as to the actual 'source' we must maintain a steady scepticism.

[22] *N* 107.
[23] Bateson, *Selected Poems*, p. 126. See also the more elaborate (and unhelpful) argument of Harold Bloom, *Blake's Apocalypse: a Study in Poetic Argument* (Ithaca, 1963), pp. 141–2, which also discounts the clear meaning of the third line.

It may be nice to think so. But the blood of the soldier is for real, as well as apocalyptic, and so is the venereal disease that blinds the new born infant and which plagues the marriage hearse. We need not go outside the poem to document the increased discussion of such disease in the early 1790s,[24] nor, to turn the coin over, the indictment by Mary Wollstonecraft and her circle of marriage without love as prostitution. The poem makes the point very literally. Blake was often a very literal-minded man.

Another fragment in the notebook is closely related to this conclusion: a verse intended as the conclusion to 'The Human Abstract' (or so it would seem) but not used in its final version. It does not, in fact, relate directly to the imagery of 'The Human Abstract' and we may suppose that Blake, when he realized this, saw also how he could transpose the concept to make a conclusion to 'London':

> There souls of men are bought & sold
> And milk fed infancy for gold
> And youth to slaughter houses led
> And [maidens: *del.*] beauty for a bit of bread.[25]

This enables us to see, once more, that 'London' is a literal poem and it is also an apocalyptic one; or we may say that it is a poem whose moral realism is so searching that it is raised to the intensity of apocalyptic vision. For the poem is not, of course, a terrible cumulative *catalogue* of unrelated abuses and suffering. It is organized in two ways. First, and most simply, it is organized about the street-cries of London. In the first verse, we are placed with Blake (if we are entitled – as I think we are – to take him as the wandering observer) and we 'see' with his eyes. But in the second, third and fourth verses we are *hearing*, and the passage from sight to sound has an effect of reducing the sense of distance or of the alienation of the observer from his object of the first verse, and of immersing us within the human condition through which he walks. We *see* one thing at a time, as distinct moments of perception, although, by the end of the first verse, these perceptions become cumulative and repetitive ('in every face . . . marks

---

[24] As for example the long review of Jesse Foot, *A Complete Treatise on the Origin, Theory, and Cure of the Lues Venerea etc.* (London, 1792 – but based on lectures read in Dean Street, Soho in 1790 and 1791) in *Analytical Review*, XII (April 1792), 399, and XIII (July 1792), 261. See also the discussion in Grant C. Roti and Donald L. Kent, 'The Last Stanza of Blake's London', *Blake: an Illustrated Quarterly*, XI: 1 (Summer 1977).

[25] *N* 107.

. . . marks'). We *hear* many things simultaneously. Literally, we hear the eerie, almost animal cadence of the street-cries (and although we may now be forgetting them, if we were to be transported somehow to eighteenth-century London, these cries would be our first and most astonishing impression), the cries of the children, the "weep, 'weep' of the chimney-sweeps, and, led on by these, we hear the more symbolic sounds of 'bans', 'manacles', and the soldier's 'sigh'. This second verse is all sounds and it moves through an acceleration of generalization towards the third. If 'charter'd' is repeated, and if 'marks' falls with a triple beat, 'every' falls upon us no less than seven times: a single incidence in the first verse prepares for five uses in the second and a single incidence in the third ties it into the developing structure. 'Cry' also falls three times, carrying us from the second verse to the first line of the third. But in the third verse there is a thickening of sensual perception. Until this point we have seen and heard, but now we 'sense', through the sounds (the 'cry' and the 'sigh'), the activities that these indicate: the efforts of the chimney-sweep, the blackening walls of the churches, the blood of the soldier. We are not detached from this predicament; if anything, this impression of 'hearing' giving way to 'sensing' immerses us even more deeply within it.

—We have been wandering, with Blake, into an ever more dense immersion. But the opening of the fourth verse ('But most thro' midnight streets I hear') appears to set us a little apart from this once more. 'I hear' takes us back from ourselves to Blake who is a little apart from the scene and listening. Nothing in the earlier verses had prepared us for the darkness of 'midnight streets', unless perhaps the 'blackning Church': what had been suggested before was the activity of the day-time streets, the street-cries, the occasions of commerce. The verse is not knitted in tidily to the rest at the level of literal organization: the 'Marriage hearse' is a conceit more abstract than any other in the poem, apart from 'mind-forg'd manacles'. Since we know that he had intended at first to end the poem with three verses,[26] should we say that the final verse was an afterthought tacked on after the original images had ceased to beat in his mind – imperfectly soldered to the main body and still betraying signs of a separate origin?

It is a fair question. Blake, like other poets, had afterthoughts and made

[26] This is emphasized by the fact that it was the first line of verse 3 which (in the notebook draft) was to begin with 'But most . . .'; 'But most the chimney sweepers cry'.

revisions which were unwise. And if we were to stop short at this literal or technical organization of the poem we could make a case against its final verse. But we must attend also to a second, symbolic, level of organization. The immersion in sights and sounds is of a kind which forces one to generalize from London to 'the human condition'. The point is self-evident ('In every cry of every Man'). But this kind of statement, of which a certain school of commentators on Blake is over-fond, takes us only a little way, and a great deal less far than is sometimes knowingly implied. For 'the human condition', unless further qualified or disclosed, is nothing but a kind of metaphysical full stop. Or, worse than that, it is a bundle of solecisms about mortality and defeated aspiration. But 'the human condition' is what poets make poetry *out of*, not what they end up with. This poem is about a *particular* human condition, which acquires, through the selection of the simplest and most archetypal examples (man, infant, soldier, palace, harlot), a generalized resonance; it expresses an attitude *towards* that condition; and it offers a unitary analysis as to its character.

Two comments may be made on the attitude disclosed by Blake towards his own material. First, it is often noted that 'London' is one of the *Songs of Experience* which carries 'the voice of honest indignation'. This is true. The voice can be heard from the first 'charter'd'; it rises to full strength in the third and final verses (appalls, runs in blood, blasts, blights). But it is equally true that this voice is held in equilibrium with the voice of compassion. This is clear from the first introduction of 'mark'. If we have here (and the triple insistence enforces conviction) the 'mark of the beast', Blake would have been entitled to pour down upon these worshippers at the shrine of false gods the full vials of his wrath:

And there followed another angel, saying, Babylon is fallen, is fallen, that great city, because she made all nations drink of the wine of the wrath of her fornication.

And the third angel followed them, saying with a loud voice, If any man worship the beast and his image, and receive his mark in his forehead, or in his hand,

The same shall drink of the wine of the wrath of God, which is poured out without mixture into the cup of his indignation; and he shall be tormented with fire and brimstone in the presence of the holy angels, and in the presence of the Lamb:

And the smoke of their torment ascendeth up for ever and ever: and they have no rest day nor night, who worship the beast and his image, and whosoever receiveth the mark of his name.[27]

But Blake indicates 'weakness' and 'woe', and the slow rhythm of the line, checked at mid-point, suggests contemplation and pity rather than wrath. Nor is this note of grave compassion ever lost: it continues in the cries, the fear, the tear: even the soldier is 'hapless'. If 'London' is that part of the human condition which may be equally described as 'Hell', it is not a hell to which only the damned are confined, while the saved may contemplate their torments; nor is this Virgil's 'Hades'. This is a city of Everyman; nor do we feel, in our increasing immersion, that we – or Blake himself – are observers from without. These are not so much our fellow-damned as our fellow-sufferers.

The second comment upon Blake's attitude is this: his treatment of the city departs from a strong literary convention. To establish this point fully would take us further outside the poem than I mean to go. But one way of handling the city, both in itself and as an exemplar of the human condition, derived from classical (especially Juvenalian) satire; and in this it is the city's turbulence, its theatre of changing human passions, its fractured, accidental and episodic life, its swift succession of discrete images of human vice, guile, or helplessness, which provided the staple of the convention. Samuel Johnson's 'London' was a place where at one corner a 'fell attorney prowls for prey' and at the next a 'female atheist talks you dead'. And the convention was, in some part, a countryman's convention, in some part a class convention – generally both: a country gentleman's convention. From whichever aspect, plebeian London was seen from outside as a spectacle. Wordsworth was still able to draw upon this convention – although with significant shifts of emphasis – in *The Prelude*.[28]

Blake's 'London' is not seen from without as spectacle. It is seen, or suffered, from within, by a Londoner. And what is unusual about *this* image of the-human-condition-as-hell is that it offers the city as a unitary experience and not as a theatre of discrete episodes. For this to be so, there must be an ulterior symbolic organization behind the literal organization

[27] Revelation xiv. 8–11. These verses immediately precede those in which the Son of Man appears with 'in his hand a sharp sickle', and which lead on to 'the great winepress of the wrath of God' (xiv. 14–20) – that vision of the last vintage which worked in Blake's imagination.
[28] See Williams, *Country and City*, chapter 14, and Glen, 'The Poet in Society'.

of this street-cry following upon that. And this symbolic organization should now, after this lengthy discussion, have become fully disclosed. The tone of compassion falls upon those who are in hell, the sufferers; but the tone of indignation falls upon the institutions of repression – mind-forg'd manacles, blackning Church, Palace, Marriage hearse. And the symbolic organization is within the clearly conceived and developing logic of market relations. Blake does not only list symptoms: within the developing imagery which unites the poem he also discloses their cause. From the first introduction of 'charter'd' he never loses hold of the image of buying and selling although these words themselves are never used. 'Charter'd' both grants from on high and licenses and it limits and excludes; if we recall Paine it is a 'selling and buying' of freedom. What are bought and sold in 'London' are not only goods and services but human values, affections, and vitalities. From freedom we move (with 'mark') to a race marked by buying and selling, the worshippers of the beast and his image. Then we move through these values in ascendant scale: goods are bought and sold (street-cries), childhood (the chimney-sweep), human life (the soldier), and, in the final verse, youth, beauty and love, the source of life, is bought and sold in the figure of the diseased harlot who, herself, is only the other side of the 'Marriage hearse'.[29] In a series of literal, unified images of great power Blake compresses an indictment of the acquisitive ethic, endorsed by the institutions of State, which divides man from man, brings him into mental and moral bondage, destroys the sources of joy, and brings, as its consequence, blindness and death. And it is now evident why the final verse is no afterthought but appeared to Blake as the necessary conclusion to the poem. The fragment left over from 'The Human Abstract'

> There souls of men are bought & sold
> And milk fed infancy for gold
> And youth to slaughter houses led
> And beauty for a bit of bread

[29] With 'Marriage hearse' we are at the point of junction with another universe of imagery which critics of the 'neo-Platonist' persuasion emphasize to the exclusion of all other aspects of Blake's thought. In this universe, for the spirit to assume mortal dress is a form of death or sleep: hence sexual generation generates death: hence (these would argue) 'Marriage hearse'. There are times when Blake uses images in this way, although often with more equivocation, inversion, or idiosyncrasy than this kind of criticism suggests. This is not, however, one of these times. The poem is not concerned with lamenting the constrictions of the spirit within its material 'coffin' but with the 'plagues' which 'blight' sexual love and generation.

is a synopsis of the argument in 'London'. As it stands it remains as an argument, a series of assertions which would only persuade those already persuaded. But it provided, in its last line, the image of the harlot, whose love is bought and sold, which was necessary to complete 'London' and make that poem 'shut like a box'. And the harlot not only provides a culminating symbol of the reification of values, she is also a point of junction with the parallel imagery of religious mystification and oppression: for if this is Babylon, then the harlot is Babylon's whore who brought about the city's fall 'because she made all nations drink of the wine of the wrath of her fornication'. For English radical Dissent in the eighteenth century, the whore of Babylon was not only the 'scarlet woman' of Rome, but also *all* Erastianism, all compromise between things spiritual and the temporal powers of the State, and hence, very specifically, that extraordinary 'Erastian' formation, the Church of England. One recalls Blake's annotations to Bishop Watson (throughout), and his polemic against 'The Abomination that maketh desolate. i.e. State Religion which is the Source of all Cruelty' (E607/K393). Hence the harlot is able to unite in a single nexus the imagery of market relations and the imagery of ideological domination by the agency of a State Church, prostituted to the occasions of temporal power.

To tie the poem up in this way was, perhaps, to add to its pessimism. To end with the blood on the Palace walls might suggest an apocalyptic consummation, a revolutionary overthrow. To end with the diseased infant is to implant life within a cycle of defeat. And yet the poem doesn't *sound* defeated, in part because the tone of compassion or of indignation offers a challenge to the logic of its 'argument',[30] in part because the logic of the symbolic analysis of market relations proposes, at the same time, if not an alternative, at least the challenge that (in compassion and in indignation) this alternative could be found.

In any case, these pages of mine have been teasing out meanings from one poem of sixteen lines. And Blake's larger meanings lie in groupings of poems, in contraries, and in cumulative insights into differing states.

[30] See F. R. Leavis, 'Justifying One's Valuation of Blake', in Paley and Phillips, *Essays*, p. 80: 'the effect of the poetry [of the *Songs*] is very far from inducing an acceptance of human defeat. One can testify that the poet himself is not frightened, and, further, that there is no malevolence, no anti-human animus, no reductive bent, in his realism . . .'

'London' is not about *the* human condition but about a particular condition or state, and a way of seeing this. This state must be set against other states, both of experience and of innocence. Thus a fuller discussion would have to place 'London' alongside 'The Human Abstract', which shows the generation of the prohibitive Tree of Mystery, whose fruit continually regenerates man's Fall; and in this conjunction 'London' (when seen as hell) shows the condition of the Fallen who lie within the empire of property, self-interest, State religion and Mystery. And when the poem is placed within the context of the *Songs* it is easier to see the fraternal but transformed relationship which Blake's thought at this time bears to Painite radicalism and to Deism. Blake is both accepting a part of this thought and turning it to a new account. For while 'London' is a poem which a 'Jacobinical' Londoner could respond to and accept, it is scarcely one which he could write. The average Painite, or supporter of the London Corresponding Society, would have been unlikely to have written 'mind-forg'd' (since the manacles would have been seen as wholly exterior, imposed by priestcraft and kingcraft); and the voice of indignation would probably have drowned the voice of compassion, since most Painites would have found it difficult to accept Blake's vision of man as being simultaneously oppressed (although by very much the same forces as those described by Paine) and in a self-victimized or Fallen state. One might seem to contradict the other. And behind this would lie (if we followed this analysis into adjacent poems) ulterior differences of emphasis both as to the 'cause' of this human condition and also as to its 'remedy'.

For if Blake found congenial the Painite denunciation of the repressive institutions of State and Church, it did not follow that man's redemption from this state could be effected by a political reorganization of these institutions alone. There must be some utopian leap, some human re-birth, from Mystery to renewed imaginative life, from 'London' to the New Jerusalem of brotherhood. To examine this leap would take us very far beyond this poem. But we can't take a full view of the meaning of even this poem without recalling that Blake did not always see London in this way: it was not always to be Babylon or the city of destruction in the Apocalypse. There were other times when he saw it as the city of lost innocence:

> The fields from Islington to Marybone,
> To Primrose Hill and Saint Johns Wood,
> Were builded over with pillars of gold,
> And there Jerusalems pillars stood.
>
> . . .
>
> The Jews-harp-house & the Green Man;
> The Ponds where Boys to bathe delight;
> The fields of Cows by Willans farm:
> Shine in Jerusalems pleasant sight.

And it could also be the millennial city, of that time when the moral and self-righteous law should be overthrown, and the Multitude return to Unity:

> In my Exchanges every Land
> Shall walk, & mine in every Land,
> Mutual shall build Jerusalem:
> Both heart in heart & hand in hand. (E170, 172/K649, 650, 652)

POSTSCRIPT: SWEDENBORG AND 'LONDON'

To have discussed the matter of Swedenborg's influence upon 'London' in the body of this essay would have elevated the point to undue importance. But it does have some interest. The image of London as symbolizing a human condition, or, more exactly, contrasting conditions, one heavenly and spiritual, and the other hellish and corporeal, which could well have occurred to Blake or to any other poet at almost any moment of any cultural day, was no doubt enforced by his reading of Swedenborg's vision of London. When Blake was writing the *Songs* (*both* halves of the *Songs*) he was not 'under the influence of Swedenborgianism' but in a close, even obsessive, argumentative relation with that influence.[31] Miss Kathleen Raine has recently emphasized this once more, and she is right to insist that the lasting debt which Swedenborgian influence laid upon Blake was in habituating him to a mode of apprehension in alternating 'correspond-ences'[32] by which every experience (and every passage of the Bible) may

---

[31] The case for 'neo-Platonist' interpretations of Blake seems to me misconceived. I hope to publish shortly evidence which suggests that Blake was drawing upon more obscure and idiosyncratic traditions of radical Dissent, germane at some points to Behmenist and hermetic thought, but very differently accented.

[32] See Raine, *Tradition*, esp. vol. I, pp. 4–6.

also be seen as a code or an analogy of both spiritual and hellish states or conditions: the eye of the interpreter (who has 'received' Swedenborg's insights) sees through the appearance to an ulterior reality (or to dialectically opposed realities) which the appearance both masks and signals. All appearance (and most Holy Writ) is a code of an ulterior significance; and it is the poet's business, through the exercise of imagination, to crack that code.

This might seem to be fraught with importance, until we reflect that this is what a good part of poetry (as well as some philosophy) has always been about. All symbolism and allegory must involve some notion of 'correspondences'. Possibly this had become difficult to see within the 'single vision' of eighteenth-century polite culture, and Blake needed Swedenborg (and the company of Swedenborgian 'receivers') to renew his confidence. It is now as difficult to recover exactly why Swedenborg excited intelligent and sensitive men in the 1790s as it may be, in 150 years time, to recover why certain of the more abstruse structuralists have excited contemporary minds. For most of Baron Swedenborg's visions are monstrously pedestrian, and they are remote from experiential controls or affective reference. In certain cases they served only to irritate Blake and to provoke him, as in *The Marriage of Heaven and Hell*, to satire. But then as now we have the conviction among the initiates that a code has been cracked, giving insight into the 'internal sense' of things.

The habit of thinking in 'correspondences' certainly excited Blake and his friends at the moment of the foundation, in 1789, of the New Jerusalem Church. Swedenborg had renewed the arcane wisdom of the thrice-greatest Hermes, Hermes Trismegistos: 'All things which are in heaven are upon earth, after an earthly manner; all things which are upon earth are in heaven, after a heavenly manner.'[33] Observers of the adherents of the Church in the 1790s noted their eager attention to the reading of the Scriptures in their 'internal sense'; passages whose sexual candour offended modesty could be read and discussed, without a blush, in mixed congrega-

[33] This translation is Southey's in his 'Account of Swedenborgianism' in *Letters from England*, 3rd edn (1814), vol. III, chapter 62, pp. 116–17. Miss Raine sometimes makes this thought (which she supposes Blake may have received through Thomas Vaughan: see e.g. Raine, *Tradition*, vol. I, p. 119) seem more arcane than it was. Southey recalls Milton:

> What if Earth
> Be but the shadow of Heaven, and things therein
> Each to other like, more than on Earth is thought?

tions, since they were only a dark glass through which a divine light was refracted.[34] For the initiates, a code, or dictionary of correspondences, was learned by rote in a more literal way: 'Two legs stand for the will of God; by a small piece of the ear we are to understand the will of truth; the son of a she-ass denotes rational truth; and an ass, without any mention of his pedigree, signifies the scientific principle. . .'[35] No son of a she-ass springs to mind in Blake's poems of this decade. But we should remain alert to allusions to this code or jargon of 'pseudo-symbolism',[36] even if their intention is ironical. It is unlikely that we have exhausted them.

In this sense the notion of 'London' as symbol of the-human-condition-as-hell owed something to Swedenborgian influence. Something – but not very much. For although Blake could have read – and perhaps must have read – Swedenborg's visionary correspondences of London, we can't be sure in what form he read them, and it is difficult to see how they could have moved him to much more than ill-temper. Swedenborg often repeated himself, and it is difficult to pick up all variants of his visions. Blake could have read the source indicated by Miss Raine, in Swedenborg's *True Christian Religion* (London, 1781).[37] This would have given him a rather stilted translation of a vision of London in its spiritual sense. He could also have read *A Continuation Concerning the Last Judgement and the Spiritual World* (London, 1791), where the same vision is presented with slight variations. But it is most likely of all that he read a passage 'Concerning LONDON in the Spiritual World' which appeared in the *New-Jerusalem Magazine* in 1790.

This is a real bibliographical head-ache which would require an authority fully versed in Swedenborgiana to elucidate. It appears to me that the source of the vision is in the Baron's 'Spiritual Diary', which, however, was not published in English in Blake's lifetime.[38] But a French enthusiast, living in London, Benedict Chastanier, had in his possession extensive

---

[34] See *Analytical Review*, XIV (1792), 190–3.

[35] Southey, *Letters*, vol. III, p. 118. See also E. Swedenborg, *An Hieroglyphic Key to Natural and Spiritual Mysteries by Way of Representations and Correspondences* (1792).

[36] See Raine, *Tradition*, vol. I, p. 5.

[37] *Ibid.*, vol. II, p. 266.

[38] The first volume of the *Spiritual Diary*, trans. J. H. Smithson and G. Bush, was not published until 1846. A brief passage about London in its infernal state appeared in vol. IV (London, 1889), p. 278, section 5016: 'I . . . wandered through several of the streets . . . Men are plundered there.' But see also note 45 below. I am grateful to Mr A. S. Wainscot, the Librarian of the Swedenborg Society, for bibliographical help.

manuscripts of Swedenborg, and from this source extracts flowed into Swedenborgian publications.[39] Since Swedenborg himself had drawn upon his own diary for the visions inscribed in his own prior publications, variants proliferated.

Swedenborg's account commenced: 'There are two large Cities like London, into which most of the English enter after Death. I was permitted to . . . walk through them.'[40] The versions apparently available to Blake in 1791–3 largely concerned London in the spiritual world. But there are marked differences between the version offered in *True Christian Religion* (as cited by Miss Raine) and that in the *New-Jerusalem Magazine*. Thus *True Christian Religion*: 'The Middle . . . answers to that Part of London, where the Merchants meet, called the Exchange, and there the Moderators dwell; above that Middle Part is the East, Below it is the West; on the right Side is the South, on the left Side is the North.' And thus the *New-Jerusalem Magazine*: 'In the middle of the city is situated the *Exchange*, to the right whereof dwells a moderator, and his officers round about it. The middle street answers to Holborn; the east is in front; the west behind reaching down to Wapping . . .' Thus Chastanier's version (if this was Chastanier) is more concrete and immensely closer to the Jerusalem of Blake's later writings. But the differences reach into more subtle definitions. Thus *True Christian Religion*:

The Eastern Quarter is inhabited by those who have been particularly distinguished for leading Lives of Charity, and in that Quarter there are magnificent Palaces; the Southern Quarter is inhabited by such as have been distinguished for Wisdom . . . the Northern Quarter is inhabited by those who have been particularly delighted with the Liberty of speaking and writing; and in the Western Quarter are they who maintain the Doctrine of Justification by Faith alone.

---

[39] Benedict Chastanier was a French surgeon, who declared in 1791 that he had been living in England for twenty-six years, i.e. from 1766: see *New Magazine of Knowledge Concerning Heaven and Hell* II, (London, 1790–1), 112; C. T. Odhner, *Robert Hindmarsh* (Philadelphia, 1895), p. 10. In 1790–1 he was living at 68 Tottenham Court Road; he had been an active member of the Swedenborgian circles since the early 1780s; a number of Swedenborg's manuscripts were in his hands, including the 'Spiritual Diary', and he transmitted his translations impartially to all enthusiasts, publishing in both the (rival) journals of 1790: see *New Magazine* . . . II (1791), 248, 349 *et passim*; *New-Jerusalem Magazine* (London, 1790), *passim*, and its 'Preface', referring to many manuscripts, letters and essays; J. Hyde, 'Benedict Chastanier', *New-Church Review*, XIV (1907), 181–205.

[40] E. Swedenborg, *A Continuation Concerning the Last Judgement and the Spiritual World* (London, 1791), p. 35, section 42.

Thus the *New-Jerusalem Magazine*:

In the eastern quarter . . . dwell the best of them, where they all worship the Lord. Those who are distinguished for intelligence reside in the southern quarter which extends almost to Islington, where there is also an assembly held; such as dwell in this quarter are also prudent in speaking and writing. Towards the north dwell those who are illiterate, and who are zealous for liberty of speech in which they delight. In the west reside those who are in an obscure affection of good; and these are fearful of declaring their minds openly.[41]

It is as if we were looking through differently tinted doctrinal spectacles. There is, even, a sense of *class* emphasis in the two versions; where *True Christian Religion* is always bland and full of gentlemanly angels[42] the *Magazine* suggests that plebeian elements, even the illiterate, might also emblematize eternity.[43] But (and alas) we can't, as yet, carry this comparison further, into alternative versions of Swedenborg's vision of London in its infernal state. What we are offered, which we know to have been available when the poem was written, does not take us far:

The other great City like London is not in the middle Part of the Christian Region . . . but lies at some Distance from it in the North; and is the Receptacle of those after Death who are inwardly wicked. In the midst of it there is an open Communication with Hell, into which the Inhabitants sink down, and are swallowed up . . .[44]

This will hardly have set Blake's imagination afire.

Swedenborg had other visions of infernal cities, and of the destruction of Babylon, but I haven't located any extended vision of London-as-hell. It is not impossible that Blake could have seen an account circulated in manuscript, and now lost.[45] But if we discount this possibility, then the direct

---

[41] Compare *True Christian Religion* (London, 1781), pp. 438–9, and 'Concerning LONDON in the Spiritual World', 'From the manuscripts of EMANUEL SWEDENBORG', *New-Jerusalem Magazine* (London, 1790), pp. 247–8.

[42] On this point I agree with G. R. Sabri-Tabrizi, *The 'Heaven' and 'Hell' of William Blake* (London, 1973).

[43] Chastanier, however, was no reformer or republican: he considered that France, in 1792, was distracted by 'a spirit of *mad philosophy*': *New-Jerusalem Journal*, I (1792), 367–70.

[44] Swedenborg, *A Continuation Concerning the Last Judgement*, p. 36, section 43.

[45] This is a possibility, but not one which I can support. For the brief accounts of London in its infernal state, see note 38 above and J. F. Potts, *The Swedenborg Concordance*, vol. IV (London, 1895), entry under 'London'. The original for the *New-Jerusalem Magazine*'s version of London in its spiritual state is a manuscript dated 1762 and known to Swedenborgian scholars as 'The Last Judgement (Posthumous) MS'. This includes the full passage (with reference to Holborn, Wapping, Islington etc.) as published by the *Magazine*: it was not subsequently published again

influence of Swedenborg's vision upon 'London' is null; or, at the most, it may be felt in an inverted sense. For the Baron's complacent vision of a heavenly commercial city, purged of all spiritual evil,[46] would have appeared to Blake not as an inspiration but as an incitement to protest. Perhaps he thought of his own poem as a rebuke. And that, possibly, might be of bearing upon the poem's conception. Thus it turns out to be a trivial matter, an academicism which I have laboured for long enough, and readers would do best to return to the poem and forget about this note.

Yet perhaps it would be advisable not to forget about it altogether. For this note is preliminary. We can see at least how London was brought within the 'science of correspondences' and discussed among the New Jerusalemites of the 1790s. It is still being seen in this way by Blake in *Jerusalem*:

> I behold London; a Human awful wonder of God!
> He says: Return, Albion, return! I give myself for thee:
> My streets are my, Ideas of Imagination.
> Awake Albion, awake! and let us awake up together.
> My Houses are Thoughts: my Inhabitants; Affections,
> The children of my thoughts, walking within my blood-vessels

(E178/K665)

This is a variant – however transformed and turned to new uses – of the Swedenborgian Grand Man. And we should also remember how the concreteness of Chastanier's translation in the *New-Jerusalem Magazine*

until 1846, by J. F. Tafel, as part VII of the *Diarium Spirituale* (Tubingen): see Emanuel Swedenborg, *The Last Judgement (Posthumous)* (Swedenborg Society, London, 1934), section 268 and Preface. But Chastanier had very possibly completed a translation of the full *Diary* (and of other manuscripts) by 1790: when the *New-Jerusalem Magazine* folded up for lack of support, subscribers were circulated with *Proposals for printing by Subscription Emanuel Swedenborg's Spiritual Diary* (June 1791) (copy of prospectus bound in with *Magazine* in the volume in the Swedenborg Society's Library, London). All early accounts of the New Church show that a principal activity was listening to readings from Swedenborg's manuscripts. It is not, therefore, impossible that Blake might have heard or seen some fuller version of London in its infernal state which has not survived. For the first 148 sections of the *Diary* (also known as *Memorabilia*), which were in Chastanier's hands, subsequently have been lost: see James Hyde, *A Bibliography of the Works of Emanuel Swedenborg* (London, 1906), pp. 118–19; R. L. Tafel, *Documents Concerning . . . Swedenborg* (London, 1877), vol. III, pp. 807–8, 836–7.

46 'In a place answering to *Moorfields* and round about it, which is in the southern quarter is a promiscuous multitude; thither from the city are led all those who incline to evils, wherefore the croud there by turns is ejected and this continually, whereby the city is cleared of the evil in it, and they who are thus led away appear no more': *New-Jerusalem Magazine* (1790), 247. We would now think of Moorfields – and (just beyond) Poplar and Bow – as a gateway to the East End rather than the south. But Swedenborg's points of the compass were also not 'natural' ones, but carried pseudo-symbolic significance: 'on the right side [of London] is the South . . .'

(Holborn, Wapping, Islington) and its palpable social reference ('those who are illiterate', those 'who are zealous for liberty of speech', those who 'are fearful of declaring their minds openly') may have started Blake's imagination working towards the astonishing transformations of the epics:

> The Shuttles of death sing in the sky to Islington & Pancrass
> Round Marybone to Tyburns River, weaving black melancholy as a net,
> And despair as meshes closely wove over the west of London   (E181/K668)

Blake of course felt himself to be able, as a Londoner, to improve on the Swedish mystic's topography. He also felt able, in his millenarial and radical self, to turn the Baron's very conservative visions upside-down. Where Swedenborg had found a smug spiritual London, with a point of evacuation around Moorfields where the 'promiscuous multitude . . . who incline to evils' were ejected,[47] it was (in Blake's vision) not the evil but Jerusalem herself who was 'cast . . . forth upon the wilds to Poplar & Bow. . .'.[48] Since Swedenborg's time the terminuses for Hell had moved two or three miles further east.

[47] Above, note 46.   [48] E181/K668.

CHAPTER 3

BLAKE'S CRITICISM OF MORAL THINKING IN *SONGS OF INNOCENCE AND OF EXPERIENCE*

HEATHER GLEN

Songs of Innocence and of Experience are mostly concerned with what would usually be described as moral questions. Many of them – especially of *Songs of Innocence* – seem, at least superficially, to belong to the recognizable eighteenth-century genre of moral songs for children; and *Songs of Experience* contain several poems which look like poems of social protest. But a close reading of the poems suggests that Blake's attitude towards late eighteenth-century habits of moral judgement and instruction is by no means a simple one. Although the *Songs* display an awareness of many of the issues raised in contemporary ethical discussion, they reach beyond such discussion by questioning the very premises on which it is based.

Songs of Innocence and of Experience were initially addressed to an expanding middle-class reading public – those liberal middle classes who could be expected to pay five shillings for what was apparently an attractive example of a child's book of poems, who would take a humanitarian interest in such subjects as the plight of the chimney-sweeps or of the charity school children. Such readers did not by any means all share the same opinions, but they do seem to have shared certain very basic assumptions, assumptions natural to a dominant class which felt no really radical challenge to its attempts to impose its modes of thinking and feeling on others. To such readers, there was nothing problematic about moral judgement as such. The nature of the judgement, its fitness to the particular instance, might be debated and disagreed over; but morality itself was something universally applicable, and moral values, however difficult to grasp in real-life situations, could be rationally and unambiguously defined. The greatest eighteenth-century writers were of course not unthinking in their acceptance of these premises: both Hume and Johnson, for instance, expressed doubts as to whether the reason could ever completely control moral choice, or whether moral principles could ever be really adequately determined. But for both, moral virtue – whatever one understood it to be – remained an ideal to be striven towards, the refinement of moral judgement the best task of the rational man. Characteristically, it is Johnson who gives the clearest exposition of the nature of his contemporaries' assumptions. 'He that thinks reasonably', he wrote in the *Preface to Shakespeare*, 'must think morally': and while this is obviously a far from adequate summary of his own intimate and perceptive understanding of moral dilemmas, it is a fair indication of the belief that lay behind his whole life's work – as it lay behind the moral thinking of his age. Moral judgement was a necessary part of all experience: there was no area of life to which it did not properly extend.

Such an assumption is by no means a peculiar one; it is basic to many, perhaps most, people's thinking today. But it is one that was emphatically not shared by Blake: that seems, indeed, to have been directly challenged by him:

> Pity would be no more,
> If we did not make somebody Poor;
> And Mercy no more could be
> If all were as happy as we.
>
> . . .
>
> The Gods of the earth and sea
> Sought thro' Nature to find this Tree;
> But their search was all in vain:
> There grows one in the Human Brain.   (E27/K217)

What is being expressed here is not merely an attack on a dehumanizing social order. Nor is it a distrust of the human ability to make the correct moral discriminations. It is nothing less than a distrust of moral thinking itself.

This was not just an abstract philosophical theory: it was based on and rooted in an intimate sense of the conditions of life in late eighteenth-century England as Blake saw them. And for this reason, perhaps the most revealing of his poems on 'moral' questions are those which deal with what are usually thought of as social problems: those of the *Songs of Innocence and of Experience* which deal with some of the injustices and abuses which preoccupied Blake's humanitarian contemporaries. There will be no room in this essay to discuss the *Songs* as a whole collection. But a consideration of some of these poems does, I think, throw a good deal of light on Blake's peculiar but quite coherent and intelligible distrust of what he called 'Eating of the Tree of Knowledge of Good & Evil' (E553/K615).

Thirty-five years after it was first published, Charles Lamb sent 'The Chimney Sweeper' from *Songs of Innocence* as a contribution to a charitable volume designed to arouse sympathy for the lot of the chimney-sweeps, *The Chimney-Sweeper's Friend and Climbing Boy's Album*.[1] It is an illuminating context for the poem. The first half of the volume contains reports of contemporary enquiries into the conditions under which boys were employed: the horrific nature of the evidence is curiously at odds with the matter-of-fact way in which it is reported (often by the chimney-sweeps themselves). The second half consists of 'protest' verse, of which the following, by William Lisle Bowles, is a fair example:

> They sing of the poor sailor-boy who wanders o'er the deep,
> But few are they who think upon the friendless LITTLE SWEEP!
> In darkness to his dreary toil, thro' winter's frost and snows,
> When the keen north is piping shrill, the shiv'ring urchin goes.

> He has no father, and from grief his mother's eyes are dim,
> And none besides, in all the world, awakes to pray for HIM:
> For him no summer Sundays smile, no health is in the breeze;
> His mind dark as his fate, his frame a prey to dire disease.

The sing-song sentimentality of this is very different from the prosaic, dulled acceptance of the sweeps' courtroom speeches.[2] And interestingly, in Blake's poem, one catches echoes of both these tones: the unquestioning matter-of-factness of the sweeps, and the easy pathos of 'protest'. Blake knows, intimately, the common kinds of response to the situation he presents, and he also seems to be sharply aware of the disjunction between them.

By 1789, when Blake's poem was issued, the plight of the London

---

[1] *The Chimney-Sweeper's Friend and Climbing Boy's Album*, ed. James Montgomery (London, 1824).

[2] 'I think it was injudicious to mix stories avowedly colour'd by fiction with the sad true statements from the parliamentary records, etc. . . .', wrote Lamb to Bernard Barton, on 15 May 1824.

chimney-sweepers was already the subject of considerable humanitarian concern; was seen, indeed, by some, as a national scandal. Jonas Hanway's *A Sentimental History of Chimney Sweeps*, published in 1785 'to recommend to my fellow-subjects, particularly the inhabitants of these vast cities, the exercise of their humanity towards those who call the loudest for it, – Chimney Sweepers Climbing-Boys!', prefigures not merely Blake's ironic play upon the chimney-sweeper's familiar street-cry, but also that sense of the sweep as the blackened exposer of the pretensions of a whole society which was to find poetic expression in 'London':

it is in vain to talk of the *age being enlightened*, while the *chimnies are darkened* by their narrowness, and their tops so covered with *earthen pots*.   (p. xviii)

no other nation employs *boys* in sweeping their chimnies; it being generally done by *men climbers*, or by brushwood tied to a cord.   (p. 31)

the national disgrace is manifest: it is an offence against God; and nature cries against us!   (p. 58)

Beside this, 'The Chimney Sweeper' from *Songs of Innocence* might at first seem more remarkable for what it does not say than for what it does. There is none of Hanway's explicit protest, and none of Bowles's confident sentimentality. Instead, the poem opens with the unmediated voice of the chimney-sweeper himself, telling about his life with unemotional sobriety. The facts that he details are the familiar facts of Hanway's account:

> When my mother died I was very young,
> And my Father sold me while yet my tongue
> Could scarcely cry "weep! 'weep! 'weep!'
> So your chimneys I sweep, & in soot I sleep.   (E10/K117)

How the masters obtain these children, would be mysterious, were it not known that numbers of the least virtuous, or most necessitous among the labouring poor, part with their children at any rate . . . Orphans, who are in a vagabond state, or the illegitimate children of the poorest kind of people, are said to be sold; that is, their service for seven years is disposed of for twenty or thirty shillings; being a smaller price than the value of a *terrier*: but it is presumed that the children of poor parents, who cannot find bread for a numerous family, make up by much the greater part of the number of the *climbing boys* . . . If the boy is under a master who has constant, regular employment, as soon as his *morning's work* is done, he is generally sent to seek for further business, or, as they term it, *to call the streets* . . . We may figure to ourselves, the boy called from the bag of soot on which he slept, oftentimes walking a mile or two to his work.

(pp. 24–7)

And the unprotesting flatness of his speech is analogous to that of the court reports published in *The Chimney-Sweeper's Friend* more than thirty years later: here, as there, the sweep seems either too naïve or too apathetic to question what has happened to him. But the effect of Blake's stanza is not one of childish acceptance. If the little boy explains his life as an inescapable logical progression, one thing naturally following on from the next ('When . . . And . . . So . . .'), the *un*naturalness of that progression is emphasized by the way in which his awkwardly prosaic speaking voice prevents any regular metrical pattern being established – so that the matter-of-fact chain of cause and effect ending in 'So your chimneys I sweep' has none of the feeling of conclusiveness that, for instance, Bowles's more explicitly protesting lines do. This is a state of affairs that the child accepts, apparently uncritically, but the verse does not.

And the unease created by the rhythm is reinforced by the bald directness of the boy's own speech. The polite reader is unemphatically but inescapably implicated as the childish catalogue continues – 'So *your* chimneys I sweep': he is allowed no easy indulgence in sentimental pity, for he is denied any position from which he might unhypocritically direct it. Nor is there any trace of Bowles's sweep's self-regarding pathos. If the child's naïve account of his own street cry – "weep! 'weep! 'weep!' – unconsciously suggests that other, less 'innocent' perspective of pity from which the lot of the sweeps might be seen, his unconsciousness is part of the point. He was sold, he tells us, 'while yet my tongue / Could scarcely cry 'weep! 'weep! 'weep!'; before he was capable of seeing himself as an object of compassion, before he would have been likely to question the inexorable progression outlined in the stanza. Unwittingly, he 'calls for humanity'[3] but it does not seem to occur to him to see *himself* as a pitiable object at all. Instead his interest turns very quickly away from himself, towards another equally unfortunate.

And as soon as it does so, the verse takes life: it leaps from the rational

---

[3] Jonas Hanway, *A Sentimental History of Chimney Sweeps* (1785), p. ix: 'The ruling motive to my writing these pages, was to recommend to my fellow subjects . . . the exercise of their humanity towards those who call the loudest for it, – Chimney Sweepers Climbing-Boys!'

summary of the first stanza into the focus of present vision. The logical connections, which have seemed stilted and artificial, here hit the ear with a feeling of excited inevitability, as the child's colloquial speech rhythms fall naturally into metrical patterns:

> There's little Tom Dacre, who cried when his head,
> That curl'd like a lamb's back, was shav'd, so I said
> 'Hush, Tom! never mind it, for when your head's bare
> 'You know that the soot cannot spoil your white hair.'

And as in the first stanza the child's uncomplaining repetition of the cry that is the sign of his servitude releases a double meaning in the verse, so here his innocent acceptance of the terrible pragmatism that has debased them opens up a visionary perspective. His delighted feeling for the other child's beauty – 'his head / That curl'd like a lamb's back' – becomes, in a movement of unprotesting sympathy, an unconscious affirmation that in *their* sight it cannot be destroyed: on his lips, the rationalizations of the masters acquire an illogical, transcendent suggestiveness:

> 'for when your head's bare
> 'You know that the soot cannot spoil your white hair.'

There is no judgement here. Instead there is an utterly unself-regarding, unquestioning responsiveness to the world which is more positive even than trust, and which seems to be able to transform the most threatening circumstances.

The dramatic movement from the first to this second stanza is the pivot of the poem. The first – stilted, awkward, a distanced account of a whole life – shows the child trying to describe his experiences in the language of adult rationalism: the second – vivid, particular, quick-moving – registers a much more spontaneous, unselfconscious involvement in positive feeling for another. It is an entirely natural transition – the child abandoning his prosaic summary to focus on that which interests and excites him much more – but in presenting it Blake also evaluates it. The 'childish' mode of experience is felt, in the very movement of the verse, in the liveliness of its realization, to have a naturalness and a rightness that the adult mode does not. And as the poem goes on, the transforming power of that unjudging responsiveness becomes more and more apparent. Just as the first chimney-sweeper's quick intuitive sympathy creates its own natural logic, different from (and an unconscious ironic commentary upon) the self-seeking logic of rational utilitarianism which is responsible for their condition, so in little Tom Dacre's unself-pitying dream the harsh facts of their life become the components of a transcendent imaginative vision. The cramped chimneys in which the sweeps were immured and sometimes actually did suffocate are seen as 'coffins of black'; by a similar emotional logic the sky which they could glimpse beyond them as they worked is the ultimate symbol of freedom – 'They rise upon clouds and sport in the wind'. Even the luminous vision of the boys leaping down to bathe in the river has its foundation in fact: as *The Chimney-Sweeper's Friend* reveals, in a reprinted report of evidence taken before a committee of the House of Lords: 'We found that among the less respectable class of chimney-sweepers the boys were taken to the New River [for washing] on a Sunday morning, in the summer season' (p. 175). To the pragmatic adult view, the river is a place to wash in: to the little sweep, it is a place of radiant meaning, like the river of life of the Apocalypse. To the committee, the sweeps are a generalized class of unfortunates: to this boy, as to his friend, they are particular people with familiar names. His dream is no escapist fantasy: what he sees is neither a denial of nor a vague generalization of the particular details of his life, but (as is the case in all dreams) a concentration on those which are emotionally significant, a distortion which is the expression of a profound response to them. The result is a dynamic vision of joyous energy which – as the more alert of Blake's eighteenth-century readers would have perceived with a shock – is created, paradoxically, out of those very elements in the world which would seem to threaten it most.

And it is a vision which contrasts sharply with the rational, common-sense frame of reference evoked by the final moral axiom:

So if all do their duty they need not fear harm.

The child seems merely to be parroting the precepts of the morality that he has been taught and which justifies his exploitation: behind this line one hears the voice of a master telling a boy that if he works hard he will not be whipped, or that the child's soul is safe if he fulfils the 'duties' appropriate to his station. His words are very close to those which a contemporary interlocutor from the polite classes might have hoped to hear: the sympathetic Hanway, for instance, writes:

As to the boys in question, very few of them are taught anything: but we may flatter ourselves that a period of more justice is at hand. *Mr. Raikes*, a gentleman of Gloucester, has lately established what are called *Sunday Schools*, that, instead of permitting children to loiter in idleness, ignorance, and vice, as young chimney-sweepers do with us, the poorest kind of children are collected and taught their duty . . . (p. 9)

I have now before my eyes a particular object of the misery I have endeavoured to describe . . . The object in question, to judge from his discourse, has the full exercise of his reason, and all its glorious faculties; and affections not inferior to the common race of men. He is now twelve years of age, a cripple on crutches, hardly three feet seven inches in stature. . . . His hair felt like a hog's bristles, and his head like a warm cinder . . . He repeats the Lord's-prayer, and the Belief, seemingly acquired by the force of genius, or an instinctive power: he had also heard of such a thing as *Commandments*.

This boy, from a certain active spirit and goodness of heart, still performs his duty to his mistress; and though he cannot move on the surface of the earth without the assistance of crutches, and has aid from the parish, he climbs and sweeps a chimney. (pp. 77–9)

But something of the contradiction in which this lands Hanway – and which is exposed by Blake – is suggested when one turns from such passages as these to those where he appeals to religion not merely as that which helps the oppressed to bear their situation, but as something equally binding on their masters: 'Happy were it for the earth, if the inhabitants were all Christians: if they understood their duty as such, "loving the Lord his God with all his heart, and his neighbour as himself" and the precarious tenure of their present state, when "they fall they would find a stay"' (p. xxvii). Seen in the light of this, the radical irony in the 'all' of Blake's final line becomes clear: an irony that is as much an unconscious indictment as the 'your' of the fourth line of the poem. The sweep may be innocent, but the target of the verse is not. For if *all* did their duty, in the sense of loving their neighbours as themselves, there would indeed be no 'harm' such as that in which this child must live. On his lips, the 'moral' he offers is an unconscious but scathing criticism of those who have taught it him. And it is also a veiled, innocently spoken threat, prefiguring the 'blasting' new-born infant's fear of 'London'. In a society such as this, where all do *not* do their 'duty', 'they' (and the vagueness of the pronoun is significant) must indeed fear harm, for all are debased together.

This latter feeling is a very long way from the sentimental pathos of Bowles's lines, or from a simple humanitarian appeal. And it is reinforced when one considers that for the eighteenth-century reader the figure of the chimney-sweeper would have had other associations besides those of a pitiable object: associations which make Blake's choice of him as the subject of a poem such as this extraordinarily interesting. 'The Chimney Sweeper', as Kathleen Raine has noted,[4] bears a close resemblance to a passage from a Swedenborgian tract published in English translation in 1787, a passage which it is perhaps worth quoting in full:

There are also Spirits amongst those from the Earth Jupiter, whom they call Sweepers of Chimnies, because they appear in like Garments, and likewise with sooty faces . . . One of these Spirits came to me, and anxiously requested that I would intercede for him to be admitted into Heaven; he said, that he was not conscious of having done any Evil, only that he had reprimanded the Inhabitants of his Earth, and that after reprimanding he instructed them . . . I was informed that they are such at first, who are afterwards received amongst those who constitute the Province of the *Seminal Vessels* in the Grand Man or Heaven; for in these vessels the Semen is collected, and is encompassed with a Covering of suitable Matter, fit to preserve the prolific Principle of the Semen from being dissipated, but which may be put off in the Neck of the Uterus, thus what is reserved within may serve for Conception or the Impregnation of the Ovulum; hence also that the seminal Matter hath a strong Tendency and as it were a burning Desire to put itself off, and leave the Semen to accomplish it's end: Somewhat similar appeared likewise in this Spirit: He came again to me, in vile Raiment, and again said, that he had a burning Desire to be admitted into Heaven, and that now he perceived himself to be qualified for that Purpose; it was given me to tell him, that possibly that was a Token that he would shortly be admitted: at that Instant the Angel called to him to cast off his Raiment, which he did immediately with inconceivable Quickness from the Vehemence of his Desire; whereby was represented what is the Nature of their Desires, who are in the Province to which the seminal Vessels correspond. I was informed that such, when they are prepared for Heaven, are stripped of their own

---

[4] Kathleen Raine, *Blake and Tradition* (2 vols., London, 1969), vol. I, pp. 25–6.

Garments, and are clothed with new shining Raiment, and become Angels. They are likened unto Caterpillars, which having passed through that vile State of their Existence, are changed into Nymphs and thus into Butterflies, in which last state they are gifted with new Cloathing, and also with Wings of various Colours, as blue, yellow, silver, or golden; at the same Time they have Liberty to fly in the open Air as in their Heaven, and to celebrate their Marriages, and to lay their Eggs, and thus to provide for the Propagation of their Kind . . .[5]

Miss Raine concentrates on the spiritual significance of the image: the way in which the desire of the sweep to be rid of his 'vile Raiment' is a metaphor for the soul's desire to cast off the body. And in his rendering of the little sweep's dream – at once realistic as a dream-transmutation of elements in his life, and suggestive of exactly this kind of spiritual transcendence – Blake is certainly evoking something of the same metaphoric resonance. Yet his poem – with its patent concern with actual, contemporary social reality and its problematic last line – is clearly not simply a metaphor for a spiritual experience. I think that it is worth considering the not-so-spiritual suggestions of Swedenborg's passage a little more closely. It certainly seems likely that Blake had read this passage,[6] and the closeness of some of its imagery to his suggests that he was very familiar with it. But to all but a small group of his readers it would obviously have been unknown. Its interest, as far as this poem is concerned, lies less in any direct borrowings that Blake may have made from it than in what it suggests about the potency of the sweep as an image of 'burning' and subversive 'Desire'. And such suggestions would have been very familiar to Blake's late eighteenth-century readers, whether or not they were Swedenborgians.

Humanitarian concern for the chimney-sweeps was in 1789 a phenomenon of fairly recent date: until about 1760, Dorothy George points out, 'chimney-sweepers . . . had been regarded as villains ripening for the gallows rather than as objects of compassion'.[7] Because of the seasonal nature of their work, they were often left to beg – or forced to turn to

---

[5] E. Swedenborg, *Concerning the Earths in our Solar System* (London, 1787), section 79. I am grateful to Edward Thompson for pointing out the relevance of this passage.

[6] In his annotations to Swedenborg's *Heaven and Hell*, written about 1790, Blake alludes to section 73 of this work (E591/K939). Noted by David Erdman, *Blake: Prophet against Empire*, revised edn (N.Y., 1969), p. 132.

[7] M. Dorothy George, *London Life in the Eighteenth Century* (Harmondsworth, 1966), p. 242.

crime – during the summer; in the winter, they were sent to call the streets for trade, and because of this had much greater freedom (along with greater hardship) than most other apprentices.[8] Hence their popular image was one of lawlessness and disorder (and, oddly, idleness): mill-owners objecting to Peel's 1802 act for the protection of apprentices in cotton-mills argued that such apprentices were 'composed of the children of beggars, chimney-sweepers and others accustomed to live in total idleness and not infrequently addicted to stealing, swearing and other vices'.[9] It was perhaps this image of unruliness that had made the sweeps constant symbols of subversion in the Wilkite riots of the 1760s and 1770s. John Brewer suggests some other possibilities:

It is difficult to see why chimney-sweeps were so important. Possibly they were regarded as 'liminal' people [i.e. outside the hierarchical structure of the society and representing the values of *communitas*, an egalitarian social order], occupying a twilight world of their own. Both their appearance and their activities would reinforce this view. Hanway certainly thought of them as a group that operated outside the usual mechanisms of social control, but he had his reasons for wanting to exaggerate their unruly and supposedly callous nature. For obvious reasons they were difficult to identify, and this seems to have been a genuine cause for concern on the part of the London magistracy (e.g. *Old Bailey Proceedings*, 1768, 360). Persons described as chimney sweeps may not have been sweeps at all, but simply those who dressed as sweeps, both for the purposes of disguise, and to emphasise the peculiarity of the situation.[10]

The feeling that the sweep was a marginal figure unsubservient to the laws of the society, combined with the obvious sexual symbolism of his trade of pushing his way up chimneys (pointed to by Swedenborg, but also acknowledged in popular folklore in England well into this century, in the custom of a chimney-sweep kissing a bride to bring good luck upon the marriage),[11] made him a very potent image of subversive passion. It is an image which could not have failed to be present in the minds of readers to whom the Wilkes riots were a recent memory, and one which

[8] *Ibid.*, pp. 239–42.

[9] *Ibid.*, p. 252.

[10] John Brewer, *Party Ideology and Popular Politics at the Accession of George III* (Cambridge, 1976), p. 308. For a discussion of 'liminality' see Victor W. Turner, *The Ritual Process* (London, 1969).

[11] Enid Porter, *The Folklore of East Anglia* (London, 1974), p. 26, quotes a case in Suffolk as late as 1969.

would have complicated any simple feelings of humanitarian concern for such a figure. An incident cited by Brewer is extremely suggestive:

on April Fool's day 1771, effigies of the Princess Dowager, Lord Bute, the Speaker of the House of Commons and the two Fox brothers were placed in two carts preceded by a hearse, and taken through the streets of London to the properly constituted execution place of all traitors, Tower Hill, where they were decapitated by a chimney-sweep who also doubled as the officiating minister; they were then ceremoniously burnt.[12]

This chimney-sweep is very different from Blake's innocent child. But the fact that such associations could cluster around such a figure, the closeness of Blake's images to Swedenborg's imagery of 'burning Desire', and the veiled warning of the poem's final line – 'So if all do their duty, they need not fear harm' – make it difficult to see the 'Innocent' chimney-sweeper simply as a wronged victim, whose passive presence is intended to stir the conscience of the polite reader. His dream is too potent, too dynamic for that. He may be unconscious of it, but he hints at the possibility of an avenging energy at work within the society.

And in his innocence he also represents a human potential for an unjudging wholeness of vision, an unself-seeking love, that is unrealized by the social structure within which he must live. For in repeating the platitudes of the morality that allows and even justifies suffering such as his, he is not merely exposing the hypocrisy of those who would maintain the *status quo*. He is also giving expression to the radical implications of the Christianity which has been taught to him. For in another sense, he activates a real truth in the moral cliché he offers. He *does* do his duty, if duty is to be conceived of as the kind of spontaneous and quick-witted and understanding love he shows towards another frightened little boy: in a similar way, little Tom's dream focusses on the release of *others*. And even in conditions of the most unequivocal 'harm' they do seem to find no cause for fear, but a visionary life. For them, tenderly seen particulars – 'his head / That curl'd like a lamb's back', 'thousands of sweepers, Dick, Joe, Ned & Jack' – take on an imaginative dimension that transcends that of 'fact', creating a world of warmth and happiness and mutual concern that is more vivid, and in poetic terms, more real, than the world of

---

[12] Brewer, *Party Ideology*, p. 184.

darkness and coldness and exploitation within which they must live. It is, indeed, exactly the opposite of the outlined 'reality' which surrounds it. But the mainspring of their vision is not escapist fantasy. It is an impulse of imaginative empathy that creates a *shared* transcendent reality:

> 'Hush, Tom! never mind it, for when your head's bare
> 'You know that the soot cannot spoil your white hair.'

Their vision is a vision of possibility released by that impulse, a vision which is not a fantasy-alternative safely insulated from the real world in which they must live, but one which comments unanswerably on what their society accepts as reality, on its failure to actualize the values it purports to hold. In attesting that 'If *all* do their duty, they need not fear harm', Blake's sweep is exposing the essential radicalism of Christianity, a religion of love, not of obedience within an immutable *status quo*, of the spirit, not of the law, of equality, not of subordination.

And it is a vision which cannot be communicated in the debased moral language of this society. The eighteenth-century reader of such a poem would have expected to find it resolved by a summarizing moral. But the moral tag with which this child tries to sum up his story remains, as we have seen, disturbingly ambiguous: on one level, an unconsciously ironic echo of the ideology of subordination which seeks to keep him contented with his lot, on another, charged with a newly radical meaning. The reader is deliberately left uncertain as to which is the correct interpretation – and is forced into a disconcerting awareness of the emptiness of the generalizing, moralizing, aphoristic approach to experience. For the enigmatic abstraction of that echoed moral – 'a Moral like a sting in the tail' (E267/K778) – contrasts tellingly with the little sweep's unjudging, unanalytic, plastic liveliness of vision. The difference between the child's innocence and the rationalizing, generalizing Experience whose words he parrots is not a difference between two moral attitudes towards the world, one good and the other bad, but a difference between two states of being, one within the universe of moral discourse and the other out of it. He is not outlining a superior morality: he is affirming a way of seeing which is not that of the moral law, which was alive before the moral law was constructed upon it, and which questions the pretensions of that law as well as apprehending a reality towards which it can only point. If the poem articulates a religious position, it is not, whether seriously or ironically, that of quiescent Methodism – 'the best available defence of the *status quo*'[13] – but that of antinomianism.

Blake may or may not have been connected with actual antinomian sects in eighteenth-century London.[14] He certainly seems to have been familiar with antinomian ideas – and in particular with those which held that the moral law is a mystifying block to understanding, the result of 'the Sleep which the Soul may fall into in its deadly dreams of Good & Evil when it leaves Paradise following the Serpent',[15] that the divine potential exists in every human being, and that heaven and hell are spiritual states rather than places beyond this world. The connection of such ideas with the kind of vision presented in this poem (as in many other of the *Songs*) is clear enough. Yet 'The Chimney Sweeper' is not a theological tract, nor does it expound even an unorthodox doctrine. It springs from and articulates a whole sense of a society, and its antinomian implications are of interest, less because they point towards Blake's possible connections with or more distant debts to such thinkers, than because of the way in which the poem itself illuminates the complex nature of antinomianism and its relevance to the society which Blake knew.

Blake is not simply exposing suffering and exploitation which had hitherto gone unremarked: as we have seen, others had protested at the condition of the chimney-sweeps, and even within the children's books of the period one finds little poems deploring their lot. By writing what would superficially have appeared to be such a poem, Blake was deliberately engaging with the polite morality of his day in one of its simplest forms, arousing expectations of clear-cut moral instruction in his readers. And 'The Chimney Sweeper' would have forced the more alert of such readers to recognize – not as an abstract idea, but as a difficulty felt in the very act of reading – that their own familiar moral terms, when really located within the social situations to which they were usually so confidently applied, could seem disturbingly double-edged. This is not a simple

[13] Nick Shrimpton, 'Hell's Hymnbook: *Blake's Songs of Innocence and of Experience* and their models', in R. T. Davies and B. G. Beatty (eds), *Literature of the Romantic Period 1750–1850* (Liverpool, 1976), p. 33.
[14] cf. A. L. Morton, *The Everlasting Gospel* (London, 1958).
[15] 'A Vision of the Last Judgment', E553/K614.

'protest poem'. It implicates the reader directly, and refuses to allow him any uncontaminated moral perspective (e.g. of pity, of clearly defined duty) such as conventional 'protest' verse would assume. And hence it offers not a theology, but a dramatization of that conflict between actual social experience and 'official' justifying morality of which the antinomian rejection of the moral law is a natural theological expression. The closing moral platitude by its very unsatisfactoriness exposes the way in which a morality abstracted from the social experience on which it is based can become a radically problematic thing. It is not just that its terms (such as the 'duty' of which Hanway writes) have become devalued, or that it can simply be dismissed as the hypocritical ideology of an exploiting class. It is not entirely meaningless: it can, as we have seen, be turned with devastating meaning on those who profess to hold it. In Blake's own words, 'The Wicked will turn it to Wickedness, the Righteous to Righteousness.'[16] But its meaning depends quite radically on the lips from which it is spoken, and its abstraction (the abstraction necessary to generalization) means that it is always less than – at best a mere pointer towards, at worst a mystifying block to – the reality of vision.

Blake's chimney-sweep (like the other innocent speakers of *Songs of Innocence*) testifies to a human *potentia* which transcends all the distortions and the devaluations which the social experience of his time has left embedded in the language of ordinary moral discourse: his dream is not a vague, unfocussed private aspiration, but a vivid articulation of possibility, activated by an unjudging love, which leads naturally into a sense of how 'all' might be. Again and again, in different ways, the *Songs of Innocence* present such a vision: the finest poetic expression in our language of that sense of the divine within the human which was the inspiration of the seventeenth-century antinomians and which informed their social thinking – the 'Divine Vision' which Blake kept in time of trouble.[17] But it was never for Blake an escapist vision. It was born out of and defined against a painfully intimate sense of all that threatened it most – not merely the suffering and exploitation manifest in late eighteenth-century English society, but the powerful patterns of thinking and feeling which determined and were determined by that society, and towards which contemporary consciousness was inevitably pulled. And to Blake, as the

[16] *Jerusalem* 27, 'To the Jews', E169/K649.　　[17] *Jerusalem* 95.20, E252/K742.

scathing implicit criticism of moral precept in 'The Chimney Sweeper' suggests, the attempt to order experience according to an abstracted moral law was one of the cruxes of the social disaster he saw around him.

Why he felt this can be seen most clearly, perhaps, if one turns to two of the *Songs* which seem to have been designed as companion pieces, the two 'Holy Thursday's. The first, from *Songs of Innocence* (E13/K121-2), is in many ways very similar to 'The Chimney Sweeper'. Like that poem, it deals with a typical object of eighteenth-century charitable concern: like that poem, it would have appeared to its first readers to be an exercise in the popular convention of the moral song, with an improving moral 'tag' at the end. And like 'The Chimney Sweeper', it is a great deal less simple than it at first appears. There is the same curious intermingling of 'vision' and realism: the speaker, like the little sweep, registers a great deal about the actual circumstances he is describing,[18] but seems equally unconcerned with complaining about them. His view of the children's procession is the reverse of escapist: like the little sweep's dream, it is composed of the ordinary, not-very-graceful elements of the scene before him. Indeed, here 'reality' is even more insistently present in the poetry, not merely in the obvious details of the beadles' 'wands' and the regimented seating arrangements, but in the continuous rhythm of marching feet – created by the length of the lines and the large number of short jostling syllables in each, and curiously at odds with the transcendental vision of 'Thames waters' flowing. The plate itself suggests that Blake meant to emphasize the difficult, hobbledehoy movement of the children. In design it is unlike any of the other plates, with its straight horizontal lines of children at top and bottom – children who move stiffly and awkwardly, not at all like the little sweeps in the plate for 'The Chimney Sweeper'. And it is the only

---

[18] cf. the report of the 'Anniversary Meeting of the Charity Children at the Cathedral Church of St. Paul' in Mrs Trimmer's *Family Magazine* for June 1788:

> At half past ten o'clock yesterday morning the doors were opened, and before eleven the church was crowded with as respectable an audience as St. Paul's ever witnessed . . .
>
> The children, to the amount of ten thousand, were seated on a circular scaffolding erected from the organ round the dome of the church, and the children rising and singing the hundredth psalm, with great judgement, had a most solemn effect.
>
> The service was listened to with much more attention than could be expected from so numerous an audience; the singing and chaunting parts being most delightfully warbled by the gentlemen of the choir, the children joining in the Gloria Patria and the Hallelujah.
>
> The sermon, which was excellent, and very apposite, was preached by the Bishop of Norwich.

plate in *Songs of Innocence* which has curling lines and tendrils between every line, and in some places between the words, making the song deliberately difficult to read, and emphasizing its jerky difficult rhythm. There is nothing evasive or escapist about this poem: the vision it presents is rooted in an acute sensitivity to an actual, living situation – a sensitivity which informs and yet does not destroy the larger, more sweeping movement of natural process that is suggested by the imagery.

'Holy Thursday' is unlike 'The Chimney Sweeper' in that the speaker is not himself exactly an innocent. He watches the scene with some consciousness of its implications; he labels the children as 'innocent', where innocence itself would be unselfconscious; he knows that there are other 'multitudes' (this is London in the 1780s) than 'multitudes of lambs'. But he is not the kind of speaker that the reader accustomed to reading children's verse about the poor would have expected. He is not standing back and moralizing over what he sees: to him it is a marvellous spectacle with a life and colour that have nothing to do with moral judgement. His voice has something of the same unmoralizing, unpitying empathy as we catch in the chimney-sweep's picture of Tom Dacre and his dream: as that child is able excitedly to enter into the logic of another's vision, so this watcher registers the jog-trot rhythm of the children's procession with wondering sensitivity, and moves on an expansive echo of their own song:

> Now like a mighty wind they raise to heaven the voice of song,
> Or like harmonious thunderings the seats of heaven among.

And although, like the little sweep's dream with its 'coffins of black' and its 'clouds' of freedom, his vision underlines the inner significance of the everyday – the beadles who carry their wands like snow, the children who sit above their guardians, the radiance which is 'all their own' – it does not moralize it in a knowingly superior way, turning it to a self-congratulatory or protesting purpose. Instead, he makes out of the most disturbing elements of the situation (the visible hierarchy which is suggestively overturned in the seating arrangements, the regimented marching of the children) a quite a-moral vision of beauty and harmony, based in but not confined to a specific scene (as the tenses waver between past and present, to give an effect both of timelessness and particularity).

Like 'The Chimney Sweeper', 'Holy Thursday' ends with a 'moral': a 'moral' which is at once less clichéd than but just as equivocal in tone as that of the other poem:

> Then cherish pity, lest you drive an angel from your door.

One feels here an appeal to a shared tradition of charity, that has its roots in the experience of a more-than-natural dimension in life: the energy of that 'angelic' vision of the children still informs the line (cf. Hebrews xiii.2: 'Be not forgetful to entertain strangers, for thereby some have entertained angels unawares'). Yet there is the same sense of platitudinous flatness in comparison to what has gone before; and the same curious ambiguity of import – an ambiguity which, like that of the other poem, is focussed in the abstract moral term, 'pity'. In one sense, it could be argued that in genuinely seeing the children as 'angels', the poem has defined a radical new meaning for the word (as the chimney-sweep has defined a radical new meaning for 'duty'). And, as in the other poem, this radical new meaning carries with it an implied threat to the polite reader who falls short of it. But in another sense – and especially in the context of what was apparently a child's book – this conclusion is merely a parrotting of an expected platitude that falls far short of summing up what has been imaginatively realized. The charity children were favourite subjects for middle-class self-congratulation: what better example to the child of the 'pity' which his elders so patently practise?

That the song *was* taken thus – as a quite unambiguous appeal to clearly established polite standards – is indicated (as also, incidentally, is its fidelity to fact) by its inclusion in Priscilla Wakefield's children's guide-book, *Perambulations in London, and its environs*, published in 1809. A prominent philanthropist, and one of the earliest promoters of savings banks and friendly societies for the poor, Mrs Wakefield was a practising member of the Society of Friends, and came of a distinguished Quaker family (she was the aunt of Elizabeth Fry, and grand-daughter of the seventeenth-century author of *The Apology for the Quakers*, Robert Barclay). She might thus be taken as a fair example of a certain kind of not-quite-conventional humanitarian concern. But that even such as she did share the fundamental modes of thinking of their class, its habit of appeal to secure general moral standards, is suggested by the way in which she presents Blake's song:

My uncle was present at a most affecting solemnity at this church [St Paul's] last year, and he has promised us that we shall be indulged with the same sight the next summer vacation. About six thousand children, dressed in uniforms of different colours, are assembled here, on benches raised to a great height one above the other, circularly, round the dome. The order with which each school finds its own situation, and the union of so many voices, all raised at one moment to the praise of their great Creator, as they chaunt the hundredth psalm, on the entrance of the clergyman, caused the most delightful and affecting sensation my uncle ever remembered. The solemnity of the place, and the hope that so much innocence, under such protection, would be reared to virtue and happiness, must add greatly to the effect on the minds of the spectators.

This uncommon scene is so well described in the following lines by Mr. Blake, that I think you will forgive me for adding to the length of this letter, though drawn out so far on one subject. [She then quotes 'Holy Thursday' from *Songs of Innocence*.][19]

This introduction, which takes no account of the ironies which twentieth-century critics have found in the final line, reveals a great deal about Blake's radical difference from his contemporaries. For to Blake, a moral term such as 'pity' is clearly problematic, in a way in which to Mrs Wakefield it is not. Where she speaks confidently of 'virtue', and of the 'affecting sensation' such a scene can give to the benevolent observer, Blake offers his curiously double-edged maxim:

> Then cherish pity, lest you drive an angel from your door.

And the effect of the implicit warning is to make the reader question what he sees as 'pity', in a way which Mrs Wakefield's book certainly does not prompt him to do. Indeed, nine years earlier, in her *Reflections on the*

---

[19] Priscilla Wakefield, *Perambulations in London, and its Environs . . . in Letters. Designed for Young Persons* (London, 1809), pp. 181–2. 'Holy Thursday' ends the letter, much as it silences its original hearers in *An Island in the Moon* (E453/K59). This early publication of 'Holy Thursday' has apparently not been noted by Blake scholars. The punctuation Mrs Wakefield inserts is (with one or two minor deviations) the same as that of the only earlier reprinting of the song, in Benjamin Heath Malkin's *A Father's Memoirs of His Child* (London, 1806), pp. 31–2. Blake's plate has only one mark of punctuation (in the last line), which Mrs Wakefield alters in the same way as Malkin. This suggests that his volume, rather than Blake's own, was the source from which she took the song.

It seems to me likely that Mrs Wakefield's volume, rather than an original copy of the *Songs*, is the source from which Jane and Ann Taylor took 'Holy Thursday' for inclusion in the third edition of *their* children's guide to London, *City Scenes, or A Peep into London* (1st edn 1809, 3rd edn 1818). This reprinting of the poem (though not Mrs Wakefield's) is noted in G. E. Bentley and Martin Nurmi (eds), *A Blake Bibliography* (Minneapolis, 1964).

Present Condition of the Female Sex: with suggestions for its Improvement (as its title suggests, a progressive book by late eighteenth-century standards), she had explicitly defended the kind of moral instruction which Blake's line seems to be evoking ironically:

The establishment of schools for the education of the infant poor, is an encouragement to matrimony, and one of the most certain means of promoting a reform in the manners of the lower classes, if they are regulated upon principles adapted to this design; the children, (girls only are here considered) should be instructed with plainness and simplicity in the doctrines of christianity, enforcing by remarks, within the reach of their capacity, the moral precepts it enjoins, and illustrating them by familiar examples, which come home to their own bosoms, and the circumstances of their lives ... The books provided for the instruction and amusement of charity-schools, should be written for the purpose: short lessons of morality, or concerning the inferior obligations of civil life, in clear language, unembarrassed with difficult words, and rendered entertaining by the interest of simple narrative are best adapted to convey the knowledge required by the readers for whom they are designed.[20]

But in offering his 'short lesson of morality' in a context which emphasizes its inconclusiveness and ambiguity, Blake is awakening the same uneasiness about such 'moral precepts' as he does in 'The Chimney Sweeper'. He seems deliberately to be contrasting the substantiality and liveliness of an unmoralizing vision with the distanced (subjunctive) and potentially mystifying abstraction of the expected – in late eighteenth-century terms the quite natural – attempt to order experience according to a generalized moral code.

This suspicion of moral thinking extends not merely to that which seeks to justify the *status quo*, but to that which seeks to oppose it. This is perhaps the most difficult aspect of Blake's poetry, the one in which the foreignness of the antinomian vision strikes the modern reader most

---

[20] Priscilla Wakefield, *Reflections on the Present Condition of the Female Sex: with suggestions for its Improvement* (London, 1798), pp. 184–7. The comparatively progressive nature of Mrs Wakefield's view of education is suggested by a passage following this, which provides an interesting commentary on Blake's 'wands as white as snow':

The cane and the rod are banished, by the refinement of modern manners, from female seminaries of a superior order, it is earnestly wished, that they were likewise excluded from all others, as the use of them serves rather to indulge the angry passions of the teacher, than to produce reformation in the scholar; for where reason & kind treatment are ineffectual, blows are never likely to prevail. Severity hardens the heart and depresses a meritorious emulation. (p. 190)

sharply. And it is one which becomes particularly evident in the second 'Holy Thursday' (E19–20/K211–12). This is a puzzling poem. In one way, as David Erdman points out,[21] it clearly seems closer than its 'Innocent' counterpart to Blake's real attitude towards such events as the charity children's procession: in that sense, it is much less 'roseate' (Erdman's term) and more 'realistic'. And yet in what sense is one to define 'realistic'? The first poem, as we have seen, registers a very great deal about the particular details of the scene it depicts: in the second, we would scarcely know what the speaker was reacting to, did we not have the first 'Holy Thursday' for reference. His consciousness seems to be the subject of the poem.

The difference of this from the poetry of straightforward social concern is evident when one considers Crabbe's contemporary lines on a similar subject:

> Theirs is the house that holds the parish-poor,
> Whose walls of mud scarce bear the broken door;
> There, where the putrid vapours, flagging, play,
> And the dull wheel hums doleful through the day;
> There children dwell who know no parents' care;
> Parents, who know no children's love, dwell there!
> . . .
> Here too the sick their final doom receive,
> Here brought, amid the scenes of grief, to grieve,
> Where the loud groans from some sad chamber flow,
> Mix'd with the clamours of the crowd below;
> Here, sorrowing, they each kindred sorrow scan,
> And the cold charities of man to man:
> Whose laws indeed for ruin'd age provide,
> And strong compulsion plucks the scrap from pride;
> But still that scrap is bought with many a sigh,
> And pride embitters what it can't deny.
>
> (*The Village* (1783) I. 228–49)

Crabbe tells the reader something about what his workhouse is like, but it is not in wealth of detail that the force of the poetry lies. Rather, it is in his generalizing capacity that the reader senses Crabbe's intimacy with the abuses he is describing. It is true that these sufferers are not individualized, nor is their workhouse a clearly depicted place, but the poetry would lose

---

[21] Erdman, *Prophet against Empire*, p. 122.

a good deal if they were. Crabbe is directing attention not towards a vivid realization of a particular scene, but to a much larger crescendo of human misery, whose surge into rage and sinking back into impotence is conveyed through generalization:

> There children dwell who know no parents' care;
> Parents, who know no children's love, dwell there!

The strong syntactic patterning mimes the working of a circular social process in which all these sufferers are hopelessly locked: and because of this we are interested less in the speaker and his local responses than in that of which he speaks.

Exactly the reverse is true of 'Holy Thursday'. In a sense, it seems to spring from the same impulse: an angry response to social abuses which is transformed, by its very intensity, into a much more generalized protest. Yet the difference is startling:

> Is this a holy thing to see
> In a rich and fruitful land,
> Babes reduc'd to misery,
> Fed with cold and usurous hand?

This has none of the powerful, indignant surge of Crabbe's couplets, none of his sure grasp of dynamically shifting relationships. Despite the indignant hiss with which it opens, it seems curiously lacking in confidence, its rhythms disjointed and hesitant. And as the poem goes on, it becomes clear that its speaker is a much more complex and changing creation than is Crabbe's enraged observer. We move from the bitter abruptness of the opening stanza to the plangent echoes of the second, from the dulled monotony of the third to the oddly uncertain stasis of the last. And what is being presented is less a deplorable situation than a psychological process.

Instead of focussing, as Crabbe does, on the perfectly valid reasons for his speaker's anger, Blake dramatizes his progression from the immediate, passionate response of the first stanza to a position of shocked withdrawal – a gradual rigidifying of stance which at length blocks out the possibility of any kind of fruitful interaction with the world which he confronts. From the very opening it is clear that this protesting speaker is not at all like the speaker of the first 'Holy Thursday'. Here there is none of the ready movement of lively responsiveness which one finds in the earlier poem, none of the openness of vision that rejoices as much in 'the grey-headed beadles' with their 'wands as white as snow' as in the children dressed in 'red and blue and green'. This is a judging mentality, which reduces things to their moral qualities, and robs them of their rich reality. The luminous country in which the little children flow along like a river has become merely 'a rich and fruitful land', the venerable and ambiguously awe-inspiring beadles are reduced to 'cold and usurous hand'. And the warmly spontaneous sympathy of one little sweep for another – a sympathy which escapes such moral categorizings as 'pity' – has been replaced by a consciously moralizing protest. This speaker is not noticing things which the other speaker ignored: he is seeing in quite a different way.

By the second stanza, his first reaction of horrified outrage has become a doubting unwillingness to see anything in the world which does not answer to that feeling:

> Is that trembling cry a song?
> Can it be a song of joy?
> And so many children poor?

He hears a dim echo of that larger world of innocence, but his incredulous perception wavers into disbelief, and finally hardens into flat denial:

> It is a land of poverty!

By the third stanza, he is deliberately building up for himself a world in which the worst is the case, a world exactly the opposite of that of the first 'Holy Thursday':

> And their sun does never shine,
> And their fields are bleak & bare,
> And their ways are fill'd with thorns:
> It is eternal winter there.

This has none of the movement and energy of the 'Innocent' song: the active verbs have been replaced by a series of flat copulas, linking stereotyped ideas rather than expressing particular perceptions. There is certainly no sense here, as there is in the earlier poem, that this is a rendition of a real scene, the expression of a moment when the speaker saw what was before him with more than usual vividness and clarity. Yet in spite of its (in one sense) static quality, this stanza dramatizes another stage in its speaker's progression – his growing elaboration of and belief in a totally negative world. The final stanza takes the process to its logical conclusion:

> For where-e'er the sun does shine,
> And where-e'er the rain does fall:
> Babe can never hunger there,
> Nor poverty the mind appall.

For this speaker, a more positive state than that which he confronts and towards which effort might be directed is almost unimaginable. It can be envisaged only in terms of negatives – as the inconceivable opposite of what is.

It is impossible not to feel that these last two stanzas – addressed to readers much more deeply familiar with the Bible than we are today – are meant to evoke and offer an ironic reversal of Revelation vii.16–17:

They shall hunger no more, neither thirst any more; neither shall the sun light on them, nor any heat.

For the Lamb which is in the midst of the throne shall feed them, and shall lead them unto living fountains of waters: and God shall wipe away all tears from their eyes.

Where Revelation images a transcendent state, not bound by the laws of the natural world, Blake's speaker, searching for a positive vision, can only offer the flattest gesture towards the order of nature. And where Revelation goes on to realize a magnificent vision of hope and comfort, Blake's speaker ends with a chilling, self-reflexive confession:

> Nor poverty the mind appall.

For as well as indignation, the final line of this poem expresses a horrified self-awareness, as the speaker realizes the extent to which his own outrage has paralysed him. There is a submerged pun in 'appall', which takes up and recognizes the logic of that withdrawal from reality which the rest of the poem has dramatized. For the statement that hunger and poverty cannot exist in the *real* world is not just a pathetic fallacy: it is also a dim apprehension of that truth which is demonstrated in the first 'Holy Thursday'. If this speaker *could* approach the world in a spirit of trusting, unjudging acceptance, if his mind were not 'appalled' by 'poverty' (and the suggestion is that it is its own poverty which casts a 'pall' over it, as much as the suffering to which he is responding), perhaps he would see a different world, a world at once more real and more beautiful, a world in which 'cherishing pity' would be at least potentially meaningful. But the moralizing, abstracting indignation within which he is locked cuts him off from any such reality.

Blake does not mock his speaker's dilemma. Indeed, one feels the force of his own direct anger – an anger which is registered again and again in his marginalia – in that first impassioned outburst. The protest is partly his own. Yet the poem is clearly not, as one of the best of Blake's critics has claimed, 'a direct moral comment on the London world of his time, using . . . simple metres to give force and emphasis':[22] it is a subtle dramatization of the psychological process initiated by 'direct moral comment'. As Blake would put it, 'If you go on So, the result is So.'[23] If the speaker's first angry protest is understandable, the colourless world to which his judgement leads seems like a hopeless withdrawal from any possibility of alleviating the situation. Blake pushes his 'protest' to its logical conclusion, and implicitly evaluates it at every stage. For him, such moral outrage, however justified it may seem, is not liberating, but ultimately a sterile, egocentric trap: its end is an immersion in subjective feeling which reduces reality to a series of self-produced abstractions, and cannot convincingly imagine any possibility other than what is.

What is it that makes this outrage – which to the modern reader may well seem a more right-minded reaction to the sight of the charity children than exclamations at their beauty – so disastrously limiting? Blake's fullest answer to this is in 'London' (E26–7/K216), one of the greatest of the *Songs of Experience*, and one which is often seen as a poem of 'social protest'. It certainly does offer a powerful vision of what is wrong with the society it depicts. But it is significantly different from other protest poems of its time, not merely because of its richer imaginative sense of the inter-relationships that make up that society, but also because of the self-reflexive consciousness that informs it.

Blake begins not with a confidently public voice, but as a lonely wanderer at a remove from and 'marking' the life about him. As in the second 'Holy Thursday', it is on his consciousness rather than on the evils

[22] D. W. Harding, *Experience into Words* (Harmondsworth, 1974), p. 36.
[23] Annotations to Watson, E607/K392.

he confronts that the opening stanza focusses: the distinction becomes clear when one compares Johnson's satiric portrait of London, published fifty years before:

> Here malice, rapine, accident, conspire,
> And now a rabble rages, now a fire;
> Their ambush here relentless ruffians lay,
> And here the fell attorney prowls for prey;
> Here falling houses thunder on your head,
> And here a female atheist talks you dead.[24]

Johnson's active verbs direct attention to the varied, distinctive life he sees before him. But there is little such life in the Blake: his speaker wanders apart and 'marks' the same message everywhere:

> I wander thro' each charter'd street,
> Near where the charter'd Thames does flow,
> And mark in every face I meet
> Marks of weakness, marks of woe.

He appeals to no obvious audience, for he cannot assume, as Johnson does, that there is a generalized yet familiar 'you' on whom he can rely to share his feelings. His sense of the city is a thin and obsessive one, and it is deliberately dramatized as thin and obsessive.

For if in the first two lines he registers the man-made constriction not only of the streets, but also of the flowing river, by the second half of the stanza he is recognizing something similar in his own activity:

> And mark in every face I meet
> Marks of weakness, marks of woe.

The relentless categorizing which stamps the Thames as surely as it does the streets is like his own mode of relating to the world. The pattern of the stanza is one of harsh monotony bearing down upon the hopeful iambic rise of that opening 'I wander': by the final line, the trochaic substitution at the opening of the second has become an established trochaic rhythm. And in each line the strongest stress falls on the sound-linked delimiting words, 'mark' and 'charter'd', which cut short the possibilities for spontaneous action registered in 'wander', 'flow' and 'meet'. The speaker's imaginatively bankrupt repetition of these words drives home the sense of a harsh,

---

[24] 'London' (1738), vol. II, pp. 13–18.

restrictive categorizing which seeks to contain all within its own mould. If he can see 'marks' in the faces around him, 'marking' is what he does.

David Erdman[25] and Edward Thompson[26] have both pointed to the way in which, by 1793, 'charter'd' had become a central word in political debate, as a result of Paine's ironic demystification of its old Whig meaning:

It is a perversion of terms to say, that a charter gives rights. It operates by a contrary effect, that of taking rights away. Rights are inherently in all the inhabitants; but charters, by annulling these rights in the majority, leave the right by exclusion in the hands of a few . . . all charters have no other than an indirect negative operation. They do not give rights to A, but they make a difference in favour of A by taking away the right of B, and consequently are instruments of injustice.[27]

Blake's opposition of man-made 'charters' and flowing river suggests that he means his readers to take up this newly acquired ironic sense of the word. But the reader of 1793, however familiar with *The Rights of Man*, would also have been pressingly aware of its more positive resonances – resonances on which Wordsworth was to draw, four years later, in 'The Old Cumberland Beggar':

> to the heart
> Of each recalling his peculiar boons,
> His charters and exemptions . . .   (117–19)

And in the same notebook in which 'London' was first drafted, we find Blake playing on the sound-link between 'charter'd' and 'cheating':

> The cheating waves of charter'd streams.   (E464/K166)

It is a suggestive entry. For in using 'charter'd' in 'London', Blake is not simply emphasizing its new, reversed meaning: he is forcing his reader into a disconcerting sense of the 'cheating' nature of the word, its capacity to act as a mask for hypocrisy. Paine's demystification of the term is a magnificent piece of polemic. But Blake moves beyond polemic to a dramatization of what it is like to live within his 'chartering' society, and to try to apprehend the world through its categories. The speaker of 'London' repeats the word in a way which registers little sense of difference

---

[25] Erdman, *Prophet against Empire*, pp. 276–7.
[26] cf. chapter 2 above.
[27] Thomas Paine, *Rights of Man* (Harmondsworth, 1969), pp. 242–3.

between the objects to which it is applied – the man-made streets, the freely flowing Thames. And his mode of seeing is exactly like the political system of chartering, which must distance and reduce to abstraction the human realities on which it operates. Within this society, where political strategies are at a remove from real human meanings, the very effort to make sense of experience is tainted. Language has ceased to be the vehicle for these meanings, and become disturbingly ambivalent and 'cheating'. As Blake elsewhere said, 'In Equivocal Worlds Up & Down are Equivocal' (E668/K785).

And nobody within such a society is free simply to comment or protest: all are implicated. In the first stanza of 'London', Blake's speaker turns from a contemplation of the 'charter'd' streets and the 'charter'd' Thames (the only way in which he seems able to see them) to reflect on his own activity:

> And mark in every face I meet
> Marks of weakness, marks of woe.

The abstracting division by which the 'chartering' society works is, he recognizes, equally a function of his own consciousness. And the sense of an inevitable and imprisoning relationship between the 'facts' he sees and the way in which he sees is reinforced by the use of 'mark' as both verb and object.

Edward Thompson, in pointing to the mingling of apocalyptic vision and acute social observation in this poem, has suggested some of the associations which the noun 'mark' would have had for those moving, like Blake, in the radical religious groups of eighteenth-century London – associations which throw the 'buying and selling' imagery of the poem into sharp relief.[28] 'And he causeth all, both small and great, rich and poor, free and bond, to receive a mark in their right hand, or in their foreheads: And that no man might buy or sell, save he that hath the mark of the beast' (Revelation xiii. 16–17). I think it is worth exploring some of the other resonances which readers intimate with the Bible would have felt in the word. For in a passage of which Blake is curiously reminiscent,

[28] cf. chapter 2 above. Thompson points out that this passage refers to 'marks' of salvation, but I cannot accept his argument that this destroys its relevance. Blake *is*, as Thompson says, depicting a universal process, in which all are equally involved: and therefore he seems to me to be deliberately evoking the resonance of Biblical passages such as this in order to question their judging separation of damned from saved. 'Marking' is of the same order as 'chartering'.

'marking' is a strategy of judgement: 'And the LORD said unto him, Go through the midst of the city, through the midst of Jerusalem, and set a mark upon the foreheads of the men that sigh and that cry for all the abominations that be done in the midst thereof' (Ezekiel ix. 4). And this marker of those who sigh and cry in the city is, significantly, 'a man clothed in linen, with a writer's inkhorn by his side' (ix. 3). It is not merely the external rottenness of his society that Blake is concerned with, but the function of those within it who try to judge it.

He sees it as a deeply ambiguous function. In the Swedenborgian circles with which he was familiar, Revelation xiii. 16 was commonly glossed as referring symbolically to the beast's 'prohibition against anyone's learning or teaching anything but what is acknowledged and received in the doctrine'.[29] And the doctrine of the beast was the doctrine of salvation by faith alone; a withdrawal from any responsibility for alleviating suffering in the world. In other words, to 'mark' was to be locked within a mystifying ideology which served as an apologia for and preserver of the *status quo*.

Both these kinds of suggestion lie behind Blake's use of 'mark'. On the one hand, the 'marks' that he sees are the external signs of a rotten society, the brands on the faces of the damned. On the other, the 'marking' that he does is the internal logic of that society, a paralysing mental strategy which cannot 'learn or teach anything' but the same proclamation of weakness and woe. If his speaker is a lonely wanderer, pointing to the evils he sees before him, he is more deeply and consciously implicated in the abstracting modes of his society than anyone else. One catches here also an echo of Lamentations (of which there are many other echoes in 'London'): 'For the sins of her prophets, and the iniquities of her priests, that have shed the blood of the just in the midst of her. They have wandered as blind men in the streets, they have polluted themselves with blood, so that men could not touch their garments' (Lamentations iv. 13–14). As the judge of his society, this speaker is not free of the taint he sees: he is polluted.

He wanders as a blind man in the streets. For in the second stanza, the nature of his relation to the world becomes steadily more apparent:

> In every cry of every Man,
> In every Infant's cry of fear,

---

[29] E. Swedenborg, *Apocalypse Explained*, section 840.

> In every voice, in every ban,
> The mind-forg'd manacles I hear.

The constant repetitions suggest the meagreness of his grasp on reality: in marked contrast to Johnson, with his vigorous feeling for the different noises of the city, he seems to have little sense of the multifariousness of the world before him. Like the speaker of the second 'Holy Thursday', he hears but one message in everything, and cannot hear anything clearly. And the regular metrical beat, from which the speaking rhythm scarcely varies, adds to the impression of trapped claustrophobia. It is an impression that is perhaps most strikingly rendered by the syntax: the long piling-up of one object after another, the active verb at the end overwhelmed by the inversion. This 'I' is not in control: he is dominated by what he hears. He is trapped within the world he is trying to judge.

And he recognizes the nature of his entrapment: the self-reflexiveness implicit in the first stanza is taken up and extended in the image of 'mind-forg'd manacles'. 'Manacles' is suggestive both in its figurative and its literal sense: these are fetters, but fetters which very specifically bind the hands that might help one another (and one is reminded again of the paralysing doctrine of salvation by faith alone which the Swedenborgians saw as the mark of the beast). And 'forg'd' has both concrete associations of the blacksmith's shop, and its other meaning of fraudulent fabrication: these 'manacles' are both devastatingly real and cheatingly equivocal. Blake is not simply diagnosing the repressiveness of his society. True, the image can be seen partly in this way: as Erdman notes, there is a contemporary parallel for such a diagnosis in Imlay's praise of the Ohio for its freedom from the priestcraft which elsewhere 'seems to have forged fetters for the human mind'.[30] But on the opposite side of the political debate, and in one curious way closer to Blake (whose fetters are after all forged not for but by the mind) Edmund Burke had written in his 1791 *Letter to a Member of the National Assembly*, 'Society cannot exist, unless a controlling power upon will and appetite be placed somewhere; and the less of it there is within, the more there must be without. It is ordained in the eternal constitution of things, that men of intemperate minds cannot be free. Their passions forge their fetters.'[31] Blake's 'mind-forg'd', whether an

[30] Erdman, *Prophet against Empire*, p. 277n.
[31] Edmund Burke, *Writings and Speeches* (London, Beaconsfield edn, n.d.), vol. IV, pp. 51–2.

explicit echo or not, reads like an ironic commentrary on both sides of the debate, on the very terms in which the debate has been conducted. The radical would trace the ills of society to the 'objective' manacles of repression, the Old Whig to the 'subjective' failings of human nature. But for Blake the dispute over which is to blame is meaningless, for both are inextricably fused. The mechanisms of repression which are audible and visible around him are intimately present in the 'mind' itself. And there is, significantly, no direction as to *whose* mind is meant – because Blake is pointing to a condition from which no member of this society, including his speaker, is exempt. He cannot, like Johnson, simply stand apart and judge its workings, for they are shared by and focussed in himself.

The two opening stanzas of 'London' explore the nature of the predicament which is recognized at the end of the second 'Holy Thursday': they dramatize a speaker whose mind is 'appalled' by 'poverty', and show how even in his efforts to protest at what he sees he is part of the 'cheating' abstraction from felt human values that has produced it. Yet his is a far more self-reflexive consciousness than that portrayed in the second 'Holy Thursday': he recognizes his own implication increasingly at every stage, and not just in a final moment of paralysed horror. And the recognition leads, in the third stanza, to a startling dramatic shift:

> How the Chimney-sweeper's cry
> Every black'ning Church appalls;
> And the hapless Soldier's sigh
> Runs in blood down Palace walls.

The marking 'I' of the opening has disappeared; the syntactic structure in which he is nominally in control is abandoned. And the result is that the social interconnections obscured by his abstracting consciousness become manifest. The generalizing sameness of 'every . . . every . . . every', the dimly realized cries and voices of the second stanza give way to sharply specific images; the regularity of the iambic beat changes to the heavy crushing physicality of the trochaic. No longer are we offered a succession of passive signs of generalized 'weakness' and 'woe': the separated marks and cries have become active forces within a mutually interdependent, mutually damning, network of relationships. And the reader is made suddenly, sharply aware that the essential strategy of this society is, when exposed, the same as that which has been manifested in the consciousness of the man who seeks to judge it. It is, very exactly, one of *marking* – blackening, daubing with blood, blighting with plague. This is the speaker's mode of experience – isolated and at a remove from any positive human reciprocity, yet imprinting his own damning stamp on everything, like the abstracting legal process of chartering, like the sweep and soldier, outside of and marking the walls of church and palace, like the harlot cursing in the streets at midnight. There seems to be no other way for human beings to conceive of or relate to one another in this society; 'protest' is infected at its source.

Yet this poem is very different from the second 'Holy Thursday'. And as I have suggested, the difference seems to lie, most crucially, in its speaker's relentless self-awareness. He does not assume a position of righteous indignation: from the very beginning he recognizes his own implication in that which he sees: 'I . . . mark.' It is a recognition which seems, as the poem progresses, to paralyse his judgement, for the realization that any attitude he can adopt towards his society is tainted makes it impossible for him to take up any attitude at all. He simply 'hears'. Yet the effect of the two final stanzas is the reverse of quietism or passive acceptance, and their apocalyptic tone is very different from the thin, enclosed desperation of the opening. For as he ceases to assume the controlling perspective of judgement, the reader becomes aware not of his protesting voice, but of an unavoidable logic in the society that does not depend on him at all. We have moved from his opening 'marking', where the diversity before him was analytically abstracted to his own terms, to a much more immediate vision of society as human beings in relationship. It is an exploiting relationship, a distorting relationship, and felt more directly as such: the reversal of norms, which was obliquely recognized in his ironic use of 'charter'd', focusses finally in the concretely shocking image of 'Marriage hearse'. And the dynamics of the society, no longer filtered through his distancing consciousness, have a power and a reality of which his own 'marking' can be but a thin echo. Its cries and sighs and curses are no longer simply things which strike his ear, but tangible signs of shame, and by the end, active forces for destruction. The 'marking' of the protester has given way to a sense of a certain retribution coming from forces far more potent and overwhelming than his own isolated consciousness; a retribution that, as the uncompromising present indicative tense asserts, cannot be distanced into some future, but is implicit in what is.[32]

The self-reflexiveness of 'London' has its counterpart in the double-edged maxims of the 'Innocent' 'Holy Thursday' and 'The Chimney Sweeper': all convey a radical uneasiness with the secure moral judgement which their readers would have expected. We are left not with protest, but with something less distancing and more immediately disconcerting – a sense not only of the instability of any moral judgement within the society that has been depicted, but of its active implication in that which it seeks to condemn. Such moralizing, Blake implies, dehumanizes by abstracting from and distancing the actuality of experience: it erects a law which, because abstracted, can all too easily be used to justify the powerful and mystify the powerless. And – as the diagnostic 'I mark' of 'London' suggests – it is something which man does, for which he is actively responsible.

One sees Blake approaching and worrying over this intuition in the notebook drafts of his most explicit poetic statement about moralizing, 'The Human Abstract'. The first of these drafts (K164) contrasts the singing of an Angel:

> 'Mercy, Pity, Peace
> 'Is the world's release.'

with the curse of a Devil:

> 'Mercy could be no more,
> 'If there was nobody poor,
>
> 'And pity no more could be,
> 'If all were as happy as we.'

Morality, Blake argues, is enabled by the very unsatisfactoriness of the social system: the Devil is given the last word. And the poem proceeds to its sardonic conclusion:

> Down pour'd the heavy rain
> Over the new reap'd grain,

[32] For a fuller discussion of this poem, see my article, 'The Poet in Society: Blake and Wordsworth on London', in *Literature and History*, 3 (March 1976), and Stan Smith's reply to it, 4 (Autumn 1976).

> And Mercy & Pity & Peace descended
> The Farmers were ruin'd & harvest was ended.

This is a satiric exposure of the kind of apologia for the *status quo* common enough in the eighteenth century, and exemplified in writers such as Soames Jenyns: the doctrine that all evil somehow tended towards and was an essential part of a general scheme of good. The implication of this view was that poverty and unhappiness were designed by God to call forth the desirable virtues of mercy and pity in those who were fortunate enough not to suffer them. But, as Blake scathingly suggests, the worm's-eye view of such 'moral virtues' is very different from the 'official' one. The very notion of an objective morality is ironically questioned.

But the notebook entries do not end there. Blake continues to worry over his moral terms, re-working and re-wording his 'Devil's' intuition:

> And by distress increase
> Mercy, Pity, Peace . . .

> And Miseries' increase
> Is Mercy, Pity, Peace . . .

Finally, several pages later, he works these speculations into 'The human Image' (K174). The opening stanza is, in fact, the Devil's curse, but Blake has crossed out the second line, and replaced it with a more active statement:

> Pity could be no more,
> If *we* did not *make* somebody poor.

> (my italics)

The question at the root of his thinking has finally become clear. He is no longer simply stressing the double-edged nature of moral terms within an inegalitarian society, but he is pointing to their active role in creating and justifying and maintaining such a society. And it is no longer an external system of social interconnections that he is describing, but a process in which 'we' – the polite reader and author of the *Songs*, in our humanitarian (even, in eighteenth-century terms, progressive) concern for 'the poor', the chimney-sweeps, the charity children, the little black boy – are crucially implicated. It is not just that the poem accuses its readers of being the beneficiaries of an exploiting social order – 'your chimneys I sweep'.

Much more immediately, it suggests that their very modes of thought – even those which seem most praiseworthy – manifest the same abstracting, distancing strategies which have produced the social consequences that they seek to condemn. The counterproductive process operates within the mind, as well as within the society.

There is an obvious logical and psychological truth in what Blake says: unless we regard somebody as poor, then we cannot feel 'pity' for him; unless we regard somebody as less happy than ourselves, then we cannot feel 'mercy'. The insight is one which is developed in Swedenborg's *Heaven and Hell*, which Blake annotated in 1790:

That every good has an opposite evil, and every truth an opposite falsity, may be known from this, that there is not anything that has not reference to its opposite, and that its quality and degree is known from its opposite, and degree; and this is the origin of all perception and sensation.[33]

Freud was to make a similar point, over a hundred years later:

Were it always light we should not distinguish between light and dark, and accordingly could not have either the conception of, nor the word for, light . . . It is clear that everything on this planet is relative and has independent existence only in so far as it is distinguished in its relation to and from other things . . . Since every conception is thus the twin of its opposite, how could it be thought of at first, how could it be communicated to others who tried to think it, except by being measured against its opposite?[34]

But for Blake, the problem is not merely a metaphysical or a psychological one: it is informed with a dialectical consciousness of its social determinants and dynamics. And it is on the latter that he focusses. For Swedenborg, the interdependence of good and evil is an unquestionable fact of philosophy; for Freud, it is a necessary condition of conscious thought. But for Blake, it is something which man *does*, for which he is responsible. And the implication of his stanza (as in 'London', a positive implication, which seems to be released by the unsparing self-reflexiveness of 'we . . . make somebody poor') is that he has freedom to do otherwise,

[33] E. Swedenborg, *Heaven and Hell*, 2nd edn (London 1784), section 541.
[34] Quoted from Karl Abel by Freud, in '*The Antithetical Sense of Primal Words*, a Review of a Pamphlet by Karl Abel, *Über den Gegensinn der Urworte*, 1884' (1910), *Collected Papers of Sigmund Freud*, trans. Joan Riviere (Randon, 1925), vol. IV, p. 187.

to create an almost unimaginably different world, in which the other-belittling mystification of 'moral virtue' would be impossible:

> Pity *would* be no more
> If we did not make somebody poor.

Such a world is not, of course, created in 'The Human Abstract'. Blake traces the counterproductive process of moral reasoning to its logical conclusion, showing how the self-created, abstracted moral law can take on a pseudo-life of its own, and turn against man and enslave him; and presenting the same double-layered vision of the interpenetration of dehumanizing mental and social strategies as is implicit in the second 'Holy Thursday' and 'London'. Even the second couplet has retreated from the direct self-accusation of the first:

> And mercy no more could be,
> If all were as happy as we.

And as the poem proceeds, an uncontrollable social and subjective drama is unfolded, a drama in which moral terms are reified and the ambiguities which the *Songs of Innocence* revealed in them are made active and manifest. 'Moral Virtues', Blake later wrote, in his catalogue to 'A Vision of the Last Judgment', 'do not exist; they are allegories and dissimulations' (E553/K614). But the process of 'allegory and dissimulation' to which the creation of an abstracted moral law gives rise is a frighteningly real one, and has its own uncontrollable and contorted logic – a logic which works both in the society[35] and the mind. And it leads inevitably to the monstrous reification of that Tree which 'grows in the Human Brain', the 'Tree of Knowledge of Good and Evil' against which Blake fulminated all his life:

> Shooting out against the Light
> Fibres of a deadly night,
> Reasoning upon its own dark Fiction,
> In doubt which is Self Contradiction?
> Humility is only doubt,
> And does the Sun & Moon blot out,
> Rooting over with thorns & stems
> The buried Soul & all its Gems.
>
> . . .

---

[35] Erdman, *Prophet against Empire*, pp. 271–2.

'Am I not Lucifer the Great,
'And you my daughters in Great State,
'The fruit of my Mysterious Tree
'Of Good & Evil & Misery[36]

'The Everlasting Gospel', from which this comes, is Blake's fullest poetic presentation of the antinomian theology which seems to have lain behind his thinking. But that theology – with its vision of a coming Apocalypse, its attack on the moral law, and its valuing of the divine *potentia* within the human – informs all of his writing, and can be seen in the *Songs* to be the coherent expression of a sophisticated sense of the interior and exterior workings of his society: of what is wrong with them, and of how they might be transcended. One traces it in them in many ways – in the vision of an unmoralized, unhierarchical, reciprocity and harmony presented in such *Songs of Innocence* as 'Nurse's Song' and 'The Shepherd' (both Songs whose central figures would be expected to represent guidance and instruction); in the ironic stress in others of them on the double-edged ambiguity of moral precepts which their readers would never have thought to question; in the more subtle, less apocalyptic sense of a moral frame which will not quite fit conveyed by the echoes and half-rhymes of 'The Divine Image':

> For Mercy has a human heart,
> Pity a human face,
> And Love, the human form divine,
> And Peace, the human dress.   (E12/K117)

But one traces it above all in the self-reflexiveness which will not allow Blake to assume a position of superiority to or separateness from the dynamics of the society of which he is a member –

> Pity would be no more
> If *we* did not make somebody poor.

– and which leads, in *Songs of Experience*, to a profound uneasiness with any moral attitude (even a protesting one) which speakers within this society can adopt. It is an uneasiness which gives way, in 'London' to an apocalyptic sense of a quite different kind of judgement: not the tainted dehumanizing judgement of moral abstraction, but the surrealistically concrete

[36] E512/K753 and K759.

vengeance implicit in the exploiting mechanisms of society itself. 'The tygers of wrath', said Blake, 'are wiser than the horses of instruction'. And it is surely significant that the only one of the *Songs of Experience* to present a speaker who does not constrict what he beholds to his own limiting terms is one in which he is not confidently judging what he sees, or fitting it into some abstract pre-established pattern; but one composed entirely of a series of halting questions, in which he half-fearfully contemplates energies which his own consciousness cannot contain, which challenge any standards of judgement he can bring to them:

> What the hammer? what the chain?
> In what furnace was thy brain?
> What the anvil? what dread grasp
> Dare its deadly terrors clasp?
>
> When the stars threw down their spears,
> And water'd heaven with their tears,
> Did he smile his work to see?
> Did he who made the Lamb make thee?   (E25/K214)

CHAPTER 4

EMBLEMS OF MELANCHOLY
FOR CHILDREN:
THE GATES OF PARADISE

FRANK M. PARISI

Trembling & pale sat Tharmas weeping in his clouds

Why wilt thou Examine every little fibre of my soul
Spreading them out before the Sun like Stalks of flax to dry
The infant joy is beautiful but its anatomy
Horrible Ghast & Deadly nought shalt thou find in it
But Death Despair & Everlasting brooding Melancholy

Thou wilt go mad with horror if thou dost Examine thus
Every moment of my secret hours Yea I know
That I have sinnd & that my Emanations are become harlots
I am already distracted at their deeds & if I look
Upon them more Despair will bring self murder on my soul
O Enion thou art thyself a root growing in hell
Tho thus heavenly beautiful to draw me to destruction

Sometimes I think thou art a flower expanding
Sometimes I think thou art fruit breaking from its bud
In dreadful dolor & pain & I am like an atom
A Nothing left in darkness yet I am an identity
I wish & feel & weep & groan Ah terrible terrible
The Four Zoas i, page 4 (E298/K265)

The Gates of Paradise occupies a special place in Blake's work for two reasons: because it was his first attempt at a work which would convey its meaning primarily by pictorial means and because it was the only work of his early years which he chose to reissue in a substantially altered form during the period of the later prophetic books. Unfortunately, the meaning of the earlier series has remained largely obscure. Commentators have dealt at length only with the later issue and indeed have chosen to concentrate almost exclusively on what it shares with the prophetic books. The purpose of this essay is to bring to light the meaning of the *Gates* as Blake originally intended it in his first issue of the series.

In 1793 William Blake issued his 'book of small engravings', entitled *For Children: The Gates of Paradise*. Death, in one form or another, is the subject of seven of the designs. The worm appears in two of them, and the grave in three. There are scenes of imprisonment, torture, murder and suicide; the faces of the characters tell of grief, fear, dread and despair. These designs may seem religiose or morbid today, especially in light of the title, but in Blake's own time the series would have appealed to a widespread taste for melancholy themes.[1]

In the visual arts melancholy had for quite some time a major part in the emblem tradition, culminating with the immensely popular *Emblems* of Francis Quarles (1635). When the *Emblems* eventually went out of print, the bleak outlook, the complaining tone and the mist and gloom of the graveyard became the breeding ground for a school of morbid contemplation, dominated by Young, Blair and Hervey. In this school melancholy continued to be seen as the condition of mind inherited from the fall and manifested as a kind of spiritual starvation or even demonic possession. At the same time melancholy was associated, in elegies, odes, laments and descriptive poems, with reflection, solitude and delight in nature.[2] And in yet another way, melancholy was associated with fancy and, to some degree at least, in Collins and Warton, with the creative imagination.[3]

[1] Contemporary references were few and varied. J. T. Smith referred to the *Gates* as 'a pretty little series of plates', while Allan Cunningham thought that Blake's object had been to 'represent the innocence, the happiness, and the upward aspirations of man', and that the 'mysterious halo' of the *Gates* would raise 'feelings of devotion'. Frederick Tatham, on the other hand, may have had a closer acquaintance with the series, for he presented his copy (copy F) of *For the Sexes: The Gates of Paradise* to Edward Bird following the funeral of Catherine Blake (references repr. G. E. Bentley Jr, *Blake Records* (Oxford, 1969), pp. 460, 486, 411). Reproductions of *The Gates of Paradise* are readily available in the two modern editions of Blake's writings (G. L. Keynes (ed.), *The Complete Writings of William Blake* (Oxford, 1966); and D. V. Erdman (ed.), *The Poetry and Prose of William Blake* (N.Y., 1965). See also figs 8, 15 and 16 below. For the purposes of this essay, the differences between the plates used for these reproductions, copy B of *For the Sexes: The Gates of Paradise*, and the plates of *For Children: The Gates of Paradise* are not significant.

[2] See E. M. Sickels, *The Gloomy Egoist* (N.Y., 1932).

[3] See for instance, Collins, 'The Passions. An Ode for Music'; and Warton, 'The Pleasure of Melancholy' and 'Ode to Solitude'. Burton's and Dürer's conceptions of melancholy also retained a certain currency. See Milton, *Poems on Several Occasions*, ed. Warton (1785, revised edn 1791), in which Warton explained how Milton had not abandoned the idea that Melancholy was the

All of these poets appealed to their audiences more through sympathetic attachment than through argument. They were concerned with the wretched unhappiness of the present – that is, with man after the fall and, more importantly of course, with his redemption. Whatever one thinks of their success, it is unquestioned that Young, Blair and Hervey were trying to answer the discontent of their times with prophetic and apocalyptic messages, just as Collins and Warton were trying to bring back to life a bardic and prophetic character who would signify that the nation was headed for greater accomplishments.[4] If Blake's series surpasses the achievements of these poets, one should not forget that the *Gates* begins by sharing many of their premises and aims.

The *Gates of Paradise* also appears to have many things in common with the emblem books of the eighteenth century. But upon closer examination it can be seen that the similarities lie only on the surface.[5] By the middle of the century emblems had long since ceased to offer a viable medium for the combination of text and design and books of emblems were by then addressed only to children. Blake's correspondent, Dr Trusler, for instance, published a book in 1790 entitled *The Progress of Man and Society*, which superficially resembles the *Gates* in its use of the mime of the cycle of life, the oratorical tone of the text, the subjects of the worm and the caterpillar, the four primary elements, the traveller, and the terrors of the imagination. Yet Trusler's book does not come close to the achievement of the *Gates*. Trusler's main concern was how to get on in the world; just as in another of his publications, *The Way to be Rich and Respectable* (1775), he converts every jot of information to that currency.

So also, the similarity between Plate 7 of the *Gates* and the many emblems of boys chasing butterflies turn out to be less significant than

daughter of Genius. He also explained Milton's debt to Dürer for the motifs of the black visage, the 'looks commercing with the skies', the 'sable stole of Cypress lawn', and the 'Cherub Contemplation'. And he suggested Burton's 'Author's Abstract' as another of Milton's sources. My understanding of the importance of Warton in this matter is due to a number of discussions with Michael Phillips.

4 See Northrop Frye, 'Toward Defining an Age of Sensibility', *Journal of English Literary History*, 23 (1956), 144–52.
5 For a general discussion of the emblem literature see Mario Praz, *Studies in Seventeenth Century Imagery* (Rome, 1964); Rosemary Freeman, *English Emblem Books* (London, 1948). For the connection with Blake, see Piloo Nanavutty, 'Blake and the Emblem Literature', *Journal of the Warburg and Courtauld Institutes*, xv (1952), 258–62; and Jean Hagstrum, *William Blake, Poet and Painter* (Chicago, 1964).

they may appear to be at first. Books such as Trusler's[6] did not provide Blake with models in the usual sense of that term. Indeed, *The Gates of Paradise* did not imitate the emblem books of the eighteenth century so nearly as it mimicked them. One may see in Blake the standard emblem of a youth chasing a butterfly, but Blake's meaning is completely different from the usual theme of 'vain pursuits'. The butterflies are probably the female aspect of nature for Blake, and according to his original motto, the boy is not a foolhardy youth, but the child of Mordant and Amavia who cannot wash the blood of his parents from his hands.

Despite the fact that the major artists in Blake's day had rejected the emblem for their serious work, the emblem still held a certain attraction in theory. From the time of Alciati until the end of the eighteenth century, emblem-makers defended themselves against charges of obscurantism with the legend that emblems originated in the 'hieroglyphicks' of the Egyptians. The history of language was seen as a devolution from the pristine communion of Adam and God, to the 'hieroglyphicks' of the Egyptians, then to the parables of the Hebrews, and finally to the rational, discursive language of classical times. The emblem was a witty and esoteric attempt to revive what had not been lost forever of the symbolic language of God, the language of prophecy in the Old Testament, and indeed the language of Christ himself.[7] Such a mode of expression, though it had lain fallow for so long, could not fail to attract a certain group of poets, who, with their backs to Augustan standards, were looking for a new idiom. In choosing to work with emblems, then, Blake was deliberately choosing that mode which offered the best chance of accommodating a prophetic message.

This essay[8] examines each of the plates of *The Gates of Paradise* in

---

6 See also J. H. Wynne, *Choice Emblems* (1772) and *Tales for Youth* (1790); and T. Bewick, *Select Fables* (1784). See also Erdman's discussion of the similarities between Blake's sketches in the notebook and those in Wynne's *Choice Emblems* in D. V. Erdman and D. K. Moore (eds), *The Notebook of William Blake* (Oxford, 1973), p. 9.

7 See, for instance, Bacon, *Wisdom of the Ancients* (1619), for the standard formula, and H. Estienne, *The Art of Making Devises*, trans. Blount (1640) for a typically long-winded elaboration. For a penetrating discussion of the entire subject, see E. H. Gombrich, 'Icones Symbolicae', in *Symbolic Images* (London, 1973).

8 This essay is part of a larger study of *The Gates of Paradise, Illustrations of the Book of Job*, and the emblem tradition. The most significant critical works on the *Gates* are: J. Sampson, *The Poetical Works of William Blake* (1905), pp. 366–78; C. B. Tinker, *Painter and Poet* (Cambridge, Mass., 1938), pp. 100–20; N. Frye, 'The Keys of the Gates' in J. V. Logan *et. al.* (eds), *Some British Romantics* (Columbia, 1966); John Beer, *Blake's Humanism* (Manchester, 1968), appendix 2; G.

comparison with traditional and contemporary analogues. My conclusion is that the *Gates* presents the life of fallen man as a melancholy cycle turning on frustration, defeat and despair, the more insidious for being self-renewing. At the same time the *Gates* goes far beyond contemporary analogues, for it points unequivocally to a way one may break out of the cycle into a visionary and creative state.

THE FRONTISPIECE

The story of the caterpillar and the butterfly had been seen as an allegory of life after death since medieval times, but by the late eighteenth century that meaning had been lost to all but the devotional writers. James Hervey wrote of the 'silkworm in her cell' who 'prepares for her own internment' when she is 'cloyed with pleasure and weary of the world'. But when the period of sleep has elapsed, 'she wakes from a death-like inactivity, breaks the enclosure of her tomb, throws off the dusky shroud, assumes a new form, puts on a more sumptuous array, and from an insect creeping on the ground, becomes a winged inhabitant of the air...'.[9] Among the emblem-makers, on the other hand, the story was reduced to little more than a cautionary tale. In John Wynne's *Tales for Youth* (see fig. 1), for instance, one reads of an earth-worm who, wishing to fly, climbs a tall flower only to be pitched to his death by a bee. As the 'Application of the Tale' explained, 'One thing is plain to the youngest and least experienced, namely, that those who do not climb, can never fall...' In a similar version by Thomas Bewick, Wynne's obsequious morality is mercifully eschewed and there is a suggestion of one of Blake's favourite motifs. As the butterfly explains, 'The circling shield I broke, nor knew / How long my safety hence I drew'. The motif of an imprisoning shell, so feeble in Bewick, stands over *The Gates of Paradise* from beginning to end, and shows once again how Blake could impart far more to a standard allegorical device than could any of his contemporaries. Once he establishes the

Keynes, *The Gates of Paradise*, Blake Trust Facsimile (Clairvaux, 1968); Erdman, *Notebook*. See also G. W. Digby, *Symbol and Image in William Blake* (London, 1957); Gail Kmetz, 'A Reading of the Gates of Paradise', *Blake Studies*, 3 (1971), 171–85; and M. L. Johnson, 'Emblem and Symbol in Blake', *Huntington Library Quarterly*, XXXVII (1974), 151–70.

[9] James Hervey, 'Descant Upon Creation', *Meditations and Contemplations* (1746), reprinted in *Works* (Edinburgh, 1779), vol. I, p. 246.

1. T. Bewick: engraving for J. H. Wynne, *Tales for Youth*,
'Tale of the Earth Worm' (1790)

importance of the imprisoning shell as the home of the worm, he follows
the associated images throughout the series, continually playing off one's
expectation that man will burst once and for all the 'ambient azure shell'.[10]

The motto of the frontispiece also has an interesting history. On the one
hand the phrase 'What is Man' was held to derive from the Book of Job,
and was used as a pessimistic evaluation of man's earthly achievements,
especially those of the scientific community exemplified in Blake by
Newton. On the other hand the phrase was held to derive from Psalm 8
and was used to celebrate man's dominant place in creation. Although the
derivation from the Book of Job was the more common usage, the derivation from the Psalm was the decisive one, for it was the one to which Paul
had referred in the Epistle to the Hebrews. It was also the one which
Hervey had popularized in his gloss of Young. Hervey tried to carry his
audience with him as he wrote,

My soul, fired by such noble prospects, weighs anchor from this little nook . . .
the immensity of things is her range, and an infinity of bliss is her aim . . .when
I consider thy heavens, even the works of thy fingers, the moon and the stars
which thou hast ordained; I am smitten with wonder at thy glory, and cry out
in a transport of gratitude, Lord, what is man, that thou art mindful of him . . .[11]

The tone of this passage (if little else about it) is the tone Blake intended to

[10] Edward Young, *Night Thoughts* I.132.
[11] Hervey, 'Descant Upon Creation', p. 274.

75

suggest in the motto of the frontispiece. When he first sketched the idea in his notebook, he may have had only the Jobean context in mind, but in the engraving he shortened the phrase to its more ambiguous form and punctuated it not as the complaining query it had been in the Book of Job, but as the joyful exclamation of the Psalm. With motto and design united as an emblem one can see that Blake has not suggested either the Jobean context in isolation, or the context of the Psalm in isolation, but has encompassed both of them. First, he has portrayed man's mortality and his limitations by depicting the worm, which is never without morbid associations. But instead of quoting in full the phrase from Job, and asking why God magnified man, Blake has, in effect, magnified his own picture of a reptilian-man. This strange creature, which Blake has portrayed with the exacting detail of an ornithological display, is no longer the gnawing worm of eighteenth-century moralizing, but rather a human being who is a worm only because he is asleep. For him to become a butterfly will not be a matter of pruning his 'vain desires', but simply of awakening. Notice too, that next to the human worm is a worm without any human features, who is feeding intently on the leaf. The two together suggest that transcendence is neither necessary nor universal, but depends on a certain degree of aspiration – which for the sleeping child could only take the form of dreaming. If the child bursts his cocoon, and rises to his full stature, he will stand in the same position as Albion in *Albion rose*. One supposes then, that the distance between the condition of man in the frontispiece, and his fulfilled, beatific condition in *Albion rose* is the subject matter of *The Gates of Paradise*. The frontispiece announces the beginning of that journey, and the motto announces that the success of the journey depends entirely on the traveller himself.

PLATE I

Plate 1 depicts a woman kneeling to pluck a child out of the soil. In her skirts she holds another infant. The two separate motifs, the maternal figure bending to pluck, and the child growing out of the ground, probably came to Blake through Philip Ayres's *Emblemata Amatoria* (1683). But just as in the frontispiece, Blake has used conventional motifs freely, with little deference to their usual context.[12]

[12] The similarity between Ayres and Blake was noticed independently by Johnson, 'Emblem and Symbol', p. 153.

In 1818 Blake added 'The Keys of the Gates', which for the first time identified the child as a mandrake, but it may be possible that he had this identity in mind all along. In the Bible the mandrake was associated with an aphrodisiac or an aid to conception, as it sometimes was in the herbals, and there were a host of arcane superstitions attached to it. These make interesting reading, but Blake was probably not alluding to them. For him the mandrake motif was useful mainly because the mandrake root resembles the lower half of a human torso,[13] and thus the child could be pictured as a vegetable being generated from the base world. The picture of a child growing out of the ground would have been quickly recognized as the standard representation of man's physical limitations. In *Emblemes ou Devises Chrestiennes* (Lyon, 1571),[14] for instance, one finds a similar design in which man is compared to a briar which sends its shoots back into the ground.

In the first plate of the *Gates*, the mandrake is able to escape the clutches of the soil only by being harvested, not, as in Blake's startling illustration to Young (see fig. 2) by pulling himself through his own evolutionary cycle. He is torn out of the soil by a woman, and the scene as a whole is set under the boughs of a yew or a willow tree, details which remind one of Donne's 'Progress of the Soul', in which the soul begins his journey as the forbidden fruit, becomes a mandrake, and is picked by Eve. Blake's earliest version of the motto, 'I found him beneath a Tree in the Garden', also suggests that the scene was intended to be set in Eden and that the tree is the Tree of the Knowledge of Good and Evil.[15] The identity of the scene is important, for it shows that the first real movement in the series is not a step in the direction of paradise, but a repetition of the old pattern of the fall. This pessimistic movement coincides with Bede's explanation that the mandrake, as a plant without a head, represents humanity without Christ. The mandrake, 'this living buried man' as Donne called him, is a creature without higher faculties, which in the context of the *Gates* means

---

[13] In 'The Mental Traveller', however, Blake applied the penalty for picking the mandrake – a withered arm – to anyone who dared to touch the female babe. And in *Jerusalem* 11.22, when Blake used the mandrake motif to describe Scofield, he was probably alluding to Donne's line 'he's short-lived, that with his death can do most good'.

[14] Reprinted in the Scolar Press series (Menston, 1973).

[15] The allegory based on the worm, the apple, and the butterfly was one of Blake's favourites. See his 346th design for *Night Thoughts*.

that he lacks the imaginative ability to change himself, and is doomed to follow forever the endless cycle of nature. As an organism which is rooted in the ground and yet shows some trace of human affections, he recalls, as Frye has suggested, Blake's frustrated sunflower.[16] The sunflower too was

2. Design for Young's *Night Thoughts*, no. 257 (unpublished, 1795–7). Watercolour

16 Frye, 'The Keys of the Gates', in *The Stubborn Structure* (N.Y., 1970), p. 194.

rooted in the ground and yet longed to reach 'that sweet golden clime /
Where the traveller's journey is done'. But it remained rooted, an emblem
of endless aspiration. Just so, the mandrake child is rooted and grounded
not in love, but in the deterministic world of the natural order, and this
distinction was, for Blake, the axis on which the identity and uniqueness
of man turned. It is the distinction, as Milton put it, between an 'elemental
life', and 'that ethereall and fift essence, the breath of reason it selfe . . . an
immortality' (*Areopagitica*, p. 4).

PLATES 2, 3, 4, AND 5

The four cosmic elements constitute one of the sets within the tetradic
categories, an orderly system which from ancient times was thought to
describe the composition and behaviour of all things in the universe. By the
eighteenth century, with the rise of a more empirical natural science,
schematism was no longer accepted as completely valid, and the real
opportunity which the schematic world-view offered a poet was not
whether he could show it to be true or false, but whether he would see in it
the justification of a conservative and hieratic view of life and politics, or
whether he would use it imaginatively, as a means of organizing conceptions of great scope.

Most of the Augustans either gave a half-hearted assent to the former,
or simply avoided the issue. In eighteenth-century poetry schematism had
become either outmoded or conventional, and for the most part the four
elements were used in the same way as Johnson used 'observation's'
'extensive view'. In the face of this sort of gloss, Blake had to assert that the
schematic mode was worth reviving, and he replaced the blindness of the
astronomical view with one which came close enough to see the elements
in human form. But having done so, he did not adopt yet another popular
view, such as Lavater's, of four equally bland types. On the contrary, each
of Blake's four elements seems to be monstrously deficient. Each element
is still unique and self-contained, and therefore still a kind of basic particle,
but that very condition precludes them from ever partaking of a larger
whole until they surrender their tragic identities. In this sense they do not
appear to be elemental *qualities* as such, or to correspond to the humours,
temperaments, ages, or seasons. Rather, each appears to be a kind of

anarchic hypostasis of an isolated part of the tetrad. As separate parts, the four elements cannot be united. And the old solution to this problem, the intervention of love, is no longer a viable one. Blake gives us no reason to think that, as in Spenser's 'Hymn of Love', the warring elements will be brought together in fit harmony. In *The Gates of Paradise* the elements are shown to be permanently at odds with man.

From the frontispiece one learned that the progress of life *could* be toward a beatific state, and from the schematic organization of the *Gates* as a whole one expects that this beatific state will take the form of an ideal type. In ancient and medieval times the ideal type had been formed on the model of the sanguine, but in the *Gates* the sanguine, 'Air', has abandoned himself to groundless speculation and worry. The importance of Plates 2, 3, 4, and 5 seems to be to show that the ideal type can no longer be formed from the sanguine, or for that matter, from any combination of natural qualities. Indeed, the natural qualities appear to be the principal obstacles to fulfilment. They are the images of frustration in the same context that the mandrake and the sunflower are forever tied to the earth. The four elements represent, as John Beer has said, 'man's condition under the natural law'.[17] In this condition shuffling the cards makes no very great difference. One can remain, as Pope put it, 'Like a plant on his peculiar spot', or one can try to burst out like Blake's 'Fire'. But is there so great a distinction between a man's remaining half-buried in the life of this world, like the mandrake, and his becoming 'meteor-like', flaming 'lawless thro' the void, / Destroying others, by himself destroyed' (*Essay on Man* II. 65. 6)? Is not the latter simply a reactionary consequence of the former? And do not both remain in the same chaotic state?

Insofar as he has given us portraits of the elements, Blake has re-humanized the world of the elements in a scientific age – but he has done so by showing how inhuman and deranged they have become. One cannot find a desirable place in the world of the *Gates* – not because that world is too intricately organized, or because all the good seats have been taken, but because that world is off its axis, and there is no longer a place for anyone.

Thus far in the *Gates* life has been portrayed as submerged in a terrestrial

17 John Beer, 'Blake, Coleridge, and Wordsworth: Some Cross-currents and Parallels, 1789–1805' in Morton D. Paley and Michael Phillips (eds), *William Blake: Essays in Honour of Sir Geoffrey Keynes* (Oxford, 1973), p. 244.

cycle, which may allow one to speculate that the dominant one of the four elements is the element earth.[18] Each plate can be seen as simply a different view of the same melancholy affliction. In this case Blake is not departing from tradition, but developing Milton's distinction between the four terrestrial elements, and the fifth 'quintessential' element of rationality[19] – so fully, indeed, that the best description of Blake's elements can be seen in a reading, from his point of view, of *Il Penseroso*, in which the elements are

> demons that are found
> In fire, air, flood, or under ground,
> Whose power hath a true consent
> With planet or with element.   (*Il Penseroso*, 93–6)

In other words Blake's demonic elements are simply four different faces with which the fallen order has disguised itself, an order which one can now see to be manifested psychologically in the melancholy humour. Blake has used the schematic system to portray man divided against himself. But he has also made it clear that one cannot simply put the pieces back together. One has to formulate a new ideal type, which is not part of, but greater than the system.

PLATE 6

All of the commentators agree that the figure of the winged child bursting from his shell symbolizes the birth of something new and wonderful, and the only question has been who the child represents. John Beer has shown that despite previous interpretations one's only real clue is to follow the allusion to Orphic sources, in which the winged figure is Eros – so long as it is clear that Eros is neither good nor bad in himself, but more a kind of cosmic animation which finds its character only in its objects.[20]

The motto 'At length for hatching ripe he breaks / the shell', derives from Dryden's modernization of 'The Knight's Tale' (*Fables*, 1700), where it described the birth of man. Blake used the phrase in order to suggests that the world of *The Gates of Paradise* was identical with the world

---

[18] The design of Blake's 'Earth' seems to be based on two sources, Dürer's iron etching of 'The Man in Despair' (Bartsch 70), and the generic treatment of the same subject in the iconologies. See for instance, 'Ame' in J. B. Boudard, *Iconologie* (Paris, 1759).

[19] See for instance, *Areopagitica*, p. 4; and *Paradise Lost* III. 713–18.

[20] Beer, *Blake's Humanism*, pp. 234–40.

of 'The Knight's Tale', and that this world was fallen under a specific star, the star of Saturn. As the aged god explains his rule in 'The Knight's Tale':

> Wide is my Course, nor turn I to my Place
> Till Length of Time, and move with tardy Pace.
> Man feels me, when I press th' Etherial Plains;
> My Hand is heavy, and the Wound remains.
> Mine is the Shipwreck in a Watry Sign;
> And in an Earthy, the dark Dungeon mine.
> Cold shivering Agues, melancholy Care,
> And bitter blasting Winds, and poison'd Air,
> Are mine, and wilful Death, resulting from Despair.
> The throtling Quinsey 'tis my Star appoints,
> And Rheumatisms I send to rack the Joints:
> When Churls rebel against their Native Prince,
> I arm their Hands, and furnish the Pretence;
> And housing in the Lion's hateful Sign,
> Bought Senates, and deserting Troops are mine.
> Mine is the privy Pois'ning; I command
> Unkindly Seasons, and ungrateful Land.
> By me Kings Palaces are push'd to Ground,
> And Miners, crush'd beneath their Mines are found.
> 'Twas I slew *Samson*, when the Pillar'd Hall
> Fell down, and crush'd the Many with the Fall.
> My Looking is the Sire of Pestilence,
> That sweeps at once the People and the Prince.   (III, 397–419)

Saturn's description of his dominion shows that in Plate 7 Blake has taken the theme of melancholy in its full traditional sense. Can it be that even Plate 6, which depicts the most hopeful event in the series, belongs in the melancholy cycle, under the star of Saturn?

PLATE 8

Plate 8 depicts a young man threatening to throw a spear at an old king who languishes on a crude throne. Salviati's 'Saul' is probably the source of the extreme contrapposto of the son,[21] but he can also be seen generic-

---

[21] As pointed out by A. Blunt, *The Art of William Blake* (New York, 1959), p. 38; and Hagstrum, *Poet and Painter*, p. 35.

ally, as the type of 'rebellio' in the iconologies.[22] The identity of the old king, and the motifs used to depict him, derive almost entirely from traditional depictions of melancholy and of Saturn. The monumental research of Klibansky, Panofsky, and Saxl[23] has enabled one to see in Dürer's *Melencolia I* both the fulfilment and redefinition of long-standing pictorial and intellectual traditions. For instance, the motif of the drooping head, which in ancient art belonged to Saturn, and which had been the sign of the sin of 'acedia' in medieval art, and also of the grief of St John, of the fatigue of the apostles in Gethsemane, of meditation, and many other things, came in Dürer's engraving to symbolize the simultaneous and petrifying effect of the triad of grief, fatigue and creative thought. And the motif of the clenched fist, which originated in medieval illustrations as the sign of certain delusions, like that of a 'madman who thinks that he holds a great treasure, or the whole world, in his hand', came in Dürer's engraving to signify both the 'tight-fisted' avarice of the melancholic and a 'fanatical concentration of mind which has truly grasped a problem, but which at the same moment feels itself incapable either of solving or of dismissing it'.[24] In the same fashion, many more details in Dürer's engraving fit an unusually precise and wide-ranging reinterpretation of melancholy.

While Blake was not aiming at so penetrating a resolution or so wide an application as Dürer, his design still belongs to the tradition which Dürer revitalized. Between the fifteenth and the late eighteenth century there were any number of attempts to develop the ideas and the combination of motifs which Dürer brought to so fine a pitch, and these works can give one an idea of the uses to which Dürer's engraving had been put, hence of the range of meanings available to Blake. In some works the intellectual content had only partly survived, as in Q. *Horati Flacci Emblemata* (Antwerp, 1607), where van Veen used the posture of the melancholic to illustrate 'mentis inquietudo'. In other cases the associations were more directly through Burton, as in Salvator Rosa's *Democritus Deep in Thought* (ca 1650). In others, Protestant homiletics took a leading role, as in the standard frontispiece to *Pilgrim's Progress*. And in others still, all the motifs were

---

22 See for instance, [Ripa], *C. Ripa allerley Kunsten und Wissenschaften . . .* (Augusburg, 1760–4); rpt in Edward A. Maser, *Baroque and Rococo Pictorial Imagery* (New York, 1971).
23 Raymond Klibansky, Erwin Panofsky and Fritz Saxl, *Saturn and Melancholy* (London, 1964).
24 *Ibid.*, pp. 286–90, 317–21.

diffused under a gothic fog or were sublimated to the retirement theme, as in the frontispiece to Roach's *Beauties of the Poets* (1794).

But more important than these for the present discussion is John Sturt's treatment of the figure of 'the law' in the frontispiece to a Bible (1722) (see fig. 3). For this figure Sturt combined two distinct elements, the theme of the 'veiled Mosaic Law', and one of the typical representations of Saturn. Instead of the staff or sword on which the saturnine monarch often leaned, and instead of the rod of Moses, Sturt has substituted an elongated cross. Instead of the dragon of time biting its tail, he has substituted the serpent from Genesis. Instead of a transparent veil over the face of Moses,[25] he has drawn the cloak completely over the face of 'the law'. Life under the law is, then, life under the influence of Saturn, and the law, with its covered eyes, is now incapable of discerning anything at all, while Saturn remains the figure of a cruel and officious tyrant whose politics lead nowhere.

In Plate 8 Blake has used the motifs of the drooping head, the clenched fist, the averted gaze, and the seated posture in their original melancholic context. So also, the king's resignation in the face of revolution is not only the reaction of David to Absolom that most of the critics have noted, but also a symptom which typifies the melancholic's despair and predilection toward suicide. In addition, Blake has incorporated something of Sturt's antinomianism. The saturnine tyrant in Sturt, unable, beneath his cloak, to see either the world or the gospel, was a figure of rule by blinkered principles of legality. Blake's king had just as effectively blinded himself by averting his head. And just as Sturt's tyrant represents the Old Covenant which had to be superseded, so Blake's monarch represents the Old Regime that has to be thrown out of office whenever it implants itself.

But Blake's design is not really bound by the compass of traditional and neoclassic icononography. As a matter of course he employed that symbolic language; it was the heritage of every artist. But he had his own ideas about the meaning and coherence of the tradition. Janet Warner has shown how Blake used another of the typical representations of the melancholic, 'a seated, pensive figure, often viewed from the front', as the basis for his own, more radical vision of despair. And, over the course of his lifetime, it seems that Blake was striving to create, as Frye has suggested

---

[25] As Sturt had done once before in the title page to Samuel Wesley, *The History of the Old and New Testaments attempted in Verse* (1704).

THE

Holy Bible

M.ᵗ Tabor. Matt. 17. 5.

Law. Gospell.

Printed *and Sold by* Richard Ware *at y͂* Bible & Sun *in* Amen Corner
Iust Published fitted to Bind up with all Sorts of House Bibles a Brief Concordance for the
more easy finding out of the useful Places therein Contained. by I D onname B D

3. J. Sturt: engraving for R. Ware's Bible, frontispiece (Oxford, 1722)

with respect to the Job engravings, an alphabet of human forms.[26] If the stature of the fulfilled man is like that of *Albion Rose*, the posture of the melancholic can be seen as the beginning of a collapse into a haphazard position in which all the parts of the body are in disarray. The hand clenches into a fist, stopping only at the 'limit of contraction'. The fist must support the languishing head. The chair must support the torso. And even then, the knee must be raised to prevent the body from falling to the ground. And so it goes. Blake's posture of despair – the posture of 'crowding', to use the phrase of the singer of 'Mad Song' – is the furthest compression of all, the final state before dissolution, the retreat into catatonia, like the figure in Plate 16. In Plate 8 the king is not this far gone, but he has begun to lose his grip, and there is little which can prevent his complete collapse.

From the early watercolour sketch for this design we know that Blake had originally considered a heroic context, and although he changed a number of details prior to engraving the design, it still retains some of that grandeur. By depicting both king and son naked, and by giving the son not a realistic lance but a dart such as Death carries in Blake's own illustrations to *Night Thoughts*, Blake has suggested the legendary context of the *Theogony* and the epic context of *Paradise Lost*. From the *Theogony* Blake took the permanent state of regicide and revolution. So long as there are fathers like Saturn, there will be sons like Zeus. And the lengthening shadows, so far from suggesting that the cycle is about to end, remind one of Blake's portrait of 'Fire', and of Milton's Satan. When Satan appears he seems to exude a 'disastrous twilight', which 'sheds / On half the nations, and with fear of change / Perplexes monarchs' (I. 598–9).

PLATE 9

It is evident that in Plate 9, which depicts a youth climbing a ladder to the moon, Blake intended to say something about desire, but one wonders whether he was urging the young man on, or satirizing the pitfalls of enthusiasm misdirected. For the former position David Erdman has argued that Blake was answering Gillray's cynical caricature 'The Slough of

[26] Janet Warner, 'Blake's Figures of Despair', in Paley and Phillips, *Essays*, pp. 208–24; Northrop Frye, *Fearful Symmetry* (Princeton, 1947), p. 417.

Despond', which used the figure of a ladder too short to reach the moon, by lengthening the ladder until it spanned the entire distance, and by 'providing a youthful pilgrim energetic enough to climb it'.[27] But it is open to question whether these changes alone are able to invert the tone of the design. Just because the young man will make it to the moon does not mean that going there was a good idea.

Perhaps one can find a clue to Blake's satiric intent in the incongruity of the two perspectives, the one human and the other astronomical. The minuteness of the climber with his feeble engines of assault can be seen as ludicrous when set against the cosmic scale of the heavens. The climber and the moon are literal to the point of absurdity, when the scene as a whole could have been an occasion for the sublime. The climber is not mounting on bright pinions, nor winging his way in contemplation, but climbing an ordinary slater's ladder. He is the kind of concrete-minded fellow who cannot tell the difference between Cynthia and the moon – a builder of castles in the air, as Burton put it in his 'Author's Abstract'. As for the moon itself, it is hardly pictured in the fashion one would expect if Blake intended to urge the climber on. Instead of depicting the moon 'objectively', by drawing a globe which only *appeared* to be a crescent, due to a portion of reflected light, Blake has treated the moon as if it actually were a shiny little metal crescent, with the ladder resting on the imaginary inside edge. At the same time, he has not gone completely to the opposite pole and treated the moon in the fantastic and lyrical manner he used in the *Night Thoughts* designs, where the crescent became the barge on which Cynthia floated through the stars. Thus Blake's moon can neither be the stellar body viewed by the Royal Society, nor the female body of Cynthia, Diana, Artemis, or Luna. Rather, Blake's treatment of the moon places it partly in both contexts, which makes it appear ironic, out of place, perhaps absurd.

If indeed this was what Blake was attempting, he was not first to do so. The most outrageous burlesques of all came from that 'Gothick' poet, Ariosto, for whom the moon became the repository of all things lost on earth, most notably the wits of men. When Astolfo went in search of Orlando's wits, he saw how other men had lost theirs:

[27] D. V. Erdman, *Blake: Prophet against Empire* (Princeton, 1954), pp. 203–5. See also Erdman, *Notebook*, pp. 7, 8, n. 40, and repr. of Gillray, p. 90.

> One, while he loves; one, seeking fame to gain;
> One, wealth pursuing through the stormy main;
> One, trusting to the hopes which great men raise,
> One, whom some scheme of magic guile betrays.
> Some, from their wits for fond pursuits depart,
> For jewels, paintings, and the works of art.
> Of poets' wits, in airy visions lost,
> Great store he read; of those who to their cost
> The wandering maze of sophistry pursu'd;
> And those who vain presaging planets view'd.[28]

Now Blake could not have intended to suggest everything Ariosto went on to enumerate. But who, borrowing from this most inventive artist, can ever match his fertility?

Blake's *An Island in the Moon* owes at least a nod to Ariosto, but the moon in *The Gates of Paradise* might also derive in some degree from Milton's transformation of Ariosto's Limbo of Vanity into his own Paradise of Fools. That was the place where

> pilgrims roam, that strayed so far to seek
> In Golgotha him dead, who lives in heaven;

where to the deluded and superstitious

> Saint Peter at heaven's wicket seems
> To wait them with his keys, and now at foot
> Of heaven's ascent they lift their feet, when lo
> A violent cross wind from either coast
> Blows them transverse ten thousand leagues awry
> Into the devious air;

where the Papists and all their paraphernalia

> Fly o'er the backside of the world far off
> Into a limbo large and broad, since called
> The Paradise of Fools   (*Orlando Furioso* III. 445–97)

Milton probably took some of his imagery from Burton,[29] and Blake too was probably interested in Burton's portrait of Religious Melancholy,

---

[28] Ariosto, *Orlando Furioso*, trans. Hoole (1785), 653–67.
[29] S. W. J. Grace, 'Notes on Robert Burton and John Milton', *Studies in Philology*, LII (1955), 578–91.

88

for Burton united the ridiculous activity of the superstitious with the polarity of hope and fear. As he explained it, 'To these advantages of *Hope* and *Fear*', the devil infected men with 'stupidity, canonical obedience, blind zeal'. Or if they thought themselves learned, he 'puffs them up with a vain conceit of their own worth . . . or else out of too much learning [they] become mad, or out of curiosity they will search into God's secrets, and eat of the forbidden fruit; or out of presumption of their holiness and good gifts, inspirations, become Prophets, *Enthusiasts*, and what not. . . '. Or if they feel themselves neglected, 'they begin presently to rage and rave, *coelum terrae miscent* . . .' (*The Anatomy of Melancholy* III. iv. 1. 2).

This kind of mentality, which confuses heaven with earth, and which Burton describes as one of the prime manifestations of religious melancholy, could be the key to the mentality of Blake's climber to the moon. In a more perceptive form that same zeal which drives him up the ladder might allow him to remain on earth and let the eye of his fancy glance from heaven to earth and earth to heaven. But the danger is that his imagination can become indiscriminate. In this state of mind one can hunger with an insatiable appetite for toys, trinkets, puffs of air, even the moon itself. In such a condition one may well begin scaling a ladder to the moon, and this would not be so nearly an enlargement of desire as a mistaken choice. As Johnson put it, 'the human imagination is potentially boundless in what it desires, and yet will fix itself hypnotically on a single aim or object'.

The success of Plate 9 as a satire depends to a great degree on the ability of Blake's contemporaries to relate the design to similar images. The use of the ladder to connect the mundane and the supernal was a standard device in emblematic art, and Blake, like Gillray, could have found it in such sources as *Emblemes ou Devises Chrestiennes* (Lyon, 1571), in which the climber is able to remain on his precarious ladder because his hope in God is firm.[30] But if in his treatment of the ladder, Blake intended to suggest vain and fruitless desire in search of an impossible object, then perhaps he did not borrow the motif only from the emblem tradition, and the inversion of it from Gillray, but instead was meditating on a work where it had already assumed both roles. In Dürer's *Melencolia I* the ladder had been seen as 'the symbol of an all-embracing, but often ineffectual, if not

---

[30] Reproduced in the Scolar Press series (Menston, 1973).

absurd, mental search'.[31] And by the time of *Il Penseroso* the mental search, if no longer absurd, was still all-embracing, and directed toward the

> wandering moon,
> Riding near her highest noon,
> Like one that had been led astray
> Through the heaven's wide pathless way
>
> (*Il Penseroso*, 65–70)

The ladder motif is perhaps as pedestrian a means of transport as one could find. Certainly Longinus would have preferred a more splendid carriage. Yet when one considers Plato's ladder of love in the *Symposium*, and the story of Jacob's dream (Genesis xxviii. 12), the heavenly ladder seems the perfect emblem for transcendence, and compared to it, the ladder to the moon is a ridiculous imitation. When Jacob awoke after his dream, 'he was afraid, and said, How dreadful is this place! This is none other but the house of God, and this is the gate of heaven.'

PLATE 10

The drowning man depicted in Plate 10 is unambiguously presented, but the significance of the design as a whole is still unclear. What is the meaning of drowning with respect to the rest of the series? Many commentators have suggested that Blake invested the ocean itself with a special meaning. Blake's ocean is for Keynes and others the image of materialism, and for Digby an image of 'the conditioned past'. But in eighteenth-century poetry the ocean was an image of many other things too. Elizabeth Carter found the sea to be 'Expressive of the human mind', especially of its mutability, for as she put it, 'In thy forever varying form, / My own inconstant self I find'. And for Young the ocean could be at one time, 'eternity's vast ocean', and at another, 'Death's capital', a 'too faithful mirror', which reflects 'the melancholy face of human life'.[32]

However one interprets the ocean as a poetic figure, the important point is not its significance *per se*, but the fact that one foundered in it. This was

---

[31] Philip Melanchthon, *Pictura Melancholiae*, quoted by Klibansky *et al.*, *Saturn and Melancholy*, p. 320 n. 21.
[32] G. L. Keynes, *The Gates of Paradise* (3 vols., London, 1968), vol. I, p. 17; Digby, *Symbol and Image*, pp. 42–3; Elizabeth Carter, 'Written Extempore on the Sea-shore', in *Works*, p. 377; Young, *Night Thoughts* VIII. 174–5.

the central conceit in many homiletic tracts, where one could be saved from drowning only by the hand of Christ. In Hugo, Arwaker, and Quarles the soul was depicted as being rescued from drowning by the Christ child,[33] and in one of the most popular religious works of the eighteenth century, *Theron and Aspasio* (1755), James Hervey used the motif to introduce Quarles' description of Christ as the 'Rock of Ages'. Hervey compared faith to a 'shipwrecked mariner, labouring to gain some place of safety', who cried earnestly, 'Lord, save me, I perish! and HE, who commandeth the winds, and the waves, will be sure to put forth his beneficent hand, and rescue him from the devouring sea.'[34]

This is the context in which Plate 10 belongs, a point which cannot be missed if one is to recognize that Blake inverted the meaning of the 'Rock of Ages', and left his drowning man without a rescuer. Just as the mandrake has no faculties, just as each of the fallen elements is trapped within itself, and just as there is no one to prevent the usurpation in Plate 8, so in the world of the *Gates* there is never any possibility of a *deus ex machina* for the drowning man. The whole problem with that world is the self-contained nature of its general affliction: melancholy. In this sense Plate 10 expresses the state of mind which was both the cause of drowning and the reason that one could not be saved by an external agent. This was the state of mind Cowper had described as leading toward suicide. The castaway survived a while, but finally 'he drank / The stifling wave, and then he sank' (47–8).

PLATE II

Plate 11, which depicts an old man with large spectacles clipping the wings of a youth, makes use of two motifs in the emblem literature, the spectacles and the shears. The first of these can be seen in a depiction in Q. *Horati Flacci Emblemata* (Antwerp, 1607) of a helpless, nearly blind old man seated on a stool.[35] The verses explain that such a man will be happier when he is less active, for although his senses may dull, yet his inner sense, the sight of his mind as it were, will grow more acute. In accordance with

---

[33] Hugo, *Pia Desideria* (Antwerp, 1624); Arwaker, *Pia Desideria* (1686); Quarles, *Emblems*, bk III, emblem 9. The similarity between Quarles and Blake was first noticed by Tinker, *Painter and Poet*, p. 105.

[34] James Hervey, *Theron and Aspasio* (1755), XII.

[35] Reproduced in Johnson, 'Emblem and Symbol'.

such changes, Father Time drives Sleep, Gluttony, and Lust from him, and ushers in Prudence and Temperance, who more properly belong to a dignified old age. Blake's old man in Plate 11 resembles the old man in van Veen, but Blake's treatment of the spectacles motif is nothing like van Veen's. It would be pointless for Blake to argue that in advancing years a man's mental life would become more satisfying despite the aging of his body, for it was a self-evident proposition to Blake that age was a matter of perception. And while this may sound peculiarly Blakean, one must also recall that the figure of a man whose years hung heavy with learning, and who was yet ignorant of the meaning of his life, had been a standard object of satire in the neoclassical complaint of life. In 'The Vanity of Human Wishes' (1749), Johnson told the aspiring scholar to 'pause awhile from Letters to be wise'. And when poets addressed Contemplation, they were often searching for a place and a time far from the distractions of days in the city, where one could commune with nature and oneself. But retirement could also be an excuse for mental sloth. Young mocked 'Grey-haired authority':

> in volumes deep you sit;
> In wisdom shallow: pompous ignorance!
> . . .
> Your learning, like the lunar beam, affords
> Light, but not heat; it leaves you undevout,
> Frozen at heart . . .

> (*Night Thoughts*, v. 739–40, 754–6)

In the same tone Blake intended to contrast the old fool in Plate 11 with the blind bards. Legend had it that Homer, Tiresias, and above all Milton, found in their blindness the freedom to sustain a piercing concentration. As the wall of flesh decayed, the eyes of faith grew more acute, and in comparison with the world revealed by the spirit, the physical world became no better than a fitful distraction. Thus *Samson Agonistes* was read in Blake's time largely as a commentary on events in Milton's own life, and if one looks to Blake's 'Samson', and 'Mad Song', it is clear that he saw the growth of his own powers in the same terms.[36] One who had the ability to form grand conceptions, to use the phrase of Longinus, would not regret the creeping blindness of old age, for his inner vision would

---

[36] Michael Phillips, 'Blake's Early Poetry', in Paley and Phillips, *Essays*, pp. 1–28.

ever be expanding, sharpening. But the old fool in Plate 11, as a personification of Lockean epistemology, is a bitter denial of this. He wears spectacles in order to magnify the world, for within himself he has nothing. He is the perfect observer, and his mind is as empty as a *camera obscura*. Because he requires spectacles, he shows that his knowledge derives solely from the impressions registered by his senses. Yet he does not look at the world with any determination. Indeed, Blake has depicted him with eyes closed, so that his spectacles can have only a pedantic, ceremonial significance. As Locke put it, 'in bare, naked perception, the mind is, for the most part, only passive; and what it perceives it cannot avoid perceiving' (*Essay* II. 4. 1). In Plate 11 Blake sardonically replies to this that the notion of passive perception is tantamount to wilful blindness. Even worse, the consequences of a lack of vision do not remain in the perceiver alone. Because the old man has *refused* to see beyond his own nose, he typifies a predilection to prohibit others from mental travelling.

The second motif, of the shears, also derives from the emblem tradition. In the books of Otto van Veen, for instance, the shears belonged to God, who cut the silver cord. In Boudard's abbreviation of Ripa (Paris, 1759) the figure 'Reformation' wielded a pruning knife with the motto 'castigo mores'. In Quarles, the shears belonged to Sense, who clipped the wings of Faith. And as late as 1751 Nathaniel Cotton was still following Quarles and writing of 'Sense (that Tyrant!)', who 'holds the empress, Soul, in chains'.[37] But more important for the present discussion is the old man, Saturn, who was often represented in ancient art brandishing a sickle, with a cloak pulled partly over his head. In some commentaries the sickle was thought to derive from the *Theogony*, where it was the instrument Saturn used to castrate his father, and with which Saturn himself was paid in kind. In others, it was interpreted as the harvest sickle of the aged god, who, having been banished by Zeus, had come to Latium to teach agriculture to the Romans. Among the many variations his portrait was to undergo before he came to resemble the old man clipping the wings of youth, the most important, as Panofsky has traced in detail,[38] was his identification with Chronos, rather than Kronos, and the former's transformation into Father Time. The picture of this character curtailing

[37] N. Cotton, 'Death', in *Visions in Verse* (1751).
[38] Erwin Panofsky, 'Father Time', in *Studies in Iconology* (N.Y., 1939), pp. 69–93.

the wings of Cupid[39] in van Veen's *Amorum Emblemata* (Antwerp, 1603) was probably the central analogue for Blake's design.

For obvious reasons there appeared many ghastly portraits of this old man devouring his prey, and the two distinct identities as we know them, Father Time and Saturn, were often run together[40] so that the character was at once the destroyer, the revealer, the one who castrated, and the one who was castrated. It was this kind of explosive and contradictory material which Blake was turning to shape time and again in the notebook sketches[41] which depict a giant crunching a human body between its jaws.

PLATE 12

Plate 12 (fig. 9 below) depicts a scene from the thirty-third canto of the *Inferno*, in which Count Ugolino explains to Dante how he and his four sons were starved to death in the tower of Pisa by Archbishop Ruggiero. This story was the single most popular section of *The Divine Comedy* in eighteenth-century England, and the Ugolino episode was seen not in the allegorical context of *The Divine Comedy*, nor even in the political context which explained why the Count had been imprisoned. Rather the Ugolino episode became an isolated moment of pathos, a heart-rending story of undeserved suffering inflicted by the Church. For the eighteenth century the story of Ugolino became the sentimental, even pathetic account of a Whig unjustly deprived of his freedom, while Dante became one with Shakespeare and Milton, whose capacity for depicting passion at its fullest freed them from the tyranny of classical restraint.[42]

Blake's treatment of the Ugolino episode begins in this context. The anti-clericism is stated explicitly in the motto, 'Does thy God O Priest take

[39] Reproduced in Panofsky, 'Father Time', plate XXXI.

[40] One could easily find evidence in classical sources which appeared to support the identity of the two: e.g. Ovid, *Metamorphoses*, XV. 234–5. Blake's friend George Cumberland, for instance, described an engraving which we now know as 'The Allegory of Time' as 'Saturn Devouring the Rock' (*Anecdotes of Julio Bonasoni* (1793), p. 72, no. 192). The similarity between Blake's Plate 11 and the one in *Amorum Emblemata* was first noticed by Tinker, *Painter and Poet*, p. 105; and the similarity between Blake's plate and the one in Quarles' *Emblems* was first noticed by Nanavutty, 'Emblem Literature'. Johnson, 'Emblem and Symbol', suggests interpretation of this plate antithetic to the one presented here.

[41] Erdman and Moore, *Notebook*, pp. 15–17.

[42] My understanding of this material depends on two works, Paget Toynbee, *Dante in English Literature* (1909); and Frances Yates, 'Transformations of Dante's Ugolino', *Journal of the Warburg and Courtauld Institutes*, XIV (1951), 92–117.

such vengeance as this?' Blake's dislike of the norms of classical presentation can be seen in the way he has removed any trace of the equiposed emotion which Reynolds had made so didactic in his version of the scene. And the theme of the denial of liberty, expanded from the purely political to encompass liberty of imagination, is amplified in Blake's having placed the Ugolino scene immediately following the picture of Aged Ignorance clipping the wings of youth. In the later addition to the series, 'The Keys of the Gates', Blake explicitly joins the two scenes together, as the work of the same agent:

> Holy & cold I clipd the Wings
> Of all Sublunary Things
> And in depths of my Dungeons
> Closed the Father & the Sons

Even without this explicit admission in 'The Keys', it is clear that the god of imprisonment is identical with the man who clips the wings, the one whose influence is felt in shipwrecks, suicides, and usurpations. Just as his father before him, Saturn's response to the unforeseen birth of his children was to imprison them deep within the earth from the moment they saw light. And when he was finally deposed and his son Zeus took the throne, he too buried everyone who dared to challenge him. In Hesiod[43] the imprisonment of the children was always portrayed as an automatic reaction by the father, just as the child's hatred of the father was almost a part of his birthright. For Blake this conception was the main thematic link between the Ugolino episode and the other events depicted in the *Gates*. He incorporated, of course, the pathos, the anti-clericism, and the Whig stance which the eighteenth century read into the story, but he also organized all of these within the theme of Saturn's baleful influence. Blake's treatment of the subject reaches beyond the limited context in which his contemporaries viewed the story, and he uses the essential themes of bondage and parasitism to form a large historical and legendary pattern in much the same way that Dante originally conceived the story.

Blake's extensive use of the theme of melancholy and of the character of Saturn is evident at many points outside of *The Gates of Paradise*; and although a full discussion of these is beyond the scope of the present essay, one is too important not to be mentioned. In *Melencolia I* Dürer had

[43] Cf. Hesiod, *Theogony* 135–6; 156–7; and 461–72.

depicted Dame Melancholy as the embodiment not just of Melancholy, but also of the nexus Saturn–Melancholy–Geometry. The traditional connection between Saturn and Melancholy has already been explained. The connection between Saturn and Geometry was ready to hand because the activities proper to one under the influence of Saturn, such as farming, building, and accounting, were also associated with the domain of Geometry, which included the arts of measurement and construction. Geometry and Melancholy, on the other hand, were connected by Dürer in the context of creative art. He saw Melancholy, following Ficino and Petrarch, as the spring of genius and of artistic inspiration; and he saw the arts of measurement, which belonged to Geometry, as expressive of the mastery of technique. In pictorial terms the figure that embodied this threefold intellectual content seemed to be constructed mainly on the figures of Melancholy and Geometry, with Saturn serving in a minor capacity. But following Dürer, the important nexus of Saturn–Melancholy–Geometry was revived by Goltzius and Jacob de Gheyn in a portrait of Melancholy.[44] In this picture Saturn is once again a classical god. He sits astride his sphere in the midst of the starry heavens, a background which not only underlines his power and the depth of his concentration, but also the coldness and isolation of his position. His cloak covers the top of his head, and his head rests wearily on his hand. His eyes are closed in deep contemplation and sorrow.

With respect to *Melencolia I* this engraving is enormously important because, as Panofsky has explained,[45] it makes explicit what Dürer had only inferred: 'the essential unity of Melancholy, Saturn, and Mathematics'. With respect to Blake, the engraving is no less significant, for it establishes the similarity, if not the identity, of the aged god Saturn, his melancholy condition of mind, and Blake's embodiment of these in Urizen. When one looks at these three side by side – *Melencolia I*, de Gheyn's portrait of Melancholy, and the frontispiece to *Europe* – one can see that Blake's interest in Saturn and in melancholy did not end with *The Gates of Paradise*, but rather became for him the basis for Urizen, his finest mythographic and satiric creation.

---

[44] Reproduced in Klibansky *et al.*, *Saturn and Melancholy*, plate 143. Blake certainly knew of this work, for de Gheyn had engraved it after Goltzius, whom Blake had commended in the highest terms in his *Descriptive Catalogue*.

[45] Klibansky *et al.*, *Saturn and Melancholy*, p. 399.

PLATE 14

The melancholy traveller was a familiar figure in the poetry of natural description, and while this character was not depicted heading toward the door of death, like Blake's traveller (see fig. 17 below), he was still the kind of man whose unfailing lassitude left him wandering through the church-yard wrapped in an indolence as intractable as death itself. In the poetry of the graveyard, on the other hand, the motif of a weary traveller had a less emotional and more heraldic function. For Blair it served as the exordium to *The Grave*, and for Young as the coda to *Night Thoughts*.

These travellers are all familiar, but Blake's traveller is rather ambigu-ously defined in relation to them. What kind of man is Blake's traveller? Is he a wanderer, lost and forlorn, whose melancholy derives from his contemplation of the mutability of nature; or is he a pilgrim, marching away from the distractions of this world, and hurrying to his goal in the next? In the broad mythographic scheme of 'The Keys of the Gates', the traveller may well have become a pilgrim, but in the early version of the series with which we are concerned the traveller is treated differently. It is clear at any rate that Blake did not intend to allude to Bunyan's pilgrim in this version, for he did not use the two identifying details of the knapsack and the book,[46] nor did he depict the traveller as an admirable, honest character. Indeed, the details of the traveller's face are so indistinct that one cannot determine whether he is simply troubled in mind, whether he fears some unseen pursuer, or whether his glum and uneasy expression is only a measure of his haste. Whatever the cause of his disturbance, he has become an unsettling figure, who is more nearly fleeing something than approaching his goal.

This figure, popular in later Romantic poetry,[47] was also the character-type of a number of earlier works in the age of sensibility. Goldsmith's traveller, who wandered 'remote, unfriended, melancholy, slow', said, like Kafka's hunger artist, that he 'kept his course along', despite the pain, because he was never able to find any satisfaction. He had spent his life 'Impell'd with steps unceasing, to pursue / Some fleeting good, that mocks

[46] See G. L. Keynes, 'Pilgrim's Progress', in *Blake Studies* (Oxford, 1973), pp. 162–4.
[47] See for instance, B. Blackstone's *The Lost Travellers* (London, 1962), which borrows its theme from the Epilogue of *For the Sexes: The Gates of Paradise*.

me with the view' ('The Traveller' (1760), 25–6). And in James Beattie's 'Triumph of Melancholy' (1766), the traveller who 'through many a lonesome path is doomed to roam' finally abandoned himself to solitude:

> Ah Melancholy! how I feel thy power!
> Long have I laboured to elude thy sway
> But 'tis enough, for I resist no more   (213–15)

Pictorial treatments of this traveller were also popular. Even in the emblem books for children there were stories of wandering men, lost at night. Tale XXVII of John Wynne's *Tales for Youth* (1790), for instance, tells the story of the Benighted Traveller (see fig. 4), who is led astray by 'a

4. T. Bewick: engraving for J. H. Wynne, *Tales for Youth*,
'The Benighted Traveller' (1790)

glimmering flame', which he mistakes for a 'faithful guide'. In this emblem the traveller, wearing a large black hat and leaning on his walking stick, is lost in the darkness, but he spies a light afar off, and to this he directs his steps. These details remind one of Blake's traveller (despite the fact that Wynne's emblem deals with physical, not mental travelling), for just as Wynne's traveller is led astray by Will-of-the-Wisps and Jack-O-Lanthorns, so Blake's traveller may well have been led astray by a figment of his imagination, a manner of deception which was given a special value ever since Milton had used it in *Paradise Lost* (IX. 631–45) to describe Satan tempting Eve.

Between the time of Milton and Blake, the motif of the lost traveller was put to many uses which find echoes in *The Gates of Paradise*. For Quarles it described the soul, lost and forlorn: 'Like a strange Trav'ller by the Sun forsook, / And in a road unknown by night o'ertook'. For Dryden it was a weapon to be used against the Deists. Reason was to the soul, 'Dim, as the borrow'd beams of Moon and Stars / To *lonely, weary, wandring Travellers*' (*Religio Laici* (1862), 1–2). And for Johnson, in 'The Vanity of Human Wishes', it characterized the melancholy condition of man where

> Hope and Fear, Desire and Hate,
> O'er spread with Snares the clouded Maze of Fate,
> Where wav'ring Man, betray'd by vent'rous Pride,
> To tread the dreary Paths without a Guide;
> As treach'rous Phantoms in the Mist delude,
> Shuns fancied Ills, or chases airy Good.　　　　　(5–10)

Blake's traveller shares many qualities with these melancholy travellers,[48] but at the same time Blake's traveller seems to be a kindred soul to a more famous melancholy traveller in *As You Like It*.[49] Jacques' own description of his melancholy, and Rosalind's reaction, provide diagnosis enough:

Jacques: I have neither the scholar's melancholy, which is emulation, nor the musician's, which is fantastical; nor the courtier's, which is proud; nor the soldier's, which is ambitious; nor the lawyer's, which is politic; nor the lady's, which is nice; nor the lover's, which is all these; but it is a melancholy of mine own, compounded of many simples, extracted from many objects, and indeed the sundry contemplation of my travels, in which my often rumination wraps me in a most humorous sadness.

Rosalind: A traveller! By my faith, you have great reason to be sad. I fear you have sold your own lands to see other men's. Then to have seen much and to have nothing is to have rich eyes and poor hands.

Jacques: Yes, I have gained my experience.　　　　　(IV. i. 10–24)

But what is one to make of Jacques? If one sees him sympathetically one will say that Jacques never harms anyone else in the play; and that however self-centred and incapable of affection he may be, he has learned to make the best of it. He could be more venal than he is, and his white melancholy is a source of enjoyment and instruction to others. But if one takes him

---

[48] With one major difference: whereas most of the other poets had a model of pacification in mind when they spoke of the place where 'the traveller's journey is done', Blake had in mind a model of dynamic creation.

[49] See Z. S. Fink, 'Jacques and the Malcontent Traveller', *Philology Quarterly*, XIV (1955), 237–52.

seriously, the way that Jacques has managed to avoid attachment to anyone else will be disturbing. He has already had his 'experience' by the time he appears in the play, which can only mean that he now considers himself incapable of further communication. He has always held himself in reserve, waiting on the margin. Although he manages to sound cheerful at times, and he tries to convince us that his melancholy is only an artifice, one will say of him: the truth is that he cannot help himself. He has nothing to look forward to from one day to the next, and it is this fatalism in his life which so galls him, not, as he says, the saccharine sweetness of it all. He is an inchoate personality who will age but never develop. In his description of the seven ages of man, he does not include the prime of life, as if the very idea is unknown to him. He is the kind of person who would be 'glad to find the grave', for his life has been an empty affair.

If it is true that Blake was depicting this sort of character, one must also realize that he had to make certain concessions to the emblematic mode, which required a fairly schematic creation. Thus Blake's traveller wears the large black hat of the melancholic in Marston and Burton, and hurries along in the twilight. At the same time the more vital points of similarity with Jacques have not been lost. Just as Jacques had missed that central segment of an active and satisfying maturity, so Blake's traveller, like Goldsmith's traveller, has spent the prime of his life wandering in pursuit of some fleeting good. Both Jacques and Blake's traveller appear mysteriously, without a past and without the prospect of any future worth the reckoning. In Blake's picture the traveller's scurrying isolation defines him just as Jacques is most eloquent in his reasons for not allowing himself to become intimate with anyone else. But most of all, it is the sense of futility one sees in both characters, of a life lived to no purpose, of only passing time. Blake's traveller may be hastening in the evening, but as one learns in the following plate, his activity leads nowhere but to the grave.

PLATE 15

Plate 15, which depicts an old man wearing a long-flowing gown, leaning on a crutch and stepping into a stone tomb, is Blake's treatment of a popular composition. In a few examples of this kind one can see that Blake's design owes a great deal to the revival of medieval motifs in a 'Gothick' setting. There was, for instance, a relatively standardized portrait of a long-bearded old man standing on the edge of the grave, such as Holbein used in the *Dance of Death*. Blake probably at some point studied the xylographic technique of Hanz Lutzelburger, who cut the most popular set of plates for Holbein. And in any case he could not have missed Thomas Bewick's copy after the series, published in 1789 (fig. 5).

5. T. Bewick: engraving for *Emblems of Mortality*, 'The Old Man' (1789)

Perhaps even closer to hand was a depiction of Death meeting a young gallant who leaned rakishly on his walking stick at the side of the grave. This picture was for many years preserved on the walls of the Hungerford Chapel in Salisbury Cathedral, and in Richard Gough's *Sepulchral Monuments of Great Britain* (1786–96), for which Blake engraved plates, there are two views of it (vol. II, plates LXXI and LXXII). These two characters from the Dance of Death always had an intrinsic connection with the traveller, for as Tyndale said in *The Dance of Machabree* (1658), the point of the Dance was 'to shew this world is but a pilgrimage'.[50]

Similar designs also appeared in the emblem books. In some of them

[50] See J. M. Clark, *The Dance of Death in the Middle Ages and the Renaissance* (Glasgow, 1950).

Father Time is the one who, like Blake's figure of Death in the notebook sketch, stands at the door to greet each man as he enters.[51] In others (see fig. 6), the long-bearded old man is depicted in his original costume as the allegorical figure of Winter, a traditional version which was especially

6. O. van Veen: engraving for Q. *Horati Flacci Emblemata*, no. 100 (Antwerp, 1607)

[51] Erdman and Moore, *Notebook*, p. 17; O. van Veen, Q. *Horati Flacci Emblemata*, emblems 81 and 82.

influential for it had continued to be produced in almost the same fashion since classical times.[52]

Now Blake's old man in Plate 15 cannot be seen just as an allegorical personification of one of the seasons, but at the same time the figure has not lost the trappings which would have immediately identified him as a member both of that scheme and of the Dance of Death. Blake's series as a whole thus retains a useful part of the scheme, so that, looking back on the series from Plate 15, the fourteen previous plates depict fourteen states that one is likely to pass on the way to the grave. In this sense the old man entering Death's Door is still a traveller, but he is no longer the melancholy traveller who wanders at midnight through the swamps. He has become a more neutral vehicle, a traveller who has by this time become identical with his destination.

Seen in this light the event depicted in Plate 15 is a familiar one. When Young spoke of 'Poor human ruins tott'ring o'er the grave', he wanted his readers not to 'Strike deeper their vile root, and closer climb / Still more enamour'd of this wretched soil' (*Night Thoughts* IV. 109–13), but to accept death for the release it could become. Blake's illustration achieves much the same point, but by a more direct means. By depicting the strong wind blowing the man into the tomb, and the man himself bent almost to collapse, the man and the forces of nature appear to be moving in unison. The man has shaken hands with the wind, and now they move with the rhythm of nature's cycle. Winter is the time for sleep.

When Blake redesigned this plate to illustrate Blair's *The Grave*, he elaborated many of the details, and added the figure of a radiant young man above the lintel of the tomb. In this form the design may be seen as the emblem of what the graveyard school tried, but never quite succeeded in portraying: the grief of mortality falling away at the birth of eternity. The immediate analogue of Blake's design was not Blair, but Hervey's gloss of Young. Above all, Hervey wanted to convince 'Men of hoary locks, bending beneath a weight of years, and tottering on the brink of the grave' to assent to his dearest (and most controversial) doctrine, the imputed righteousness of Christ. Hervey exhorted all men to glorify Christ, 'who, in the perfection of health, and the very prime of manhood, was content to become a ghastly corpse, that you might be girt with the

[52] Klibansky *et al.*, *Saturn and Melancholy*, p. 293 n. 46.

vigour, and clothed with the bloom, of eternal youth'. For Christ was the one who 'when He had overcome the sharpness of death, opened the gates of paradise'.[53]

In his illustration to *The Grave*, Blake followed Hervey's programme, but it is crucial to recognize that he did not follow it at all in *The Gates of Paradise*. He did not depict either Christ bursting the bars of death, or the eternal youth rising from the grave. Nor is it likely that he intended his audience to read such details into the design. To use such a design would have endorsed the standard formula of the graveyard school, which emphasized that eternity comes only *after* death. But Blake wanted primarily to depict an eternity which is both within life and beyond death. And so when he set up the association with Hervey's apocalyptic image of 'the gates of paradise', he also inverted the meaning by leaving out the resurrection. There may well be an eternity after death, in Blake's view, but he can see no reason to glorify it. If one cannot find a vision of eternity now, within life, what hope can there be that it will appear of itself at the moment of one's death?

PLATE 16

The major problem in the interpretation of this plate has always been the identity of the seated figure. One can argue, with Keynes, that the figure is the traveller himself. But this fails to account for the peculiarly feminine features in the later states of the plate. On the other hand, one can argue with Erdman that the figure is a sibyl, and offer for comparison the early watercolour drawing of a woman sitting in the same position. But the similarity of bodily postures cannot be decisive when so many other details are different. Or, in order to stress the canonical stamp of Blake's work, one can identify the seated figure with similar ones elsewhere in Blake, and argue with Frye that the figure is Tirzah, or with Kathleen Raine that it is the worm herself or Matron Clay.[54]

---

[53] Hervey, 'Descant Upon Creation', p. 252. Blake's title also owes something to Ghiberti's bronze doors on the east portal of the Baptistery of San Giovanni in Florence, called 'The Gates of Paradise'. Although Ghiberti was remote in time and place from Blake, his masterwork was beginning to regain its former popularity during Blake's lifetime. Cumberland did a series of primitivist 'outline drawings' of the gates during one of his tours. Thomas Patch published a series of engravings after them (Florence, 1772). And plaster casts of the gates decorated the library of the Royal Academy during the years when Blake, having completed his apprenticeship, was copying the masters in the Royal Academy.

[54] Keynes, *The Gates of Paradise*, vol. I, p. 19; Erdman, *Notebook*, p. 21; Frye, 'The Keys of the Gates', p. 194; Kathleen Raine, *Blake and Tradition* (2 vols., London, 1969), vol. I, p. 122.

However one identifies this figure, the meaning of the plate must ultimately be based on the sense that the traveller has now reached the end of his journey, and that the end of his journey is revealed to be both the grave and the womb from which he originally came. It makes little difference whether one emphasizes that the traveller now becomes part of the grave, or that the grave (or Tirzah), having invoked her claim on the traveller, now begins to inhabit his body. For all one can tell, Blake may have intended to depict both movements: the traveller collapsing into the grave, and the grave reaching up to grasp him. At any rate, life is now come to a standstill, waiting mutely to begin the cycle again, and nothing about such a condition has much to do with resurrection, transcendence, or even with the tradition of a peaceful death.

Like Plate 15, this plate inverts one's normal expectation. If Blake had been following his contemporaries, he would have exaggerated the importance of death, depicting it as the penultimate event in one's life, only to make the point that one can see beyond it. Nathaniel Cotton described this kind of scene in his 'Vision' of death, addressed, like the *Gates*, to children. Man with his *vade-mecum* is on the verge of death and cannot keep from trembling. When he finally plunges in, he meets 'the pale terrific King', who no longer has the capacity to frighten him:

> The Tyrant drops his hostile guise.
> He seems a youth divinely fair,
> In graceful ringlets waves his hair.
> His wings their whitening plumes display,
> His burnish'd plumes reflect the day.[55]

But in *The Gates of Paradise* this radiant youth never appears, and the morbid elements reign virtually uncontested.

PLATE 13

It is appropriate that discussion of Plate 13 (fig. 16 below) should follow discussion of the rest of the series, for this plate answers many of the questions posed by the rest of the series, and it stands somewhat at a distance from them, both in background and in meaning. In the emblem literature there were a number of deathbed scenes, just as there were a

[55] Cotton, 'Death'.

number of resurrection scenes, but they were for the most part concerned with piety, grief, and rewards and punishments, and none of them seems especially relevant to Blake's treatment of the two themes in Plate 13. In painting, however, the deathbed motif was a principle device in what Robert Rosenblum has called the 'Neoclassic Stoic', a 'viewpoint which looked toward antiquity for examples of high-minded human behaviour that could serve as moral paragons for contemporary audiences'.[56]

In Poussin's *The Death of Germanicus* (ca 1627), and in Hamilton's *Andromache Bewailing the Death of Hector* (ca 1761), the artist focussed on the dying hero at the moment immediately prior to death, and each of the mourners round the deathbed expressed a particular nuance of grief. In Poussin's composition, in the marble relief after it by Thomas Banks (1774), and in the copy after it by Heinrich Füger (1789), the mourners' gesture of pointing upward reminds one of Blake's Plate 13. In Poussin the gesture coincided with the upward-pointing lances of the soldiers, and had mainly an heroic significance. In Füger the gesture was rather one of supplication. And in Banks's relief, the gesture was again heroic, but because there were now two men pointing upward, and because Banks had displayed the scene in Attic nudity, one finds more a sense of the timeless, even collective, martyrdom to ideals than of the virtues of a particular hero.

One can see in Banks's neoclassical elimination of detail the beginnings of Blake's even greater simplification. In Blake's design all the details which had reference to the usual deathbed scene have been pared away. Instead of the complex group of mourners, each performing a specific function and each embodying a specific modulation of grief, Blake has depicted four figures who have almost nothing individual about them. They are differentiated only by sex and age. As a group they compose a family, but one can tell little else about them. Indeed, in the early copies Blake did not even bother to fill in the facial features of the two children; and in the later copies, in which he spent a great deal of effort to depict the risen father in a luminous glow, the family again received little attention. The boy's expression remained one of fear and of shock, and the mother and children never expressed anything but mute astonishment and grief.

---

[56] Robert Rosenblum, *Transformations in Late Eighteenth Century Art* (Princeton, 1967), p. 28. My discussion here is based almost entirely on Rosenblum, and all of the plates I discuss are reproduced in *Transformations*.

So too, the body of the dead man is no longer the centre of attention, as it had been in the neoclassical compositions. Instead of lying in a posture which is eloquent of his suffering, his courage, and his concern to leave this world in a proper state of mind, the man on the deathbed is depicted as already dead, his features already dissolving. The centre of attention has shifted from the dying man to the risen form of the man, and thus to the significance of resurrection.

For the figure of the risen man Blake has adopted the motif of the hand and finger gesturing upward. In Poussin and Füger the mourners were the ones who pointed to heaven, but in Blake it is the man who died and has now risen who points. While the gesture still stands in opposition to the corruption of death, it is no longer a gesture of heroism or of the dignity of martyrdom, but rather a testament to new values by one who is in a position to know.

Blake probably did not borrow this motif directly from Poussin or from Füger, for David had used it in a way which shows even greater affinities. In the *Death of Socrates* (1787) David depicted Socrates reaching out to accept the cup of hemlock, and gesturing with his upraised hand and fore-finger just before the final moment. In contrast to the stern moral fortitude of Socrates, Plato (at the foot of the bed) and the youth holding the cup turn away in grief or shame, and the mourners at the head of the bed display emotions ranging from impotent resignation at what they cannot prevent, to complete despair. The way in which Socrates in the stark white of his nakedness commands the attention of all, and the way that in rising from the bed he seems to be rising above the morality of those who condemned him, are the points at which Blake began to use David's design. In Blake's design the old man is not triumphing over conventional morality, but rather pointing to something beyond it. The radiance of his body is not emblematic of moral purity, but of a state in which righteous-ness has lost its temporal meaning. The motif of pointing to heaven is no longer meant to put death in greater relief, or to turn the dying man's thoughts to what awaits him, but rather it is a sign that a new state awaits all of us – and that death is only one, and not the best way to get there. The old man's hands are, indeed, the most articulate elements in Blake's design. He points upward with his left hand and down with his right, to indicate the different directions the fears and hopes of the living can take.

In this way Plate 13 points beyond the problematic view of life depicted in the rest of the plates. Ordinary life had been seen as a melancholy cycle turning on a downward spiral of dissociated emotions which inevitably resolved into a death-wish. In Plate 13 Blake shows that even within such a life one can find moments of epiphany.

CONCLUSION

Except for Plate 13, all of the scenes in *The Gates of Paradise* belong to a closed cycle. At one end man waits, then in rapid succession he is born of the earth, desires, possesses, exploits, dies, and ends back in the earth, waiting for the cycle to begin again. No matter how much energy he expends, he accomplishes nothing. The lack of resolution in this 'natural' life, this life without spirit or vision, is what makes it such a cramped, useless existence. According to the behaviour one sees in the *Gates*, the cycle of physical life is, from beginning to end, a perpetual state of melancholy. In this sense melancholy is not an individual ailment, but a general one, in which each person lives totally within himself and without others. Fear and hope have no objects, and one cannot maintain contact with one's intuitive or creative powers. Hope and fear, desire and restraint, are only momentary exchanges within a polarized field.

Yet even within such a life, there may be moments of great insight. In *Il Penseroso* Melancholy had been the daughter of both Saturn and Genius, as she had been in *Melencolia I*, so that 'melancholy' described not only the disposition of a saturnine person, but also the melancholy genius. He could be found 'pursuing his lonely and perilous path on a high ridge above the multitude and set apart from ordinary mortals by his ability to be "creative" under divine inspiration'.[57] But he was cursed in not being able to escape the burden of his gift. In the beginning he might be possessed of a nearly satanic energy which would provide for unsurpassed accomplishment, but as soon as he attempted to turn this energy to the demands of art, he would be betrayed. The price of genius could often become solitude, self-imprisonment, and despair.

One may see in the conception of the melancholy genius, with its

[57] Erwin Panofsky, 'Renascimento dell' Antichita: The Fifteenth Century', *Renaissance and Renascences in Western Art* (N.Y., 1970), p. 187.

permanent internecine struggle between vitality and anxiety, the germ of much of Blake's early work. And one may see *The Gates of Paradise* as Blake's expression of his own condition in precisely these terms. Each of the scenes bears down on one central problem: the struggle within a person between desire and restraint. He knows that he ought to be able to forge the image of himself and his world as he would have them, but the danger constantly facing him is that he will not be able either to take the task firmly in hand or to escape the burden of it.[58] In *The Gates of Paradise* Blake is trying to turn the inevitable war between desire and restraint into a form which will prove creative. In any particular design it may be desire or it may be restraint which has the upper hand, but overall it is the way that desire is inseparable from restraint, the way that each begets the other, which perpetuates the struggle and which must eventually be surpassed.

From a point of view outside the cycle it will appear that this struggle will never yield the least advantage either way. But to look at the cycle from a distance is precisely the point of view of 'Air', and it is clear that this astronomical perspective is of little help to him, nor can it be to anyone else. From a viewpoint within the cycle, however, each leap of desire has a momentous importance. From an imaginative point of view the timely renewals of nature will seem to be resurrections in the same way that the emergence of life and growth from the seed will always be mysterious and wonderful. From a centre which one cannot locate life begins, both in the earth, and in the mind; and the difference between an acorn and an oak, like the difference between an ovum and a living human being with the faculty of imagination, is no less than the difference between time and eternity. Thus the events depicted in Plates 6 and 13 are potential resurrections into a new existence beyond the cycle. The birth of desire in Plate 6 is, alas, immediately compromised by the cruel event depicted in Plate 7; but the glimmering vision of Plate 13 may be a true resurrection – and in his earlier years Blake could have left it at that. However, Plate 13 indicates a good deal more than the seasonal renewal of life, and because it does, one begins to see how the cycle may be broken.

The old man in the vision is trying to teach those who see him the way out of the self-perpetuating switch of hope and fear to a more permanent state of creative perception. Such a state cannot be within the bounds of an

[58] For a delineation of this view, see Phillips, 'Blake's Early Poetry'.

earthly cycle. It has only to be found for the beholder, while he holds the vision clearly, to be free. Now the more emphasis one puts on this vision- ary state, the less adequate the cycle is going to appear, no matter how capable the cycle may be of renewing itself. Because Plate 13 is the single completely prophetic plate in the series, it also becomes the most articulate event in the series, and is indeed necessary to offset the dumb despair of the rest. Once one knows that moments of melancholy can be the very occasions of epiphany, then eternity is no longer a state that exists only after death. While Blake does not develop this conception as fully as he might, and while one never sees in the *Gates* the eternal artist, one who can stand self-fulfilled and independent, yet the motto of the plate, and the fact that the mourners have indeed seen what we would, gives one a glimpse of a divine, purely creative and purely imaginative identity which does not depend on nature for anything but an occasion.

The Gates of Paradise contains, then, two visions of life. One, which derives from the majority of the plates, is of human life which though self-renewing is characterized mainly by melancholy. The other, presented in Plate 13, extends the notion of renewal to a completely different state, a state which is beyond the bounds of desire and restraint, hope and fear. Although it begins in melancholy, it is never again subject to the rhythm of the cycle. And although the struggle between desire and restraint is never permanently resolved, Plate 13 suggests how it can be surpassed.

One learns in Plate 13 that desire is not the principal thing: vision is. Desire only provides a quota of energy, which then has to be consumed. But vision is the pristine state of self-identity, the life of pure creation. In putting forward this ideal, Blake does not abandon the conception that ordinary life is more like a treadmill than a pilgrimage, nor does he do anything to make the prospect less menacing. But he does suggest that within the inevitable polarization of hope and fear, desire and restraint, there are moments of renewal, which may, if one uses them creatively, open gates leading out of such a wretched life. In this sense the title of the series is not so ironic after all. *For Children: The Gates of Paradise* is the great prologue to the pilgrimage. It does not present paradise itself, it only shows us the gates that open inward. But once he recognizes them, the reader is ready to begin the journey.

CHAPTER 5

THE BOOK OF URIZEN AND AN ESSAY CONCERNING HUMAN UNDERSTANDING

HARALD A. KITTEL

I

'Satiric poetry sets the flawed reality of the world against the ultimate reality of the ideal.'[1] In accordance with Schiller's succinct statement, portions of *The Book of Urizen* may be read as satire directed against John Locke's theory of knowledge, thus implicitly affirming Blake's own metaphysics of reality.[2] While attention is focussed in this essay on Locke, it should be understood that he represents a school of thought which Blake also associates with Bacon, Newton and, in a wider sense, with Rousseau and Voltaire. In his annotations to Reynolds's *Discourse* VIII, Blake claims to have

read Burkes Treatise when very Young at the same time I read Locke on Human Understanding & Bacons Advancement of Learning on Every one of these Books I wrote my Opinions & on looking them over find that my Notes on Reynolds in this Book are exactly Similar. I felt the Same Contempt & Abhorrence then; that I do now. (E650/K476-7)

As Blake's copy of Locke's *An Essay Concerning Human Understanding* is not

---

1 Friedrich Schiller, 'Ueber Naive und Sentimentalische Dichtung', *Saemmtliche Werke*, with introduction by Karl Goedeke (Stuttgart, 1872), vol. VI, p. 398. My translation. All references to Blake's writings are taken from D. V. Erdman (ed.), *The Poetry and Prose of William Blake*, commentary by Harold Bloom (1966; fourth printing, revised, Garden City, N.Y., 1970); hereafter cited as E. Quotations from *The Book of Urizen*, hereafter cited as *Urizen*, will be cited by plate and line number. Other references to Blake's works will be identified by the page numbers in Erdman's edition and in Geoffrey Keynes (ed.), *The Complete Writings of William Blake* (London, 1966); hereafter cited as K.

2 This paper takes its thematic lead from Northrop Frye, 'The Case Against Locke', in *Fearful Symmetry* (Boston, 1962), pp. 3–29. Further valuable information has been gleaned from Kathleen Raine, *Blake and Tradition* (2 vols., London, 1969). See especially the chapter entitled 'The Sensible World' in vol. II, pp. 101–30.

extant, this claim cannot be conclusively verified.[3] There are, however, early references to Locke in *An Island in the Moon* and in *The Song of Los*, besides numerous later ones in poems, marginalia and in one letter.[4] Mark Schorer finds such references 'consistently annoying until the symbol they compose is defined; this is possible only by locating it in Blake's cosmology. Once located, the symbol may be cracked, and the criticism it contains may then throw some light on the thought that formed Blake's cosmos.'[5] In this essay the attempt will be made to establish in *Urizen* significant symbolic correlatives with aspects of Locke's theory of knowledge, and to reveal the opposed philosophical viewpoints.

Book I of the *Essay* sets out to prove that neither *principles*, practical or speculative, nor *ideas* are innate; that the ideas of God, of Divine, Moral and Natural Law, of reward and punishment are acquired by education and retained by memory. Ideas originate in sensation and reflection.[6]

Our observation, employed either about external sensible objects, or about the internal operations of our minds perceived and reflected on by ourselves, is that which supplies our understandings with all the materials of thinking. These two are the fountains of knowledge, from whence all the ideas we have, or can naturally have, do spring.
(*Essay* II. I. 2)

Had he accepted the rationalist premise that all our knowledge is derived from experience, Blake would have had to agree with Locke's conclusion: *naturally*, there are no innate ideas. However, Blake's radical anti-rational-

---

[3] John Locke, *An Essay Concerning Human Understanding*, ed. John W. Yolton (revised, 2 vols., London, 1972). Hereafter cited as *Essay*. Quotations from the *Essay* will be cited by book, chapter and paragraph number.

[4] *An Island in the Moon*, E447/K52; E451/K57. *The Song of Los* 4.17, E66/K246. Letter to George Cumberland, 6 December 1795, K790.

[5] Mark Schorer, 'William Blake and the Cosmic Nadir', *Sewanee Review*, 43 (1935), 210. Correspondingly, Martin K. Nurmi attempts

> to show how Blake formed certain of his visionary ideas partly in reaction against philosophical enemies, or at least how the particular form in which he cast these ideas arises out of an attempt to expose the errors of these enemies by his taking some of their central concepts and reconceiving them in a visionary context. According to Blake, 'you cannot behold . . . [Satan] till he be reveald in his System' (*J* 43[29].10, E189/K653) and one of his main purposes was to display various aspects of systems of satanic thought in such a way that what was satanic about them would be recognizable.

'Negative Sources in Blake', in Alvin H. Rosenfeld (ed.), *William Blake: Essays for S. Foster Damon* (Providence, 1969), pp. 303–4.

[6] *Idea* 'being that term which, I think, serves best to stand for whatsoever is the object of the understanding when a man thinks, I have used it to express whatever is meant by phantasm, notion, species, or whatever it is which the mind can be employed about in thinking;' (*Essay* I.I.8).

ism throughout his career as an artist led him to quarrel with that very premise which renders 'Mind & Imagination' dependent on 'Mortal & Perishing Nature'.[7] In the early tractates, *There is No Natural Religion* and *All Religions are One*, his position is systematically and effectively outlined. Later, in his annotations to Reynolds, we meet the same sentiments. 'Reynolds Thinks that Man Learns all that he Knows I say on the Contrary That Man Brings All that he has or Can have Into the World with him. Man is Born Like a Garden ready Planted & Sown This World is too poor to produce one Seed' (E645–6/K471). One and a half decades before making this telling comment, Blake had incorporated in *Urizen* the tension generated by his own and Locke's opposing viewpoints. Theme, structure and symbolism of the poem clearly reflect this opposition. First, Eternity, Blake's 'ultimate reality of the ideal', is contrasted with the 'flawed reality' of Urizen. Secondly, by way of inverting Locke's methodology, Blake's attack takes the form of a genesis – presented on an epic scale and in theogonic-cum-cosmogonic symbolism – of empirical premises and their disastrous universal effects.

II

Blake's intimations of the imaginative absolute on the one hand, and of Urizen's fallen condition as revealed by his efforts on the other, gain in significance if examined in the light of Locke's epistemology. Before Urizen's withdrawal from Eternity,

> Earth was not: nor globes of attraction
> The will of the Immortal expanded
> Or contracted his all flexible senses.
> Death was not, but eternal life sprung.   (3.36–9)

While ironically alluding to Genesis, these lines are an appropriate introduction to Blake's poetic exploration of the relationship between spirit and matter and, therefore, of the metaphysics of the world of time and space. They adumbrate a universal harmony of mind and body upon which 'the limited order of a Cartesian universe has yet to be imposed',[8] and thus incorporate Blake's tentative solution to what Mitchell describes as 'the

---

[7] Annotations to the works of Sir Joshua Reynolds, *Discourse VII*, E649/K475.
[8] John Beer, *Blake's Visionary Universe* (Manchester, 1969), p. 80.

traditional paradox of attempting to represent an uncreated (or at least qualitatively different) world in language and imagery which are, by their very nature, post-creation entities'.[9] The inherent allusion to Genesis is an ironic and aesthetic device pointing to a generic relationship between the *First Book of Moses* and *The [First] Book of Urizen*, rather than a specific critique of the biblical Creation account by Blake.

Founded on principles other than energy generated by matter, Eternity does not support spheres formed by material bodies whose gravitation ensures the relative stability of Newton's universe. To the unfallen mind, Eternity offers no basis for rationalist premises and the axioms of natural science, nor is it a suitable object for accurate observation and description. Comprising matter and motion and thus involving the ideas of time and space, the image *globe* has to be associated with a number of properties or *primary qualities* as defined by Locke, such as impenetrability, extension, figure, mobility and, in a wider sense, number.[10] The globe is a most effective symbol of empirical methods of contemplating the universe, of specific conceptions or ideas of the world as manifest, for instance, in Newtonian cosmology; and, indeed, of the observer's state of consciousness.

In lines 37–8 of *Urizen*, quoted above, empirical notions of space, matter and the mechanism of sensory perception are inverted. In contra-distinction to Locke's view, the will exerts control over the senses independent of external causes or objects of experience. In Eternity, the scope of the senses is neither restricted by anatomical deficiencies nor are they dependent on the weakness or intensity of impressions received from an as yet unperceived outside world. The active mind is autonomous and instantaneously fulfils its desires. In Locke's terminology, *understanding* (the *power* of perception) and the *will* (the *power* to prefer, choose, or forbear the consideration of any idea, the motion of the body or of thought) are faculties of the mind.[11] According to Blake, in Eternity mind of its own volition determines the flexible movements of the senses, rather than

being every day informed by the senses of the alteration of those simple ideas it observes in things without; and taking notice how one comes to an end, and

[9] W. J. T. Mitchell, 'Poetic and Pictorial Imagination in Blake's *The Book of Urizen*', *Eighteenth-Century Studies*, 3 (1969), 85.
[10] Cf. *Essay* II.8.23.
[11] Cf. *Essay* II.21.5–6.

ceases to be, and another begins to exist which was not before; reflecting also on what passes within itself, and observing a constant change of its ideas, sometimes by the impressions of outward objects on the senses, and sometimes by the determination of its own choice; and concluding . . . that the like changes will for the future be made in the same things, by like agents, and by the like ways . . .

(Essay II. 21.1)

By conceiving of the will as the elective power of the mind, determining thought and action in absolute liberty, Blake repudiates the premise to Locke's theory of knowledge. In Eternity there are no *agents* distinct from *powers*. Consequently, there are no empirical *relations*.[12]

Reference to Locke's conception of the *will* also contributes toward a better understanding of Urizen's motive for withdrawing from Eternity. Urizen declares:

> I have sought for a joy without pain,
> For a solid without fluctuation
> Why will you die O Eternals?
> Why live in unquenchable burnings? (4.10–13)

Living in the flames of inspired energetic activity with its complementary potential for *joy* and *pain* is associated by Urizen with 'death' in life. Due to its aptness to produce pain, this is *evil* as defined by Locke, whereas Urizen desires joy, permanent and exclusive. Locke calls it 'a delight of the mind, from the consideration of the present or assured approaching possession of a good' (II. 20.7). In the absence of this good, Urizen lives with an 'uneasiness of desire' (*Essay* II. 21.33). Originating 'in the mind from thought' (*Essay* II. 21.41), later in the poem, from change in general, it *naturally* and 'successively determines' (*Essay* II. 21.31) Urizen's will to take deliberate and perverted action. His desire for unqualified happiness, absolute fixity and uniformity is the longing for that unknown extreme 'the utmost bounds whereof we know not' (*Essay* II. 21.41), as Locke claims. Urizen, like Locke's God, is under the self-imposed necessity of being happy.[13] Ironically, his liberty, like that of 'finite intellectual beings', consists in the 'great privilege' (*Essay* II. 21.52) of being endowed with the 'constant desire of happiness, and the constraint it puts upon us to act for it' (*Essay*

---

[12] Cf. *Essay* II.21.1–4.
[13] Cf. *Essay* II.21.50.

II. 21.50). Originating in Urizen's own mind, his idea of liberty is necessity; his idea of infinitude will be shown to be limitation. Urizen's name first suggests his identity as the horizon of the human mind and also indicates his tendency to self-limitation and introspection whether one chooses to read it as a contraction of 'your reason' or as a transliteration of the Greek verb 'ourizein'.[14]

In his fallen condition, as viewed *sub specie aeternitatis*, Urizen appears

> Dark revolving in silent activity:
> Unseen in tormenting passions;
> An activity unknown and horrible;
> A self-contemplating shadow,
> In enormous labours occupied   (3.18–22)

It is hardly coincidental that Locke's 'Pleasure and pain and that which causes them, good and evil', should be 'the hinges on which our passions turn' (*Essay* II. 20.3). At the same time, Blake's lines may be read as the qualifying poetic projection of 'thinking and motion' to which, according to Locke, all 'the actions that we have any idea of' (II. 21.8) reduce themselves. Urizen is identified with his activities – physical and spiritual aspects being metaphorically fused – which, in turn, reveal his self-centred motivations and intentions. Despite certain resemblances, the mode of transformation employed by Blake in *Urizen* and in *The Four Zoas*, where he encompasses an even wider scale of human consciousness, goes well beyond Shelley's mode of imaginative transformation as described in the Preface of *Prometheus Unbound*.

The imagery which I have employed will be found, in many instances, to have been drawn from the operations of the human mind, or from those external actions by which they are expressed. This is unusual in modern poetry, although Dante and Shakespeare are full of instances of the same kind.[15]

However, Blake's imagery and the dramatic configurations in *Urizen*

[14] Frederick E. Pierce suggests the latter possibility and correlates the meaning of the Greek word – 'to mark out by boundaries, lay down, mark out: to limit, define' – with Urizen's character. 'Etymology as Explanation in Blake', *Philological Quarterly*, 10 (1931), 395–6. Harold Bloom adopts Pierce's explanation and surmises that 'in Eternity, Urizen was the entire intellect of Man. The poem's central irony is its constant implicit contrast between what Urizen is and what he was.' Commentary on *Urizen*, E819.

[15] Percy Bysshe Shelley, *Prometheus Unbound*. Preface. Thomas Hutchinson (ed.), *The Complete Poetical Works of Percy Bysshe Shelley* (London, 1961), p. 205.

are not merely drawn from the operations of the poet's creative mind. Among other things they negatively portray the operations of the human mind as specifically conceived by Locke – and thus satirize this aspect of his philosophy. Physical actions and material events are conceived in the poem as objective expressions of these mental operations. This agrees with Blake's own definition of true poetry as 'Allegory address'd to the Intellectual powers'.[16] Originating in Blake's ontological idealism, this definition, which is also a challenge to the reader, is related to Blake's doctrine that 'All deities reside in the human breast'[17] including, as Mitchell points out, 'those *absolute* deities which the intellect constructs out of negations (*infinite, unknowable*). Urizen is the personification of the imagination striving for this illusion of the absolute and the objective.'[18]

Urizen's authority rests on 'assum'd power' (2.1). Concealing his identity,

> unknown, abstracted
> Brooding secret, the dark power hid. (3.6–7)

Significantly both Urizen's identity and his efficacy or actions are adumbrated by the same word, for Urizen is the symbol of perverted *action* and of *passion*. Their efficacy in 'intellectual agents' Locke considers 'to be nothing else but modes of thinking and willing; in corporeal agents, nothing else but modifications of motion'. Urizen is the *power*, 'the source from whence all action proceeds' (*Essay* II. 22. 11). His self-centred desire is the motivation implicit in his withdrawal from Eternity. The emergence of a fallen universe is not so much the effect as the symbolic projection of Locke's idea of power and, therefore, of relation. Or, put differently, Urizen is at once subject and object of power, cause and effect. Through his motivation, his actions and transformations, he will finally reveal himself as the principle of universal abstraction, be it Locke's *complex idea* of *substance*, or the God of the deists.

In his 'stern counsels / Reserv'd for the days of futurity' (4.8–9), Urizen claims to have sought for the fulfilment of his desires, where everything only exists in relation to him. Judging by the specific nature of his actions, and bearing in mind his reference to 'futurity', he has not realized his

---

[16] Letter to Thomas Butts, 6 July 1803, K825.
[17] *The Marriage of Heaven and Hell* 11, E37/K153.
[18] Mitchell, 'Poetic Imagination', p. 90. See *Urizen* 4.10–11.

ambition, so far. He may hope to achieve ultimate happiness by temporarily suspending execution and satisfaction of his desires. In pursuit of this distant aim, Urizen accumulates empirical knowledge by division and analysis.

> Times on times he divided, & measur'd
> Space by space in his ninefold darkness
> Unseen, unknown! changes appeard   (3.8–10)

Urizen exercises – indeed, he *is* – the presumptuous power or faculty of the mind 'to suspend the execution and satisfaction of any of its desires, and so all, one after another, is at liberty to consider the objects of them, examine them on all sides, and weigh them with others' (II. 21. 47). In this consists liberty as defined by Locke and as exercised by Urizen. His considered actions in abstraction and secrecy are perversions of the spontaneous display of imaginative activity, unfettered by reason, in Eternity. Ironically, Urizen's autocratic laws exhaust themselves in the 'contemplation of remote and future good'.[19] They predetermine the nature and direction of any future actions and anticipate their results. These actions will constitute nothing but Locke's 'chain of consequences, linked to one another' (II. 21. 52). Blake inverts Locke's order of determination. Before the will can possibly suppose 'knowledge to guide its choice', the will must have determined such a procedure.

The paradox of Urizen's chaotic world of law and order is not created *ex nihilo*. Eternity exists before its creation. Later, in 'A Vision of the Last Judgment', Blake sums up this aspect of *Urizen*:

Many suppose that before ... the Creation All was Solitude & Chaos This is the most pernicious Idea that can enter the Mind as it takes away all sublimity from the Bible & Limits All Existence to Creation & to Chaos To the Time & Space fixed by the Corporeal Vegetative Eye & leaves the Man who entertains such an Idea the habitation of Unbelieving Demons Eternity Exists and All things in Eternity Independent of Creation which was an act of Mercy.

(E552–3/K614)

In *Urizen*, Blake's attitude concerning this final point is considerably more ambiguous.

Urizen's world is a 'void' or 'vacuum' (3.4,5), 'form'd' or abstracted from the Eternal matrix. In *Paradise Lost*, Milton's God can say of himself:

---

[19] *Essay* II.21.57.

> Boundless the deep, because I am who fill
> Infinitude, nor vacuous the space,
> Though I uncircumscribed my self retire,
> And put not forth my goodness, which is free
> To act or not, necessity and chance
> Approach not me, and what I will is fate.   (VII. 168–73)

Urizen, in contrast, retires to a mere 'place' (2.3) which, ironically, becomes a 'void' or 'vacuum' because Urizen fills it. He circumscribes this 'deep world within' (4.15), himself being surrounded by Eternals, 'myriads of Eternity' (3.44) and, later, by the tent of 'Science' (19.9).

Alastair Fowler's suggestion, based on Adamson, 'that the corollary of an ex Deo theory of Creation is a deiform nature', is applicable to both *Paradise Lost* and *Urizen*.[20] In Blake's satirical adaptation of this theory, both its moral and epistemological implications are parodied. The 'ruinous fragments of life' (5. 9) and 'An ocean of voidness unfathomable' (5.11) reflect Urizen's desolate state of mind. He is an impostor, a 'Priest' (2.1), not God Almighty. He does not create. He merely abstracts in accordance with his restrictive criteria as revealed in the course of the poem. This perversion of creativity is depicted as his deliberate withdrawal into *self*, and complemented by the Eternals allocating to him 'a place in the north' (2.3). The images establishing spatial relations suggest division within Eternity, instigated by Urizen's retirement from altruistic spiritual interaction.

According to Urizen's own report, the 'fire' pertaining to Eternals forced him to retreat into his innermost self, so to speak,

> consum'd
> Inwards, into a deep world within:
> A void immense, wild dark & deep,
> Where nothing was; Natures wide womb.
> And self balanc'd, stretch'd o'er the void
>
> . . .
>
> strong I repell'd
> The vast waves, & arose on the waters
> A wide world of solid obstruction.   (4.14–23)

---

[20] Quoted from Fowler's note on *Paradise Lost* VII.168–77, in *The Poems of John Milton*, ed. John Carey and Alastair Fowler (London, 1968), p. 785. He refers to J. H. Adamson, 'Milton and the Creation', *Journal of English and Germanic Philology*, 61 (1962). My quotations from *Paradise Lost* are taken from Fowler and Carey's edition.

Regarding himself as the principle of stability and continuity, Urizen intends, aided by his 'Book / Of eternal brass' (4.32–3), to transform his sinister realm into the objective manifestation of his ideas and, thereby, of himself. The 'Immortal', whose will freely 'expanded / Or contracted his all flexible senses' in Eternity, has become a shadow of his Eternal identity. As revealed by the empirical nature of his reductive actions and their manifestations, the 'self-contemplating shadow' (3.21) and commander of 'self-begotten armies' (5.16) is both subject and object of the process of division and abstraction.

Urizen's personal transformation signifies a change of consciousness rendered explicit and qualified by being projected on a seemingly objective cosmic scale. He has come to personify the solipsistic, introspective and retentive principle visualized as an isolated world, 'Unknown, unprolific! / Self-closd, all-repelling' (3.2–3), thus safeguarding the continuity of his fallen identity. He is Blake's poetic embodiment of Locke's *self*, 'that conscious thinking thing (whatever substance made up of, whether spiritual or material, simple or compounded, it matters not) which is sensible or conscious of pleasure and pain, capable of happiness or misery, and so is concerned for itself, as far as that consciousness extends' (*Essay* II.27.17). As Urizen's actions of measuring and dividing are manifestations of 'self derived intelligence' which 'is worldly demonstration', self, or Urizen's will, proves to be its own internal circumference and external centre.[21] This theme will be further developed in connection with Urizen's awakening.

The frontispiece of *Europe* presents Urizen's view of himself as Creator. Magnificently leaning out into the abyss, reminiscent of Milton's 'vast profundity obscure', Urizen is occupied in the act of dividing and circumscribing a vacuum of dark cosmic space.[22] This illumination corresponds with, and complements, Urizen's own conception of his creative efforts in *Urizen*. However, if correlated and contrasted with Urizen's introspective brooding as presented in the narrative, the apparently *external* space or vacuum is revealed as an illusion, a projection both of Urizen's conception of the world before Creation and of his conception of the human consciousness at birth. Blake does not accept the Lockean doctrine that there

[21] Annotations to Swedenborg's *Divine Love and Divine Wisdom*, E596/K94. Cf. *Jerusalem* 71.6–9.
[22] *Paradise Lost* VII. 229.

are no innate ideas and that at birth the human mind is a *tabula rasa*; and, as has been demonstrated, Blake does not believe in Creation *ex nihilo*. Hence, this one illumination (the frontispiece) in *Europe* reveals as fallacious the orthodox Christian notion, based on Genesis, of the conditions preceding the Divine act of Creation and conflates it with the *enlightened* conceptions of an external cosmic void and of an empty mind.

Throughout *Urizen* the apparently objective phenomenon of Urizen's creation is presented as a modification of his consciousness.[23] This 'deep world within' which is soon to become to him an external object of perception, is a function of Urizen's mind or a projection of his self-awareness. Thus, for the time being, Urizen's solipsism ironically resolves the persistent contradiction between reality and ideality, thought and thing, subject and object, being and seeming, because

> What seems to Be: Is: To those to whom
> It seems to Be, & is productive of the most dreadful
> Consequences to those to whom it seems to Be: even of
> Torments, Despair, Eternal Death;

as Blake was to sum up his notions concerning *reality* in *Jerusalem*.[24] As Urizen takes his illusions for real, they are real. He thus perversely, if inadvertently, affirms Blake's own radically subjective idealism of a later period, which maintains that 'Mental Things are alone Real what is Calld Corporeal Nobody Knows of its dwelling Place [it] is in Fallacy & its Existence an Imposture Where is the Existence Out of Mind or Thought Where is it but in the Mind of a Fool' ('A Vision of the Last Judgment', E555/K617). According to Blake empiricists and deists are such fools.[25]

III

T. S. Eliot insists that 'you cannot create a very large poem without introducing a more impersonal point of view, or splitting it up into

---

[23] Mitchell, 'Poetic Imagination', p. 93, argues on similar lines.
[24] *Jerusalem* 32[36].51–4, E177/K663.
[25] Locke holds an equally determined view:

> Is it worth the name of freedom to be at liberty to play the fool and draw shame and misery upon a man's self? If to break loose from the conduct of reason and to want that restraint of examination and judgment which keeps us from choosing or doing the worse be liberty, true liberty, madmen and fools are the only freemen. (II.21.50)

various personalities'.[26] Surely Blake cannot be accused of failing to have done so in *Urizen*. The poet's invocation of his muses, with which he introduces the poem, is a case in point.

> Eternals I hear your call gladly,
> Dictate swift winged words, & fear not
> To unfold your dark visions of torment. (2.5–7)

Significantly, the 'Preludium' to *Urizen* is not conceived as a theodicy comparable to 'The Argument' of *Paradise Lost*. Blake's muses do not find fulfilment in glorifying an almighty and benevolent God. Indeed, in *Urizen* there is no indication of the existence of such a transcendent Deity, nor of any source of inspiration uninvolved in the epic conflict. Parodying Milton's thematic declaration, Blake proposes to sing

> Of the primeval Priests assum'd power
> When Eternals spurn'd back his religion;
> And gave him a place in the north,
> Obscure, shadowy, void, solitary. (2.1–4)

A detached report cannot be expected from these Eternals because they are emotionally and actively involved with Urizen's Fall and the Creation of a new universe. If – in correspondence with Blake's ontological idealism and its empiricist negation – the cosmic setting of *Urizen* may be interpreted as the symbolic correlative of the world defined as mind, both the Eternals and Urizen are actors in this now chaotic world. And as in *Urizen* there is no source of inspiration superior to the faculties of the human mind, the poet has no choice but to consult the fragmented remnants of its former universal unity. The Eternals, Blake's muses, are eternal beings whose epic struggle against Urizen is one aspect of the events related in the poem. They perceive and relate these events as 'dark visions of torment'. Urizen's point of view is a different one. The contrasting perspectives of Urizen, of the Eternals and of Los are effectively juxtaposed and even fused throughout the poem. Furthermore, familiar notions of hierarchy and the chronology of events are at once introduced and suspended. This principle applies, for instance, to Blake's treatment of the relation of cause and effect.

Mitchell points out that Urizen's 'rebellion took place *when* the reaction

[26] T. S. Eliot, *Selected Essays*, 3rd enlarged edn (London, 1951), pp. 320–1.

occurred. Before, after, or concurrently are all equally plausible interpretations of the time sequence described in the opening lines . . . In
Urizen these priorities are evoked only to be dissolved in a world which
denies their validity.'[27] The same principle applies to the relation of cause
and effect. Locke calls it 'the most comprehensive relation wherein all
things that do or can exist are concerned' (II.25.11). Only operating
within Urizen's world, it does not affect the poem's narrative sequence,
its internal structure or the configuration of the protagonists. Although
Urizen's world is the comprehensive symbol of 'all artificial things'
(II.26.2) as conceived by Locke, it has no extrinsic cause. When, in the
course of the poem, 'a sensible separation, or juxtaposition of discernible
parts' (II.26.2) is depicted, no more is signified by this than an immanent
reflection and mechanical continuation, in the linear form of cause and
effect, of a spiritual defect inherent in Urizen's world. Opposite the
Eternal absolute his barren wilderness symbolizes a world both of immanent and of supposedly transcendent relations ruled by priest, king,
god and law.

'Priest' and 'religion' are *correlative terms* (II.25.2), to use Locke's diction.
They associate Urizen with such, ultimately, *instituted* or *voluntary
relations* (II.28.3) as deity and worshippers, with *moral rules* and with a
divine law. Furthermore, Urizen becomes the first and archetypal priest
when assuming 'power', thus adopting a priestly consciousness. In the
absence of a supreme deity his authority originates in his desire for supreme
power. Yet he is an impostor, the originator of all immanent relations,
be they temporal, spatial, moral, or generally empirical. His actions ironically reveal the fallacious nature of the ideas represented by such relations
which, according to Locke, are 'not contained in the real existence of
things, but something extraneous and super-induced' (II.25.8). Urizen
himself is the Lockean *cause* 'which makes any other thing, either simple
idea, substance, or mode, begin to be' (II.26.2). He personifies the power
of abstraction, revealed by the objectified operations of his mind.

Urizen is a lawmaker. Promulgated to determine man's private and
public conduct, as well as the methods for acquiring knowledge, his rules
correspond to the consistence of the material on which they are engraved.
Like 'eternal brass' (4.33), and like the 'rock of eternity' (4.43) on which

---

[27] Mitchell, 'Poetic Imagination', p. 87.

they are placed, they cannot be adjusted to the specific requirements of the moment. As they were not conceived in consultation with those concerned, but in Urizen's 'solitude' (4.33), they do not meet the needs of individuals. By allocating to each of his laws the relative absolute of 'one habitation: / His ancient infinite mansion' (4.36–7), Urizen emphasizes his restrictive value standards. Law prevails over Eternal spontaneity; old age is considered a distinction; and everything is confined within spatial dimensions. Finally, in an overt parody of the 'Decalogue', the 'primeval Priest' announces his lore of enforced uniformity, sterility and abstraction:

> One command, one joy, one desire,
> One curse, one weight, one measure
> One King, one God, one Law. (4.38–40)

According to Locke, there is no idea 'more simple, than that of unity, or one: it has no shadow of variety or composition in it' (II.16.1). Infinitely 'repeated additions of certain ideas of imagined parts of duration and expansion' produce the 'ideas of eternity and immensity' (II.16.8). Potentially, *one* is the most particular as well as the most general unit. Applied to Urizen, it suggests his monism. The freedom of the will is severely curtailed by Urizen's conception of *proportional* (II.28.1) and *moral* (II.28.4) relations, and of uniform *desire*, as universal absolutes. These relations originate in Urizen's archetypal withdrawal into self. They terminate in, and are ultimately founded on, Urizen's imposition. 'One joy' allegedly is the reward, the morally *good*, drawn on Urizen's victims by *voluntarily* conforming to his laws from fear of punishment.[28] Blake pointedly correlates divine and civil law with the laws of proportion imposed on man and nature by the arbitrary 'decree of the law-maker' (II.28.5), be he priest or scholarly enquirer. The sequence 'One King, one God, one Law', all of these being correlative appellations, is not accidental. The personal and remote authorities of king and god terminate in the rule of an abstract law, the culmination of tyranny.

Having come to represent the blind, sterile principle of egocentric introspection, Urizen embodies his own idea of uniformity and stability. He is priest, king, god and law in personal union. He promulgates 'secrets of wisdom / ... of dark contemplation' (4.25–6) as secrets, and engraves

[28] Cf. *Essay* II.28.5.

them with illegible scrawls in his 'Book / Of eternal brass' (4.32–3), else-where referred to as 'the Book of My Remembrance'.[29] The illumina-tion on Plate 5 depicts Urizen emerging 'from the darkness' (4.42), his head surrounded by a radiant halo. He confronts the reader with his open book. Far from revealing the truth, Urizen projects his own confused state of consciousness in the form of abstract principles outside himself, so to speak, thus providing them with an apparently independent existence of their own. The foundations are laid for a world which in its *objective* particulars is as yet unknown to its deluded maker.

'When' repelling the 'primeval Priests . . . religion', the Eternals fail to squash his rebellion. They merely contain it by allocating to Urizen 'a place in the north'. As indicated by this quasi-spatial relation and by the quasi-temporal relation of simultaneity suggested by 'when', the Eternals' reaction is correlative with, rather than obstructive to, Urizen's hiding in abstraction and secrecy, and to the means designed by him for the realiza-tion of his perverted ideas. Though detached from Eternity, this 'place in the north' is surrounded by it. The expansion of Urizen's world is rendered possible when

> Rent away with a terrible crash
> Eternity roll'd wide apart
> . . .
> Leaving ruinous fragments of life
> Hanging frowning cliffs & all between
> An ocean of voidness unfathomable.   (5.4–11)

Apparently, this rupture is consolidated when Urizen, in an attempt to protect himself from 'the flames of Eternal fury' (5.18), retires under 'a roof, vast petrific around, / . . . like a womb' (5.28–9). The emergence of this monstrosity is 'View'd by sons of Eternity, standing / On the shore of the infinite ocean' (5.34–5). Due to the contrast of Eternity and 'place', and intensified by paradoxes like 'all between / An ocean of voidness' and 'the shore of the infinite ocean', the notion of spatial *relation* is at once introduced and suspended. Metaphorical projection achieves the conflation of Locke's idea of *place*, the 'relative position of anything' (II.13.10) in

---

[29] This is the caption for a separate print of Plate 5 of *Urizen* in *Legends in a Small Book of Designs*, E662/K262. See David Erdman's commentary in David V. Erdman (ed.), *The Illuminated Blake* (N.Y., 1974), p. 187.

space, and of 'uniform space or expansion' (II.13.10), 'the undistinguishable inane of infinite space' (II.13.10). Apart from revealing Blake's own metaphysics of space, the image of Eternity encompassing spatial infinitude, of the relative position of Urizen's world opposite Eternity, constitutes a satirical reinterpretation of the empirical view of space as 'only a relation resulting from the existence of other beings at a distance' (II.13.27). Urizen's 'Immensity' (3.43) corresponds to Locke's 'infinity of space . . . [which] is nothing but a supposed endless progression of the mind over what repeated ideas of space it pleases' (II.17.7). It is encompassed by Eternity, or 'space infinite, which carries in it a plain contradiction' (II.17.7) as Locke believes, implying the notion of the mind 'actually to have a view of all those repeated ideas of space which an endless repetition can never totally represent to it' (II.17.7).

Though surrounded by Eternity, Urizen's world, paradoxically, is infinitely extended, with Urizen, 'That solitary one in Immensity' (3.43), as the centre of reference. Urizen's world has *figure* (globe, womb) which Locke defines as 'the relation which the parts of the termination of extension or circumscribed space have amongst themselves' (II.13.5). In this early phase of *Urizen*, Locke's 'sight and touch, by either of which we receive into our minds the ideas of extension or distance' (II.13.10) play no part. Hence, contrary to Locke's theory of perception, Urizen's ideas of spatial relation originate in reflection, not in sensory experience. Locke's 'ideas of certain stated lengths' (II.13.4), infinitely repeated, produce the ideas of empirical *immensity* and *eternity*. Associated with *immensity* and with *eternity*, as in 'the rock of eternity', Urizen is the Lockean 'power we find in ourselves of repeating, as often as we will, any *idea* of space . . . and the *idea* of any length of duration' (II.17.5), thus producing the ideas of numerical immensity and eternity, respectively. Extension and solidity are *eternal* or infinitely continuous in the sense that they remain unaffected by mechanical division. Similarly, the continuity of 'pure space' as conceived by Locke 'cannot be separated, neither really nor mentally' (II.13.13). At the same time pure space offers no 'resistance to the motion of body' (II.13.14). In the context of *Urizen*, Locke's concepts of extension, duration and number which 'all contain in them a secret relation of the parts' (II.21.3) are identified with Urizen's consciousness. They constitute the 'wide world of solid obstruction' (*Urizen* 4.23) which excludes 'eternal life', and the 'vacuum' or 'space undivided by existence' (13.46) which horrifies Los.

The emergence of Urizen's world, eventually contained by the Eternals inside its own conceptual reflection, the equally relative 'woof ... called ... Science' (19.9), is a novel phenomenon in Eternity.[30] It is alternately identified as a 'soul-shudd'ring vacuum' (3.5), 'a fathomless void' (6.5), 'vast forests' (3.23), 'a dark globe' (5.38), a 'petrific abominable chaos' (3.26) and

> bleak desarts
> Now fill'd with clouds, darkness & waters
> That roll'd perplex'd labring   (4.1–3)

Some of these images, associated in *Urizen* with material chaos, are unequivocally identified with empiricism. In *A Descriptive Catalogue*, 'The Horse of Intellect is leaping from the cliffs of Memory and Reasoning; it is a barren Rock: it is also called the Barren Waste of Locke and Newton.'[31] A compound of chaotic flux and fixity, of voidness and matter, Urizen's world of fragments is at once a metaphorical projection and critique of Locke's distinct ideas of solidity, body, extension and motion. All these ideas require space for their existence. Significantly, Urizen's egotism manifests itself in his desire for 'solidity' which Locke defines as consisting 'in repletion, and so an utter exclusion of other bodies out of the space it possesses' (II.4.4). As Urizen's efforts of dividing and measuring mental space prove, his thinking includes the idea of extension. The modifications of thought, so far irregular, are metaphorically identified with body and motion – and thus with a materialist conception of reality – neither of which exist without space. Finally Urizen's consciousness hardens into 'the rock of eternity', a conclusion supported by *The Book of Ahania*:

> For when Urizen shrunk away
> From Eternals, he sat on a rock
> Barren; a rock which himself
> From redounding fancies had petrified
>   (3.55–8, E85/K252)

[30]   I turn my eyes to the Schools & Universities of Europe
        And there behold the Loom of Locke whose Woof rages dire
        Washd by the Water-wheels of Newton.   (*Jerusalem* 15.14–16, E157/K636)
[31] E536/K581. For further symbols of this kind and their elaborations, see *Jerusalem* 30[34].40, E175/K661; 66.1–14, E215–16/K701–2.

The ideas of space and matter are identified with Urizen when chaos speaks with his voice, proclaiming his desires, his doubtful achievements, and the tyrannic means designed to perpetuate his rule. Urizen may now be taken to symbolize Locke's complex idea of substance, the unknown, abstract 'substratum wherein . . . [simple ideas] subsist, and from which they do result' (II.23.1). In him subsist thinking, willing and the power of moving, as well as the ideas of coherent solid parts and, eventually, a power of being moved (cf. II.23.3–5). He is the unknown 'cause of their union' (II.23.6), as in him the ideas of immaterial spirit and of matter coexist. Urizen symbolizes all manner of relativity since he is, like Locke's 'ideas of particular sorts of substances', and like his remote God, only known by his accidents which Locke supposes 'to flow from the particular internal constitution or unknown essence of that substance' (II.23.3).

In *Urizen*, there is neither a linear narrative sequence nor a readily discernible 'chronology of motivation'.[32] Due to constantly shifting perspectives, successive scenes do not form logical units. They are thematic fragments forming an increasingly comprehensive and progressively detailed texture of imaginatively interrelated and mutually reflecting events.[33] Analysis of the 'Preludium' has led to the conclusion that Urizen's withdrawal from Eternity and his hiding in abstraction are correlative with the reactions of the Eternals. This central event is further elaborated with attention focussing on Los and Urizen. The 'eternal Prophet' (*Urizen* 10.7) represents the Eternals' cause in Urizen's world. His first task is to isolate, not to recover, Urizen's creation.

> And Los round the dark globe of Urizen,
> Kept watch for Eternals to confine,
> The obscure separation alone;
> For Eternity stood wide apart   (5.37–40)

'Howling around the dark Demon' (6.2), Los suffers utmost spiritual pain:

> for in anguish,
> Urizen was rent from his side;

---

[32] This term is borrowed from Rosalie Colie, 'Time and Eternity: Paradox and Structure in *Paradise Lost*', in Alan Rudrum (ed.), *Milton: Modern Judgements* (London, 1968), p. 193.

[33] For more detailed discussions of the structure of *Urizen*, see Mitchell, 'Poetic Imagination', and especially Robert E. Simmons, '*Urizen*: The Symmetry of Fear', in David V. Erdman and John E. Grant (eds), *Blake's Visionary Forms Dramatic* (Princeton, 1970), pp. 146–73.

> And a fathomless void for his feet;
> And intense fires for his dwellings. (6.3–6)

Urizen, on the other hand, 'laid in a stony sleep / Unorganiz'd, rent from Eternity' (6.7–8). His state of unconsciousness is identified with the *objective* paradox of his petrified chaos. The Eternals call him 'Death' and 'a clod of clay' (6.9,10), while Los is 'affrighted / At the formless unmeasurable death' (7.8–9). 'Death' in this context does not signify an absolute end in the temporal sense, but the fatal dissolution of mind in matter. Urizen's condition suggests the fallacious materialist conception of reality. Confused Lockean modifications of thought and motion come alive as 'direful changes' (7.6), uncontrolled and devoid of purpose. These are the only activities taking place in Urizen's nightmarish wasteland of self-imposed isolation. The atmosphere prevailing in this chaos of mind and matter is visualized by an impressive fusion of cosmic and anthropomorphic imagery, ultimately achieving the metaphorical identification of Urizen with his unfulfilled desires and with the objective projections of his disorganized state of consciousness.

The rescue operation performed by Los on the tormented 'Immortal' with whom he had been united in Eternity, is correlative with Urizen's own protective action as described on Plate 5. Prompted by pain, and with the aid of time, Los binds 'the changes of Urizen' (8.12) into a measurable anthropomorphic universe. First, Urizen has the appearance of the surface of a young planet growing older. Like the irresistible billows of an ocean

> Ages on ages roll'd over him!
> In stony sleep ages roll'd over him!
> Like a dark waste stretching chang'able
> By earthquakes riv'n, belching sullen fires
> On ages roll'd ages in ghastly
> Sick torment (10.1–6)

By destroying the dynamic balance of contraries prevailing in Eternity, Urizen, very much against his intention, has brought about monotonous flux, unpredictable mutability and tormenting instability. These are the objective manifestations of Urizen's progressive spiritual dissociation from Eternal reality.

> And Urizen (so his eternal name)
> His prolific delight obscurd more & more
> In dark secresy hiding in surgeing
> Sulphureous fluid his phantasies. (10.11–14)

So far, *duration* has no visible effect on his irregular and unpredictable 'changes'. Its uniform flux merely perpetuates the misery of Los and Urizen, until Los imposes temporal demarcations on the rolling 'Ages'. Monotonous duration is organized, and the 'changes' coordinated, when Los forges

> chains new & new
> Numb'ring with links. hours, days & years (10.17–18)

In correspondence with Urizen's reductive effort of forming relations of *space*, Los forms periods or relations of *time*, 'dividing / The horrible night into watches' (10.10). He acts in accordance with Locke's view that 'Without some such fixed parts or periods, the order of things would be lost to our finite understandings, in the boundless invariable oceans of duration and expansion, which comprehend in them all finite beings, and in their full extent belong only to the deity' (II.15.8). There is no transcendent deity in *Urizen*, only a presumptuous 'Priest' who cannot cope with infinite expansion and duration, although he caused them to exist. Los performs the tasks both of a cosmic sentinel and of a demiurge, though in a more positive sense than Urizen. Los creates the chain of time, interconnected measurable periods with a beginning and an end, and he imposes both finite duration and continuity on otherwise disconnected mental and material phenomena. He thereby provides a mechanical framework which may not reassemble the fragments of life into their former unity. Nevertheless, he arrests the process of further disintegration. Due to the labours of Los, the

> eternal mind bounded began to roll
> Eddies of wrath ceaseless round & round,
> And the sulphureous foam surging thick
> Settled, a lake, bright, & shining clear:
> White as the snow on the mountains cold. (10.19–23)

The identity of the 'eternal mind' remains equivocal in these lines. It may only refer to Urizen. But it is equally likely to refer to Urizen and Los in their Eternal aggregate.[34]

Previously, Urizen was described as 'Dark revolving in silent activity: / Unseen in tormenting passions'. This we associated with 'thinking and motion' to which, according to Locke, 'the actions we have any idea of' reduce themselves. Now, Los imposes order on the 'eternal mind' by forming Urizen's disorganized thoughts into 'a constant train of successive ideas' (*Essay* II.14.6), as described by Locke. Locke's notion of a 'constant and regular succession of ideas in a waking man' becomes to Urizen 'the measure and standard of all other successions' (II.14.12). Locke's 'waking man' is Urizen tossing in a 'horrible dreamful slumber' (*Urizen* 10.35). As the sense organs have not yet been formed, Locke's claim that the ideas of duration and its measures are derived from sensation and reflection is implicitly repudiated.[35] Los forces the preconceived idea of time and its periods upon the confused 'eternal mind'. The concept of a constant and regular succession of ideas in time is combined with the notion of cyclic patterns of thought. Together they produce the spatial metaphor of the 'eternal mind bounded' and rolling 'round & round', thereby implicitly inverting Locke's observation 'that even motion produces in his mind an idea of succession no otherwise than as it produces there a continued train of distinguishable ideas' (II.14.6). By repeating in his mind Locke's 'measures of time, or ideas of stated lengths of duration, . . . [Urizen] can come to imagine duration, where nothing does really endure or exist' (II.14.31); and thus he imagines 'futurity'. By binding the 'eternal mind', Los commits himself to maintaining the consolidating cyclic motion, thus binding himself.[36] As motion is associated with the idea of space, the imaginative limitation of his achievement is revealed.[37]

The process of Eternal energy fading, first depicted as the freezing of volcanic lava into an icy lake, is followed by a significant shift from

[34] In *The Book of Los*, for instance, Los is described as 'the fierce, raging Immortal' who is bound in by 'Coldness, darkness, obstruction, a Solid / Without fluctuation' (4.4–6).

[35] Cf. *Essay* II.14.31.

[36] In *The Book of Los*, 'The Eternal Prophet [is] bound in a chain / Compell'd to watch Urizens shadow' (3.30–1). Compare especially 4.29–36.

[37] I agree with Frye's view that the 'cycle thus becomes the basis of all future developments'. Northrop Frye, *Fearful Symmetry* (Boston, 1962), p. 257. Yet, as far as *Urizen* is concerned, Frye's claim that thus 'the essential form of Los in this world, creative time, is established' requires considerable qualification.

metaphor to simile. The implicit identification of the 'eternal mind' with
the 'lake . . . / White as the snow on the mountains cold' (*Urizen* 10.22–3)
and with the 'nerves of joy' (10.41) of the 'Immortal', rendered explicit in
The Book of Ahania,[38] is now dissolved in a discursive equation:

> Forgetfulness, dumbness, necessity!
> In chains of the mind locked up,
> Like fetters of ice shrinking together
> Disorganiz'd, rent from Eternity   (*Urizen* 10.24–7)

Ultimately consisting of an infinite number of links, the 'chains of the
mind' may be taken to symbolize Locke's 'chain of consequences' as well
as his notion of linear 'eternity, as the future eternal duration of our souls,
as well as the eternity of that infinite Being which must necessarily have
always existed' (II.14.31). 'Forgetfulness' is the most harmful defect. For
the chained mind, 'locked [sic] up' by empiricist theory of knowledge,
Eternity has not simply vanished in an obscure past. Like innate ideas, it
has never been. Consequently, there is no hope for its recovery in the
future. Separation from Eternity entails the loss of the Eternal present.

Under the restraining influence of the chain of Los the 'eternal mind'
resigns itself to inarticulate passivity. Locke describes this condition:
'Wherever thought is wholly wanting or the power to act or forbear
according to the direction of thought, there necessity takes place'
(II.21.13). The mind's submission to Urizen's 'necessity' signifies its ultimate acceptance of the mysterious power which, by its worshippers, is
believed to govern all rationally unintelligible processes in life. To Blake,
an irrational belief in mystery and fate, submission to inhumane laws of
any kind, on the one hand, and Locke's theory of knowledge with its
blind trust in reason and abstraction on the other, have their common
origin in a passive mind, a mind without creative energy. Ignorant of his
own corruption, Urizen is its origin, agent and symbolic projection.

Through seven eventful 'Ages', Los proceeds to render permanent
Urizen's 'changes'. From an amorphous mass of mind and matter, a
universal, yet finite, man is formed, imprisoned by temporal and anatomical form. While *motion* continues, Los encloses in spherical shape Urizen's
mind,

---

[38] See *The Book of Ahania* 4.11–15.

> a roof shaggy and wild inclos'd
> In an orb, his fountain of thought. (10.33–4)

The human skull is both the protecting 'roof' and the constricting 'orb'. While preventing the total disintegration of the 'eternal mind', it also limits its future scope and flexibility. When the 'vast world of Urizen' assumes human features of cosmic proportions, it incorporates its own space or 'Abyss' (11.4).

> Ribs, like a bending cavern
> And bones of solidness, froze
> Over all his nerves of joy. (10.39–41)

The former 'void', symbolizing one aspect of Urizen's consciousness, is being further encompassed by a rib cage, bones, veins and nerves from the brain to prevent the 'Abyss' from spreading.[39] First, Los forced thought in a cyclic motion, thus severely limiting the scope of the will, 'the power to prefer or choose'. Now, the once 'all flexible senses' are becoming rigid and will eventually depend on external stimuli for whatever impressions they are capable of receiving. With the will no longer determining *thought* and *action* freely, conditions congenial to Locke's theory of knowledge are about to be provided.

The complex symbolism of *orb* and *cave*, associated with the contraction of otherwise expansive potentials, is further developed with regard to the 'Immortal's' eyes ('two little orbs / . . . fixed in two little caves' (11.13–14)), ears ('Two Ears in close volutions. / . . . / Shot spiring out and petrified' (11.21,23)), nose (13.1), stomach (13.5–6) and throat (13.7). Beholding 'the deep' (11.16), his attention is captured by his own 'deep world within', 'Natures wide womb'. By identifying material nature with Urizen's mental world, poetic symbolism ingeniously solves the pervasive contradiction between material reality and ideality, the dualism of subject and object, thought and thing, being and seeming. The objective universe of things is thus revealed not as self-sustaining matter, but as a function of mind, as Urizen's and Los's creation.

Now, moderate *modes* of pain make themselves felt: 'The pangs of hope began' (11.19), hope being, in Locke's definition, 'that pleasure in the mind which everyone finds in himself upon the thought of a profitable

---

39 See *Urizen* 10.33–11.18.

future enjoyment of a thing which is apt to delight him' (II.20.9). It is just another form of the suspense of the fulfilment of desire, comparable to the exercise of reason, previously discussed. Nevertheless, this state of mind is a considerable advance over Urizen's labouring 'In despair and the shadows of death' (5.27). Traditionally despair is the sin against the Holy Spirit or, in Locke's version, 'the thought of the unattainableness of any good' (II.20.11). Confined by anatomical barriers, the 'nerves of joy' become organs of sensory perception or experience, petrified external receptacles for the *simple ideas* and *modes* of pleasure and pain of mind and body, provided by 'the deep', be they passions like hope and fear, or simpler modes such as the pains of hunger and thirst.[40]

Directed against Locke's conceptions of man's powers, modes of thinking, of pleasure and pain, Blake's satire takes the form of a parody of the seven days of Creation in Genesis. Having created heaven, earth and all living creatures, God made man in his own image. Finally, 'God saw every thing that he had made, and, behold, it was very good.'[41] In *Urizen*, however, the forming of a limited anthropomorphic universe, of prisons for thought, desire, will and senses is a perversion of creativity. Henceforth, Urizen will be unable to conceive of himself in a way transcending the boundaries of his fettered, self-centred consciousness. He is one of Blake's 'Giants who formed this world into its sensual existence and now seem to live in it in chains'.[42] Suggesting a psychological and ontological phenomenon, the spatial metaphor of the 'eternal mind' immersed in matter is satirically depicted by the illumination on Plate 6 of *Urizen*.[43] One print of this Plate in *Legends in a Small Book of Designs* bears the inscription 'I labour upwards into futurity'.[44]

This illumination conflates the neo-Platonic image of the sea of time and space with Urizen's chaotic ocean of materialism and with his spatial vacuum which is identical with his spiritual darkness. His 'fluid phantasies' induce him with the illusion of an upward motion in a spatial and, figuratively, in a temporal and an intellectual sense, whereas in truth he makes no spiritual progress and merely marks time. His stagnation is revealed by

---

[40] See *Urizen* 13.5–9; *Essay* II.20.18.
[41] Genesis i.31.
[42] *The Marriage of Heaven and Hell*, E39/K155.
[43] I adopt the plate numbering of the Blake Trust facsimile of *Urizen* (London, 1958).
[44] *Legends in a Small Book of Designs*, E662/K262.

his beard weightlessly streaming to the left and to the right which indicates that Urizen physically and spiritually floats in his pliable environment without moving in any specific direction. The futility of his physical and intellectual efforts is further exemplified on Plate 4 of *Urizen* where Urizen is depicted, with his eyes closed, being weighed down by masses of rock. One print of this plate in *Legends in a Small Book of Designs* is inscribed with Urizen's stubborn claim 'Eternally I labour on.'[45] Considered as a complementary whole, poetic text and illuminations thus reveal the fallacy inherent in the specifically Urizenic Lockean doctrine concerning the acquisition of knowledge and the advancement of learning. By suspending the fulfilment of desire in the pursuit of positivistic empirical knowledge no spiritual progress is made. Man does not truly improve his condition.

With the 'eternal mind' submersed in matter, the perceptive faculty is now confined to receiving sensations from external objects. At the same time, however, and unknown to him, Urizen is surrounded by Eternity.[46]

> All the myriads of Eternity:
> All the wisdom & joy of life:
> Roll like a sea around him,
> Except what his little orbs
> Of sight by degrees unfold.   (13.28–32)

Eternity and Urizen's world are not successive in time. They are 'discrete' or discontinuous 'degrees' or states of consciousness coexisting on mutually exclusive levels of reality.[47] Once Urizen's 'perceptions are ... bounded by organs of perception', he cannot perceive 'more than sense (tho' ever so acute) can discover'.[48] 'Organic perceptions' only produce 'natural or organic thoughts'.[49] As a result, Urizen's 'eternal life / Like a dream was obliterated' (13.33–4). Both Urizen and Los are 'rent from Eternity' and closed in by 'a cold solitude & dark void' (13.39). Having 'suffer'd his fires to decay / ... [Los] look'd back with anxious desire'. He becomes

---

[45] E662/K262.

[46] See also *Urizen* 3.1–2; *Ahania* 4.11–12.

[47] Annotations to Swedenborg's *Wisdom of Angels Concerning Divine Love and Divine Wisdom*, E595/K93.

[48] *There is No Natural Religion*, (b), E2/K97. A remedy is suggested in *The Marriage of Heaven and Hell* 14, E39/K154: 'If the doors of perception were cleansed every thing would appear to man as it is, infinite. For man has closed himself up, till he sees all things thro' narrow chinks of his cavern.'

[49] *There is No Natural Religion*, (a), E1/K97.

aware that they are 'Cut off from life & light' by 'the space undivided by existence'. Los is horrified by the sight of what may be taken to be the metaphorical projection of a 'natural Idea' in which, according to Swedenborg, 'there is Space'.[50] In contrast to the petrified, sterile, cold, dark world of primary qualities and abstraction revolving in regular motion in a wasteland of space and time, 'existence' signifies a 'spiritual Idea' of life. It 'doth not derive any Thing from Space, but it derives every Thing appertaining to it from State'.[51] Obviously, Blake takes Swedenborg's 'spiritual Idea' to correspond with his own 'Poetic idea'.

IV

In the first part of the poem Urizen becomes a 'self-contemplating shadow' by withdrawing from Eternity. He reflects and perceives in the manner described by Locke: 'the mind turns its view inward upon itself and contemplates its own actions, thinking is the first that occurs. In it the mind observes a great variety of modifications, and from thence receives distinct ideas' (II.19.1). Urizen, accordingly, proceeds to divide, measure and, generally, to compartmentalize mental 'space' and the actions of the mind. Abstract principles of law and order are correlated with a variety of objectified chaotic 'modifications' of motion ('direful changes') taking place in a perturbed mind. The consequences of Urizen's reflective 'actions are projected into the actions themselves', which is an important feature of literary satire, as pointed out in a wider context by Price.[52] Examined in the light of Blake's contempt for Lockean epistemology, the satiric character of these complex configurations becomes obvious.

Once Urizen is woken up from 'sleep' by 'the voice of the child' (20.26) he experiences sensations, 'the actual entrance of any idea into the understanding by the senses'.[53] Desire, an 'uneasiness of the mind', determines the will to act.[54] Up to this point in the poem, mental operations and material phenomena were metaphorically identified. Now, the separation of mind

---

[50] From Swedenborg's *Wisdom of Angels Concerning Divine Love and Divine Wisdom* (London, 1788), p. 7; as quoted by Erdman and by Keynes, E592/K89.

[51] *Ibid.*, E592/K89.

[52] Martin Price, *To the Palace of Wisdom: Studies in Order and Energy from Dryden to Blake* (Garden City, N.Y., 1965), p. 429.

[53] *Essay* II.19.1.

[54] *Essay* II.21.31.

and matter, of subject and object, is accomplished. All three elements in Lockean perception, the observer, the idea and the object represented by the idea, come alive, so to speak, when

> Urizen craving with hunger
> Stung with the odours of Nature
> Explor'd his dens around   (20.30–2)

He is oblivious of the existence of Eternity. At the same time, 'Natures wide womb' has become alien to its maker who displays a newly acquired sensitiveness, perverse by Eternal standards, to *secondary qualities* as defined by Locke: 'such qualities which in truth are nothing in the objects themselves but powers to produce various sensations in us by their primary qualities, i.e. by the bulk, figure, texture, and motion of their insensible parts, as colors, sounds, tastes, etc.' (II.8.10). These qualities subsist in the *substance* of matter, which, according to Locke, is 'supposed to be (without knowing what it is) the substratum to those simple ideas we have from without' (II.23.5).

Urizen adopts the role of an observer. With the will having forfeited its absolute control over the senses, Urizen is entirely dependent on *sensation* and *reflection* to determine the will to act. The chained mind passively receives simple ideas furnished by sense organs. 'It is about these impressions made on our senses by outward objects that the mind seems first to employ itself, in such operations as . . . [Locke calls] perception, remembering, consideration, reasoning, etc.' (II.1.23). The will has become a function of understanding. Formerly, Urizen divided and measured his 'deep world within'. Now, he continues on the same lines 'to divide the Abyss beneath' (20.34). For the purpose of acquiring empirical knowledge he forms mechanical tools: 'a dividing rule', 'scales', 'a brazen quadrant', and 'golden compasses' (20.35–9). Unwittingly, he deceives himself. He relies on a natural source of light, 'a globe of fire lighting his journey' (20.48). According to Locke, the will supposes knowledge to guide its choice. As, on awakening, Urizen's mind appears to be a *tabula rasa*, his will remains undetermined with regard to the fulfilment of any immediate desires. Urizen merely decides on the mode of acquiring knowledge about the immanent manifestations of his misery, but not about its true, spiritual, cause. His uninspired decision entails a rational and sensible suspension of desire and merely perpetuates Locke's 'chain of consequences'.[55] His dilemma is anticipated in *There is No Natural Religion*. As Urizen 'sees the Ratio only, he sees himself only' (E2/K98). The 'globe' is the material symbol for this Urizenic 'Ratio'. Projected on the outside world, so to speak, Urizen's condition, his deluded state of consciousness, has turned into the deceptive object of an impaired understanding. With empirical methods of enquiry leading to the accumulation of positive knowledge, Urizen merely rediscovers *accidents* of his own spiritual substance. His perceptions are 'organic', and his desires are necessarily limited by them. Both being 'untaught by any thing but organs of sense, must be limited to objects of sense'.[56] He is a prisoner of Locke's theory of knowledge:

it seems probable to me that the simple ideas we receive from sensation and reflection are the boundaries of our thoughts; beyond which the mind, whatever efforts it would make, is not able to advance one jot; nor can it make any discoveries, when it would pry into the nature and hidden causes of those ideas . . . For whensoever we would proceed beyond these simple ideas we have from sensation and reflection, and dive further into the nature of things, we fall presently into darkness and obscurity, perplexedness and difficulties, and can discover nothing further but our own blindness and ignorance.   (II.23.29,32)

Urizen acts in accordance with Locke's doctrine without attempting to elevate 'his mind above the Ideas of Thought which are derived from Space and Time', as Swedenborg claims.[57] Yet, as has been pointed out, 'worldly demonstration' is 'self derived intelligence'. And the object of Urizen's enquiry is no more than the projection of his subjective fallacy.

In turning his back on Eternity, Urizen passed from light to darkness. On waking up, he has lost sight of the Eternal 'Infinite'.[58] Consequently, he fails to question the validity of his mode of perception and his understanding of the world. Nor does it occur to him to reverse the process of degeneration suffered by mind and senses, to shake 'off the Darkness of natural Light, and . . . [remove] its Fallacies from the Center to the Circumference', as Swedenborg demands.[59] In *Urizen*, this fallacy is every-

[55] *Essay* II.21.52.
[56] *There is No Natural Religion*, (a), E1/K97.
[57] E594/K91.
[58] See *There is No Natural Religion*, (b), E2/K97–8.
[59] E594/K91.

where, in the centre as well as in the circumference. Enslaved by the results of his own imposition, Urizen is forced to follow Blake's dictum: 'When the fallacies of darkness are in the circumference they cast a bound about the infinite' (E594/K92). Urizen weaves his own 'curtains of darkness' (19.5) in a truly Lockean fashion.

The senses at first let in particular ideas, and furnish the yet empty cabinet, and the mind by degrees growing familiar with some of them, they are lodged in the memory, and names got to them. Afterward, the mind proceeding further, abstracts them, and by degrees learns the use of general names. In this manner the mind comes to be furnished with ideas and language, the materials about which to exercise its discursive faculty. (*Essay* I.I.15)

Taken to their limits of abstraction, empiricism and nominalism combine and suffocate the human mind under 'A woof . . . called . . . Science', or ensnare it in a 'Web . . . calld . . . The Net of Religion' (25.19,22).

According to Blake, there is no value in objective results provided by positivistic science because the underlying theory of knowledge is false. The exact and strictly empirical methods employed are derived from this very theory and are designed to produce results justifying and perpetuating it. In Eternity, as adumbrated in the beginning of *Urizen*, there is no basis for the premises of Locke's theory of knowledge. Simple and complex ideas come into their own only after the 'eternal mind' has reduced itself to the level of Lockean substance, bound by Urizen's premeditated laws of science, of social and religious tyranny. When this reduction has occurred, uninspired experience, ambitiously presenting itself as empiricism, becomes indispensable.

Locke believes that man cannot know for certain whether anything is represented by an *idea*. Concerning this third element in Lockean perception, Blake takes a firm stance. Neither Urizen's 'dark world within' nor the external and, supposedly, infinite 'Abyss' are *things*. They are ideas – illusions. Reliance on substances of matter and spirit is 'death'. If there is such a thing as a third element in perception, it ought to be Eternity itself, the second element being individual man's notion of Eternity, which depends on his 'reception of the Poetic Genius' or 'Spirit of Prophecy'.[60]

[60] *All Religions are One*, E2/K98.

By refusing to 'pry into the nature and hidden causes of . . . ideas', Locke takes a truly Urizenic stance. Rather than examining his own condition, Urizen unquestioningly accepts the 'boundaries of . . . thought' – now associated with the notions of space and time. Instead of being recognized as a prerogative of Eternity, infinitude has become an attribute of the material universe. The 'Abyss' is infinite only in a spatial and immanent sense. Truth, with Urizen, is 'confined to Mathematical Demonstration'; and for Los and his sons there will be 'a great deal to do to Prove that All Truth is Prejudice for All that is Valuable in Knowledge is Superior to Demonstrative Science such as is Weighed or Measured'.[61]

V

According to Urizen's doctrine, ultimate knowledge is circumscribed by 'one weight, one measure', and morality is determined by 'One command . . . / One curse'. His 'self derived intelligence', symbolized in the poem by the objective manifestations of introspective brooding, formulates its own theories of knowledge and of morals, its own boundaries of thought and action, comprising all conceivable relations. Mind renders itself dependent on the mysterious substance of matter and on an equally elusive deity. Their respective forms of worship are the pursuits of 'Science' and of 'Religion'. Knowledge is the goal of the former, ultimate happiness that of the latter. Total knowledge is supposed to be a compound of innumerable pieces of information. While the mind accumulates facts, the will has to be determined by reason to prevent it from acting rashly as Locke believes. Any systematic rational enquiry demands the suspense of desire to forestall error. This important aspect, implicit in Urizen's method of exploring 'the Abyss', provides the connecting link with his planting 'a garden of fruits' (20.41). Both activities symbolize different forms of tyranny, because both aim at the subjection of the human mind to Urizen's law.

In *Urizen*, the 'garden of fruits' is a poor, perverted substitute for Eternity and, at the same time, the natural symbol of Urizen's utopia of *joy* and permanence, founded on an implicit conception of moral dualism. It is a trap set up to catch the human spirit. In alluding to the garden of

---

[61] Annotations to Reynolds, E648/K474-5.

Eden in Genesis, Urizen's 'garden' is implicitly associated with the tree of knowledge and its fruits, *good* and *evil*, previously correlated with *joy* and *pain*. Unable to restrain their individual desires, Urizen's 'sons & daughters' (23.24) disobey his command of uniformity and are

> curs'd
> ... for he saw
> That no flesh nor spirit could keep
> His iron laws one moment. (23.23-5)

By way of punishment, Urizen's victims are inflicted with the consciousness of guilt, which is tantamount to their having lost their innocence, and with mortality. The 'garden of fruits', thus, becomes the timeless symbol of man's nostalgia for a state of permanent joy somewhere in a fictitious past.

Urizen's hypocritical 'Pity' (25.3) provides his victims with *religion* through which they hope to gain salvation. Every single one of their actions is now considered to bear some relation to a supposedly *divine* law. Depending on 'the conformity or disagreement of ... [their] voluntary actions' to Urizen's law, moral good and evil, pleasure and pain, are drawn on them from his decree.[62] The 'sorrows of Urizens soul' (25.17) weave the 'Net of Religion' (25.22). Significantly, Locke defines *sorrow* as 'uneasiness of the mind upon the thought of a good lost, which might have been enjoyed longer; or the sense of a present evil' (II. 20.8). The 'woven hipocrisy' (25.32) of Urizen's 'Net of Religion' is 'twisted like to the human brain' (25.21), enmeshing man in reasonings over the origin of his misery and the means of remedy. Also, Urizen's 'Net' is associated with his 'aged heavens' (25.8), relics of a distant past which may once have been an inspired present. They sustain man's deluded hope for a glorious future which will never come. The web of 'sorrows' also divides the 'dungeon-like heaven' (25.12) into numerous religious creeds, turning man against man.[63]

Blake emphatically agreed with Locke on several points: morality is not an innate principle. It is acquired by the exercise of reason, motivated by self-love, and instilled by education – or indoctrination. Indeed, the exercise of reason is an expression of self-love. This applies to both

[62] *Essay* II.28.5.
[63] See *Urizen* 25.43ff.

141

Urizen and his victims. Natural and moral law originate in Urizen's self-contemplation, his self-centred desires. It is reasonable for man to observe these laws in an effort to secure ultimate personal happiness. In the pursuit of happiness and in the pursuit of knowledge man has to suspend his desires, as Locke demands; be it to avoid error, be it in conformity with rules of *moral rectitude*. Thus, scientific methodology and religious practice equally render man a worshipper of Urizen and expose him to the consequences of Urizen's dualistic *Weltanschauung*. *Voluntary* observation of his doctrines averts punishment in the forms of error or curse, while allegedly securing deserved rewards in fictitious 'futurity'.

Conformity with a supposedly divine law and with moral codes in general is symbolically correlated in the poem with the shrinking of man's anatomy in seven days, analogous to Urizen's shrinking from Eternity in seven 'Ages'. Ensnared by the 'Net of Religion', Urizen's victims

> Felt their Nerves change into Marrow
>
> . . .
>
> The Senses inward rush'd shrinking,
> Beneath the dark net of infection.
>
> . . .
>
> for their eyes
> Grew small like the eyes of a man
> And in reptile forms shrinking together
> Of seven feet stature they remaind
> Six days they. shrunk up from existence
> And on the seventh day they rested
> And they bless'd the seventh day, in sick hope:
> And forgot their eternal life　　　　　　　　　　(25.24–42)

Unable to 'rise at will / In the infinite void, but bound down / To earth by their narrowing perceptions' (25.46–7), the worshippers of Urizen assume the appearance of the biblical seducer. Like him, they are forced to feed on dust, suggesting the lowest form of sensory experience. Epistemological and moral spheres are thus symbolically conflated into the image 'reptile forms'. Transformed into anthropomorphic reptiles, men become serpents to themselves. Seducer and victim are identical.[64]

---

[64] See 'A Vision of the Last Judgment', E553/K614:
　　the Reason they so appear is The Humiliation of the Reasoning & doubting Selfhood & the
　　Giving all up to Inspiration By this it will be seen that I do not consider either the Just or the

In this part of the poem, the infectious moral code is held responsible for stifling man's imaginative faculty, symbolically expressed by his becoming dependent on sensory perception. This apparent physical defect serves to account for man's inability henceforth to 'rise at will / In the infinite void' (25.45–6). However, the degenerate state of the senses merely reflects an impaired understanding which erroneously accepts the 'streaky slime' (25.33) of Urizen's hypocrisy for transparent truth. In both *The Four Zoas* and *Urizen* the victims suffer the same fate as the deluded tyrant, since 'Beyond the bounds of their own self their senses cannot penetrate'.[65] Man has become a 'finite intelligence', as described by Locke, with 'its determinate time and place of beginning to exist, the relation to that time and place will always determine to each of them its identity, as long as it exists' (II.27.2). After a man's death, 'Tombs' (*Urizen* 28.5) are built in memory of his past achievements. Symbolizing the veneration of any form of traditional authority, the building of 'Tombs' renders man blind to the possibilities offered by the present.

In contrast with the cosmic setting of the earlier plates, Blake reveals on this final plate of *Urizen* the root of human depravity in quasi-historical and evolutionary terms. Man himself 'form'd laws of prudence, and call'd them / The eternal laws of God' (28.6–7). The restraints imposed on man to curb his will and stifle his desires, are man-made, 'mind-forg'd manacles'.[66] A remote deity and the mysterious substance of matter are both fabrications of minds forgetful of 'their eternal life'.

VI

Urizen is neither a systematic nor an explicit critique of Locke's *Essay*. Nevertheless, elements of Locke's theory of knowledge affect theme, symbolism and structure of the poem. Urizen's mental universe, as has been demonstrated, is a compound of *simple* and *complex ideas*. Symbolically objectified, they harden into those *substantial* foundations from which

Wicked to be in a Supreme State but to be every one of them States of the Sleep which the Soul may fall into in its deadly dreams of Good & Evil when it leaves Paradise . . . following the Serpent.
See also *Europe* 10.16–23.

[65] *The Four Zoas* 70.12.
[66] 'London', E26–7/K216.

sensation and *reflection* deduce the very same proportional and moral *relations*, or abstractions in general, which reduced Urizen and his victims to the level of sensory perception in the first place. Following Urizen's Lockean doctrine, man forms his laws, his gods and nature in accordance with his own limited consciousness. Throughout the poem, this consciousness is satirized by its numerous manifestations. Events, actions and seemingly illogical configurations assume new dimensions of significance if interpreted as satirical projections of aspects of Locke's epistemology or implications of his doctrine that there are no *innate ideas*. The varied expressions of Blake's opposition to the consciousness he associated with Locke's theories of knowledge and morals warrant the thematic continuity and structural unity of *Urizen*.[67]

[67] This observation should supplement Mitchell's findings. With reference to 'the Eternals' reaction to Urizen's usurpation', Mitchell points out that this 'process of assimilation of various modes of consciousness to the basic form of Urizenic consciousness is the structural principle of *The Book of Urizen*, and explains the contradictions which occur when we try, . . . to explain the poem's narrative order in terms of an *objective* spatial-temporal continuum.' Mitchell, 'Poetic Imagination', p. 91.

It is significant to note that the title page of *Urizen* adumbrates in one complex design the empirical process of acquiring and retaining knowledge by Urizenic man. Blake pictorially adapts the ancient metaphor, commonplace in Renaissance literature, of man *reading* the 'Book of Nature' with his feet, and relates it to the conception of the human mind or reason as an unwritten tablet, a *tabula rasa* (see E. R. Curtius, *European Literature and the Latin Middle Ages*, trans. Willard R. Trask (New York, 1953), pp. 304ff, 319ff). While bracing the enigmatic heiroglyphs of the 'Book of Nature' with his right foot, Urizen reflects on and rationalizes (mark his closed eyes) the dissociated fragments of experience before committing them to the as yet empty tablets on his left and right. These tablets may symbolize his state of mind, or new leaves in Urizen's book of memory.

CHAPTER 6

MILTON: THE FINAL PLATES

PETER BUTTER

I wish to ask questions about the last few plates of Blake's *Milton* – partly about the meaning, but more importantly about the poetic quality. Especially in relation to the longer prophetic books, Blake scholars have, understandably, been mainly concerned with the question, what does this mean? rather than, how good is this as poetry? Partly this stems from a quite proper feeling that understanding must precede fair evaluation, but partly also, perhaps, from a rather paltry fear. 'Allegory address'd to the Intellectual powers, while it is altogether hidden from the Corporeal Understanding' (Letter to Butts, 6 July 1803, K825) is Blake's definition of the most sublime poetry. If one asks too many questions is one revealing oneself to be a person without intellectual powers, to be a fallen Urizen or even Satan? Even if so, one should still go on. If in error, one contributes something by giving form to error that it may be cast out.

I ask my questions of *Milton* because this seems to me the best of Blake's longer prophetic books, the one in which he comes nearest to creating a self-sustaining myth, an adequate surface through which the deeper meanings may be revealed. In *Milton* there is an intelligible series of actions, leading to a climax; and some of the characters and actions, at least intermittently, move and impress us by what they are, even if we do not fully understand them. In order to be specific I concentrate on the last few plates, and do not attempt an interpretation or evaluation of the poem as a whole. Nevertheless, these plates must of course be seen in context, and some preliminary consideration of what kind of poem this is and what are the relevant criteria for judging it is needed. For some readers may feel that I have already shown a misunderstanding of the nature of the poem by expressing approval of 'an intelligible series of actions' and by writing of 'characters'. Here, it will be said, speaks the mere corporeal understanding, which can grasp only events in time. In his prophetic books Blake deliberately disconcerts the corporeal understanding in order to raise us to a higher level of awareness where we may see visions of eternity. We are not to rest in the delusions of Ulro, but to become aware of that 'Moment in each Day that Satan cannot find / Nor can his Watch Fiends find it' (*Milton* 35.42–3, E135/K526), the moment less than a pulsation of the artery in which the poet's work is done. Though in *Milton* we are shown what appears to be a sequence of events – Milton listening to the Bard's song, his descent, his encounter with Urizen, his entry into Blake's garden, his encounter with Satan and with Ololon, etc. – we are also jolted into the perception of another dimension. Even after Milton's entry into the garden Ololon still sees him struggling by the banks of Arnon, and all the time those who dwell in immortality see his real and immortal self in Eden (*M* 15.11–15, E108/K496). So, it will be maintained, we shall go wrong if we praise *Milton* for being a story, or blame it for not being as well-told a story as it might be. Similarly we shall go wrong if we look for characters in the ordinary sense. The perception of separate selfhoods is another of the delusions of Ulro from which we are to be delivered by a vision of the divine Humanity; the confrontations are between attitudes, points of view, rather than between persons. All this is true; but the danger in this line of argument is that it can be used – has been by some critics of Blake – to justify almost anything. Sheer muddle is called the structure of prophecy, and all obscurities are justified as the complexity of fourfold vision. We must keep our nerve, and, with due humility about possible failure of sight, try to discriminate between passages where vision is truly created and conveyed by the words on the page and passages where it is not. And we are entitled to demand of Blake's poems, as of any others, that they should have, if not the structure of narrative, then some other demonstrable structure, that the parts should be meaningfully related to each other and should be arranged in a meaningful order. Blake himself was not a rebel against form, and claimed of *Jerusalem* that 'every word and every letter is studied and put into its fit place' (*J* 3, E144/K621).

Milton more nearly meets these demands than Blake's other major prophecies, and it does so in part because it has a clearer story line – even though the story may be only a scaffolding, even though the feeling of a succession of events may be contradicted by the vision of an a-temporal reality. Meaning may be created by frustrating expectation as well as by satisfying it; but if events are arranged in no perceptible order – as, to a large extent, happens in *Jerusalem* – no expectation is created to be either frustrated or satisfied. Furthermore, Blake succeeds best with his mythical creations when he gives them a reality which makes them moving and impressive in themselves, when, in fact, they come closest to being characters in a drama. (I am not maintaining that this happens more in *Milton* than elsewhere; it happens, fitfully, in all the prophetic books.) Los is not just a symbol for prophecy; he is the eternal prophet, a strenuous, fallible hero. Urizen cannot adequately be described by defining what he is thought to stand for; he is always an impressive, sometimes a terrible, sometimes a comic figure, sometimes a tragic one as he contemplates the ruins of his well-meant but deluded plans. Something similar may be said of some of the minor figures, though others are little or nothing more than names. Some commentators seem equally pleased with all these, provided they can scratch together from diverse, sometimes remote and dubious, sources a plausible explanation of what a name stands for. The result is that Blake is both underrated, his best creations being reduced to abstractions, counters in a system of ideas, and overrated, his supposed intentions being accepted for the deed. What disconcerts one about the prophetic books is the large amount of didactic speech-making both by the characters and the narrator. Given the profundity and the complexity of the meanings to be conveyed this was to some extent inevitable. But if Blake had succeeded in creating a self-sustaining myth, he would not need to explain himself so much. The meanings would be enacted dramatically, and conveyed by the imagery – and so they are at the best. No one denies the tremendous imaginative power displayed. Los is furiously active with his hammer and anvil and fire. But Urizen – Urizen sundered from Los – is present also. The books are emblems of the separation of powers of which they treat.

Was Blake right in opposing as sharply as he did the corporeal understanding and the intellectual powers? The most sublime writers – Dante, Shakespeare, Milton, indeed at his best Blake himself – have been able to appeal on several levels at once, to express the highest and most complex meanings in ways which have made an immediate appeal to the senses, minds, imaginations of readers. Dante, after defining the four senses according to which a text may be expounded – the literal, allegorical, moral and anagogical – insists that 'the literal sense should always come first as the one in the meaning whereof the others are included, and without which it were impossible and irrational to attend to the others'.[1] So, though recognizing that *Milton* is prophecy not ordinary narrative, one can invoke the authority (and the example) of Dante in looking, even in it, for an adequate surface to carry the inner meanings.

I start at Plate 38, line 5 (E137/K529), where Milton, 'clothed in black, severe and silent' descended 'down a Paved work of all kinds of precious stones' into Blake's cottage garden at Felpham. These lines are touching and effective, combining the familiar (the cottage garden, Milton for the first time in the poem seen in ordinary clothes as a man) with the mythical (the paved work of precious stones, recalling Exodus xxiv.10 and the law-giving God of Moses, with whom the descending Milton is both compared and contrasted). Here we have a picture both clear in itself and meaningful. But in the next lines I begin to have difficulty, both in understanding and in being able to visualize what is happening:

> The Spectre of Satan stood upon the roaring sea & beheld
> Milton within his sleeping Humanity! trembling & shuddring
> He stood upon the waves a Twenty-seven-fold mighty Demon
> Gorgeous & beautiful: loud roll his thunders against Milton

First of all, what does the Spectre of Satan mean? A few lines later Satan is referred to by Milton as 'my Spectre'; and elsewhere in this poem he is the Spectre of Orc and the Spectre of Albion. Usually in the later prophetic books Satan seems to be a state rather than a person – and a state which cannot be redeemed, though of course beings in that state can pass out of it and be redeemed. Is there confusion here, or fruitful ambiguity? Can Satan both be a being who has an emanation (Leutha) and a spectre, and be the spectre of others? Can he both be, as he seems to be in some passages, a fallen angel capable of redemption and a mere state, essentially illusory and not capable of redemption? These lines, then, about the Spectre of Satan are less easy to understand than those which went before. They are also pictorially less clear. The spectre, for instance, is 'a Twenty-seven-fold mighty Demon'. We know roughly what this means from what we have read about the twenty-seven Churches; but the phrase does not help us to

---

[1] Dante, *Convivio*, Second Treatise i.iv. Temple Classics edn, pp. 64–5.

visualize anything clearly – it has become a cliché. The inner meaning is not assisted by the depiction of externals, as in the picture of the black-clothed, silent Milton above. Does this matter? One possible answer might be that the difference in clarity between the two passages is appropriate, the human confronting the merely spectral, which is properly indefinite.

In the first part of the next section the images on the whole effectively convey the inner meaning required. Using images reminiscent of Milton's hell in *Paradise Lost* Blake evokes his state of Ulro, and by saying 'I also stood' shows that this is a state of ruin which is potential in every man, even in the prophet, even in himself. One of the attractive features of *Milton* is the overt presence of Blake himself in it (I do not mean in the Bard's song), which helps to give a sense of immediacy. The myth is the more effectively universal for being particular. Including Blake's experience in 1800–3 (when properly assimilated, which it is not always) it makes us aware that it contains ours now too.

These lines remind one of Hopkins:

> O the mind, mind has mountains; cliffs of fall
> Frightful, sheer, no-man-fathomed. Hold them cheap
> May who ne'er hung there.[2]

Hopkins' lines convey greater intensity than Blake's longer and slacker ones. The comparison is perhaps unfair, since the intensity appropriate in a sonnet could not be sustained throughout a long poem. But one wonders whether Blake was right to confine himself to his one, even if flexible, metrical form. He thought that he was able to attain sufficient variety within the one form (*Jerusalem* 3, E144/K621), but a comparison with a poem of similar character, *Prometheus Unbound*, shows that Shelley was able to do more to make sound help in conveying variations of feeling by mixing various lyric measures with the staple blank verse. Blake's long lines are suited to sustained meditation rather than to the expression of intense feeling.

The concluding lines of this section (38.23–7) play a too familiar tune without any interesting variation, and the quality of the writing falls. When we read

> Here is her Cup filld with its poisons, in these horrid vales

[2] 'No worst there is none', *Poems of Hopkins*, 4th edn, (London, 1967), p. 100.

we might be in the world of the Gothic novel. Is there not a linguistic poverty in the prophetic books – a too frequent repetition not only of the same ideas and the same images, but also of the same words, used sometimes without much precision or discrimination? Consider, for instance, the very frequent occurrence of awful, dreadful, horrible/horrid/horrors, howl/ howling, mild, terrible/terrific/terror, thunder/thunderings, tremble/ trembling.

Milton then speaks:

> Satan! my Spectre! I know my power thee to annihilate
> And be a greater in thy place

But he renounces this power:

> I come to Self Annihilation
> Such are the Laws of Eternity that each shall mutually
> Annihilate himself for others good, as I for thee.

I have the same difficulty here about Satan as I have written of earlier. 'As I for thee' seems to imply that Satan is an 'other', someone for whom it is possible to do good, who is redeemable. But soon afterwards (40.30–3) Milton says:

> All that can be annihilated must be annihilated
> That the Children of Jerusalem may be saved from slavery
> There is a Negation, & there is a Contrary
> The Negation must be destroyd to redeem the Contraries

Is not the Satan of the earlier passage a Negation which *ought* to be annihilated? In that case Milton's renunciation of his power to annihilate him, his willingness to annihilate himself for him would be a meaningless gesture, merely a means of making himself appear morally superior. This cannot be the intention. I suspect that there is a muddle here rather than a meaningful ambiguity, a muddle arising from Blake's changing conception of Satan. In *The Marriage of Heaven and Hell* Satan was Milton's Satan, the Devil of whose party Milton was without knowing it. This conception is carried forward into parts of *Milton*, where Milton is to repent of his errors, be reconciled to the passionate, instinctive part of himself, to loose Satan from the hells into which in *Paradise Lost* he had cast him (*M* 14.31, E107/K496). But by the time of writing *Milton* Blake had arrived at his conception, which is now the predominant one, of Satan as the Selfhood, and of there being negations to be annihilated as well as contraries to be married. I do not see any way of reconciling these conceptions.

Milton's speech (38.29–49) is an impressive statement of one of the main themes of the poem, but from a dramatic point of view is disappointing at this important climax. In its self-congratulatory tone it hardly embodies the self-annihilation which it recommends; and Milton is not shown doing or suffering anything to give reality to his claim that he is putting 'off Self and all I have ever and ever'. The difficulty of self-annihilation is not dramatized in any way, as it is in the later speeches of Ololon. These criticisms can in part be met by saying that Milton and Ololon express different aspects of the total situation, and that they are not two separate characters, but one. Milton in solemn and eloquent speeches enunciates the doctrine, expresses the conversion of the mind and will; Ololon in more broken and excited utterances expresses, with pain and difficulty, the conversion of the heart. Nevertheless it is a not wholly acceptable paradox that the values of self-annihilation, inspiration, etc. should be carried by one who in his four speeches (mostly he is 'severe and silent') spends most of the time commending the sublimity of his own attitudes, exhorting and denouncing. Regarded as separate from Ololon (he is not so really, but this is how he appears to us) he is an impressive, consistently presented, rather unpleasing character, with a distinctive manner of speech.

Satan appears, and makes a bombastic speech, which is dramatically effective and which Harold Bloom (E842) rightly compares to the vainglory of Shelley's Jupiter in *Prometheus Unbound*. The situation in the two poems is closely similar. In both the main protagonist (Prometheus, Milton) has scored a mental victory (casting out hatred, self-annihilation), making possible a re-integration of his own personality (reunion of Prometheus and Asia, of Milton and Ololon) and a new life for mankind. Jupiter/Satan claims omnipotence and invokes a power (Demogorgon, the Starry Seven) which he believes is on his side, but which is revealed to be against him. But, whereas in Shelley there is a fight, Jupiter is overthrown, and the Promethean day begins, in Blake the warfare is wholly mental. There is no fight, Satan is left at 39.31 in 'great trembling & astonishment', is heard again at 39.59 thundering on the stormy sea, and then fades out.

This is an example where the frustration of expectation is meaningful and effective. Satan makes a lot of din, puts on a spectacular show, but ultimately he can do nothing. His bluster is empty provided no one believes in it. Furthermore Blake, unlike Shelley, is going to stop on the brink of Apocalypse, at the moment when time is to be swallowed up in eternity. The treatment of time in the two poems is similar in that all the actions in *Milton* and all those in *Prometheus* up to the downfall of Jupiter are essentially one action, though they must necessarily be presented in words as a sequence. Shelley goes on to a bold attempt in his Act IV to do the impossible, but Blake's stopping on the edge of that which cannot be fully known also makes a powerful ending.

The splendid appearance of the Starry Seven (39.3–9) is made all the more effective by being given a local habitation 'on my Path':

> my Path became a solid fire, as bright
> As the clear Sun & Milton silent came down on my Path.
> And there went forth from the Starry limbs of the Seven: Forms
> Human; with Trumpets innumerable, sounding articulate
> As the Seven spake; and they stood in a mighty Column of Fire
> Surrounding Felphams Vale, reaching to the Mundane Shell . . .

This is the true poetry of vision, where the images work directly on the imagination even when not fully understood, and where more is conveyed than could ever be explained.

I have some difficulty, however, over the next section:

> Satan heard . . .
> . . .
> Howling in his Spectre round his Body hungring to devour
> But fearing for the pain . . .

Whom does the 'his' in 'his Body' refer to? One would expect it to be Milton; but Milton has not been mentioned for several lines, and grammatically the 'his' ought certainly to refer to Satan himself. So Satan is howling round Milton's body, or round his own body? or does it come to the same thing – in that he is Milton's spectre (38.29)? Satan has no substantial existence in himself, only has a body in so far as he possesses the body of another? If this latter answer is right it will presumably apply also to the 'his' in 38.10:

> The Spectre of Satan stood upon the roaring sea & beheld
> Milton within his sleeping Humanity!

Satan beheld Milton's humanity which is also, insofar as he is Milton's spectre, his own humanity. It may be suggested that this answer solves the difficulties about Satan which I have written of earlier, that I need not have fussed about whether Satan is redeemable because, as the spectre – of Milton, of Albion or of others – he is so. At 39.10–12 Albion is called upon to awake:

> reclaim thy Reasoning Spectre. Subdue
> Him to the Divine Mercy, Cast him down into the Lake
> Of Los

In the fires of Los the spectre will, presumably, be not annihilated, but purified. I do not think, however, that this solves the difficulties I wrote of; indeed, it creates others. If we ask what is the positive value that the spectre potentially represents we shall probably seize upon the phrase 'Reasoning Spectre', and the equation at 40.34 of 'the Spectre' and 'the Reasoning Power in Man'. In that case, if Satan is the spectre of others and the spectre is the reasoning power, Satan is essentially the same as Urizen, which may be said to be confirmed by *Milton* 10.1: 'Then Los & Enitharmon knew that Satan is Urizen.' In that case Milton's wrestling with Urizen and his encounter with Satan are essentially the same – as, indeed, some commentators have said. Satan, it is said, is a more deeply fallen Urizen; Urizen, Satan, Spectre, Selfhood are all ways of talking about much the same thing – all are to be reclaimed. I do not deny that something like this may sometimes be suggested; but it is too simple an explanation to account for the varying, and variously successful, usages of these symbols.

'Satan is Urizen' need mean no more than that Urizen is in the state Satan, as anyone may be for a time ('Luvah is named Satan, because he has entered that State' (*Jerusalem* 49.68, E197/K680)); and to regard Urizen and Satan as essentially the same is false to the overall impression created in the prophetic books. Urizen, though sometimes in the state Satan, is well and consistently presented as the fallen Prince of Light who is to be restored to his rightful position. Satan is presented, especially in *Milton*, in varying, to my mind incompatible, ways. He is the Satan of *Paradise Lost*, to be reclaimed by the repentant Milton; he is the 'Miller of Eternity' (3.42,

E97/K483) who might presumably have a proper place and function if he would stay in his mills (though the implications of this imagery are not drawn out; Satan's mills are always shown as destructive (e.g. *M* 4.17, E97/K483), and when mills are shown in use in the preparation of the final harvest they are the mills of Urthona (*The Four Zoas* ix, page 138, E391/K378)); Enitharmon makes a space to protect him from punishment, and Jesus is willing to die for him after the rest of the Seven have refused (*M* 13.12–27, E106/K494); and he also seems in some passages a mere negation. That these differences are contradictions rather than fruitful ambiguities is by implication acknowledged by Blake in that in *Jerusalem* Satan is pretty consistently presented as a mere negation. There is nothing about Enitharmon creating a space for him, nor about Jesus or anyone else dying to reclaim him. He is 'the State of Death, & not a Human existence' (*Jerusalem* 49.67, E197/K680), a 'Body of Doubt that Seems but Is Not' (*Jerusalem* 93.20, E251/K741).

The spectre also is treated ambiguously in *Milton*. In 40.33–6 it seems to be a mere negation; but in 28.10–20 spectres are treated tenderly and are given form by the beautiful hands of Antamon. One's feeling that the presentation of spectres is imaginatively successful, even if difficult to follow with one's spectrous reasoning power, is confirmed by the fact that this time the ambiguity continues into *Jerusalem*, where the Spectre of Urthona is created as one of the most impressive presences in the poem. He is compelled to do valuable work by Los, and is praised by the Sons of Eden in songs, 'Because he kept the Divine Vision in time of trouble' (*Jerusalem* 44 [30].15, E191/K655). This spectre at least, one is made to feel, is more than a negation, and must in some way be incorporated in a restored humanity in the final vision.

The Selfhood is more a mere concept, finally equivalent to Satan. Some say that when the false self is annihilated the true self will appear, but can point to no passage in Blake where the word is used in this way (except perhaps a deleted, mainly illegible, inscription at the foot of *Jerusalem* 77, where the words 'The Real Selfhood' appear). In so far as Blake has a word for what others call the true self it is identity.

Blake's thought and his mythology were continually changing and developing – not always in step. His great creations were seen first, then their meaning gradually apprehended, rather than being devised to symbolize ready-made ideas. At the best there is richness of meaning and the excitement of discovery. On the other hand his reluctance to discard myths and images after they had ceased to express his latest intuitions sometimes led, as in the case of Satan, to confusion. Always what we must attend to is what is imaginatively created for us.

Returning to Plate 39 of *Milton* – the trumpets have sounded, one might think for the Apocalypse. Satan seems in defeat. The possibility, the difficulty, the frustration of the hope of Apocalypse are well conveyed in the next section (39.32–52) in the picture of Albion stirring on his couch and sinking back. The image is an effective and appropriate one, and it is perhaps cavilling to say that the passage is too long. Not much is added to the general idea of Albion being, in one aspect, England by the naming of many places in relation to the parts of his body – the details are not given any precise meaning. Nevertheless a longish, slow-moving passage is needed to suggest the ponderous movements of the great creature.

Bloom says that Albion's 'struggles are rewarded by the sleep of Beulah, as contrasted to his former, deeper sleep in the Night of Beulah' (E842). This, it seems to me, is an example of something quite common in Blake studies, of the critic telling his own story, in this case quite a plausible one, rather than showing anything that is really created in the words before us. Where in this passage or in the whole poem is the distinction between 'the sleep of Beulah' and 'the deeper sleep of the Night of Beulah' created? If there is any intention of indicating a change in Albion's condition as a result of his struggles is it clearly enough realized in the words? At the beginning

> Albion rose up in the Night of Beulah on his Couch
> Of dread repose seen by the visionary eye

and at the end

> with dreadful groans he sunk upon his Couch
> In moony Beulah. Los his strong Guard walks round beneath the Moon

Perhaps one can attribute some significance to the presence of the moon and of the guardianship of Los being mentioned at the end (though not denied at the beginning)? But the moon is a fairly constant feature of Beulah, and the guardianship of Los is referred to elsewhere (*Jerusalem* 19.

38, E163/K642) in a passage dealing with the fall of Albion rather than with any improvement of his condition.

We now come to the final meeting of Milton and Ololon. Here even the corporeal understanding must accept that complexity is of the essence of the situation being presented – a single, many-faceted action. Milton meets Ololon, a twelve-year-old Virgin trembling in the porch of Blake's cottage at Felpham; at the same time his spirit continues the curious wrestling match with Urizen by the brooks of Arnon, a struggle in which he does not really seek to overcome his adversary, but to make a human form for him, to humanize his own intelligence and his own conception of the divine nature. The reunion with Ololon and the humanizing of Urizen are aspects of a single action. Milton is an individual – the austerely dressed seventeenth-century Puritan poet – and also representative of the prophetic function, which is part of the human totality. Milton has entered into Blake, as has also Los; so Milton–Blake–Los are one, and together a part of Albion, and Albion's wakening and stirring on his couch is another aspect of the one action. Ololon is at once Milton's three wives and three daughters, his emanation in the sense of the feminine portion of himself – his Anima, and she is his emanation in the sense of that which he has created and loved. (I am concerned with her now only as she appears in the final plates. Earlier she was not a single female nor even sixfold, but 'multitudes' (35.37) and a river in Eden (21.15). In 36.14–15 she (or they) materialized as a female: 'They could not step into Vegetable Worlds without becoming / The enemies of Humanity except in a Female Form'.) The name suggests lamentation. Through her Milton laments over his past errors; and through her the errors of the Female Will are repented of, given form and cast out. In Plates 40 and 41 the doctrine of self-annihilation is enunciated in Milton's speech, while some attempt is made to dramatize it in the speeches of Ololon. One can compare and contrast Ololon here with Leutha as she appears in Plates 11 to 13. Reading the poem simply as a narrative one is tempted to say that Leutha is the most attractive character in it, and that her action in descending to offer herself as a ransom for Satan is the most impressive (and the most Christ-like) example of that self-annihilation which is being constantly recommended. And yet she is said to represent Sin, and her descent leads, among other things, to the birth of Death and of Rahab. However we may interpret it, her penitence is moving, and in this speech she is a more impressive presence than Ololon usually is. I suppose it is part of the point that Ololon is such a shifting figure; but the unfortunate effect is that the reader tends always to be worrying about what she represents rather than being moved by her as a fully realized presence. (A comparison with Dante's Beatrice would be unfair; but one has to acknowledge Blake's inferiority to Dante in clarity and in the combining of different levels of meaning.)

The Ololon who speaks at 40.4 onwards may be thought of, I suppose, primarily as the emanation of Milton in the sense of his work, what he has created and loved. She fears that she may be the cause of the rise of eighteenth-century Rationalism and of Natural Religion. Why this should be so is not perhaps apparent from the immediate context, but more than enough has been said to explain it earlier in the poem, especially in the speech of Rintrah and Palamabron in Plates 22–3. One of the things which makes it difficult to read the prophetic books without irritation is the obsessive return to a rather small number of ideas, repeated sometimes without enough variation or addition to make the repetition acceptable. Voltaire, Rousseau, Natural Religion, cruel Moral Virtue, Rahab, Satan – this collocation has become one of Blake's obsessions. There is, however, some advance here, in that it is now Ololon, a portion of Milton himself, who is making the acknowledgement ('Is Ololon the cause?'), whereas earlier it was Rintrah and Palamabron, misunderstanding the reason for Milton's descent, who accused him ('Milton's religion is the cause'). Milton has now been brought to a recognition of his own errors, which he is going to cast out. He has of course been shown as conscious of his errors from the moment of deciding to descend ('I in my Selfhood am that Satan: I am that Evil One'); but now his recognition, through Ololon, of the errors and of their consequences is more specific. Rintrah and Palamabron in the earlier passage may be said to represent an earlier attitude of Blake himself. They have faith in Orc:

> Lo Orc arises on the Atlantic. Lo his blood and fire
> Glow on Americas shore: Albion turns upon his Couch
> (23.6–7, E117/K506)

But now Albion has stirred upon his couch because of the imaginative activity of Milton rather than because of the revolutionary activity of Orc.

Ololon's rejection of Natural Religion leads to Rahab appearing as the whore of Babylon of the Apocalypse. Error is being given form that it may be cast out.

Milton with grave self-assurance sums up the main themes of the poem. In strong contrast Ololon 'replyd in clouds of despair'. She trembles; she shrieks. This, as elsewhere in Blake, makes the consummation seem strangely abrupt. Characters continue to howl, shriek and thunder against each other, and then suddenly we find ourselves at, or on the brink of, the Apocalypse, the Great Harvest and Vintage of the Nations. But, though the language used here is not fully adequate to the theme, the general effect created is appropriate. Ololon is still self-divided. Part of her, the Female Will, resists the necessary annihilation, whereas part recognizes that by self-surrender the Void Outside of Existence may become a Womb. While Milton in the rhythms of his speech expresses the grandeur of self-annihilation, Ololon continues to the end to express the terror, the resistance to that self-giving, and a lack of full comprehension, which creates a bridge for the reader to enter the poem.

I find myself in some difficulty, however, over the meaning of the passage which follows, a very important one:

> So saying, the Virgin divided Six-fold & with a shriek
> Dolorous that ran thro all Creation a Double Six-fold Wonder!
> Away from Ololon she divided & fled into the depths
> Of Miltons Shadow as a Dove upon the stormy Sea.
>
> Then as a Moony Ark Ololon descended to Felphams Vale
>
> (42.3–7, E142/K534)

W. H. Stevenson says that the 'Six-fold Wonder' is 'Ololon's evil part, which joins the Shadow to be annihilated'.[3] In that case why does it appear as 'a Dove upon the stormy Sea' – an image which normally conjures up ideas of hope, protection, fertility? John Beer says that the dove is a negative symbol of inspiration, contrasted with the more positive one that follows, of Ololon descending as a 'Moony Ark'.[4] I find it difficult to react in this way, to find the 'Moony Ark' more positive and attractive than the dove. Harold Bloom, on the other hand, does not ask one to fight against the natural associations of the images. He interprets:

[3] *Poems of William Blake*, ed. W. H. Stevenson (London, 1971), p. 564.
[4] John Beer, *Blake's Humanism* (Manchester, 1968), p. 183.

The Ololon of Female Love joins Milton's rejected Shadow in the depths of the chaotic sea, the watery world of the Ulro. But the Ololon who has chosen Human Love appears as the Dove sent to Noah on that sea. This latter Ololon re-descends to Blake's vale as 'a Moony Ark' of salvation.   (E842–3)

This in itself seems more reasonable, but is difficult to reconcile with what Blake says in 42.5–6, where it seems that it is the portion which divides away from Ololon which appears as a dove. Is the divided off portion of Ololon still valuable after all? The association one naturally makes of dove and ark suggests that the two symbols should not be entirely in opposition. Can one say that Female Love, once put in its right place, becomes a dove, and is received back into the ark of Human Love? Is the divided off portion Rahab, who will in eternity resume her place as Vala? The passage is cryptically suggestive.

Coming to the 'Moony Ark' itself, the perennial question arises of the relevance of bringing in knowledge of other works of the author and of his possible sources. Taking the phrase in its immediate context alone it is not very clear or effective visually, but perhaps brings in the right emotional associations – love, protection through a period of danger. Referring to Kathleen Raine's *Blake and Tradition* (vol. I, pp. 231–5) we are reminded that Blake engraved in Bryant's *Mythology* a picture of an ark in the shape of a moon resting on water with a dove and rainbow above, and that in *Jerusalem*, Plates 24 and 44, there are pictures of moon-arks. The winged ark, guided by females, on Plate 44 is, Miss Raine says, 'the traditional emblem of woman as Foederis Arca (ark of the covenant) in which life travels over the sea of generated existence'. The moon-ark on Plate 24 has within it a representation of the female genitals. If we may bring all this in, we may perhaps understand the moony ark's descent into the fires of intellect as suggesting both the protective function of female love during the passage over the sea of generated existence and the impending end of that condition. The ark will be burned up in the fires of intellect; the female will cease to have separate existence; the sexual threefold will yield to the human fourfold. Is this right? Is this effectively conveyed by the words on the page?

The imagery of the next lines after the reference to the moony ark is disconcerting, but perhaps appropriately so:

Then as a Moony Ark Ololon descended to Felphams Vale
In clouds of blood, in streams of gore, with dreadful thunderings
Into the Fires of Intellect that rejoic'd in Felphams Vale
Around the Starry Eight; with one accord the Starry Eight became
One Man Jesus the Saviour. wonderful! . . .

The ark is surrounded by clouds of blood, streams of gore, dreadful thunderings – images which might as well, or better one might think, be used to conjure up a state of horror in Ulro. I think this is deliberate, and perhaps it is acceptable. The Apocalypse is not going to be presented in a comforting way; it has been won at the expense of the warfare of six thousand years, of the annihilation of the selfhood of Jesus on the Cross, which is now repeated in Ololon:

round his [Jesus'] limbs
The Clouds of Ololon folded as a Garment dipped in blood
Written within & without in woven letters: & the Writing
Is the Divine Revelation in the Litteral expression:
A Garment of War, I heard it namd the Woof of Six Thousand Years

The clouds surrounding Ololon – we remember at this point that she was 'multitudes' before appearing as an individual – in becoming the garment of Jesus unite the whole of human suffering during time with the suffering of Jesus. The garment being dipped in blood and written over with words unites the act of self-annihilation, of Jesus and of any man, and the act of giving expression to imaginative vision, of Blake himself in writing this very poem and of any poet. The garment is, rather shockingly, a garment of war since Jesus and the prophets are warred upon, and must themselves engage in mental fight to build Jerusalem. (Is enough done in the words, here and elsewhere, to distinguish the good spiritual warfare from the evil warfare?) The great themes of the poem, cosmic and personal, are brought together in images which work well – on the symbolic level at least, if not quite consistently in the literal expression.

The Apocalypse seems at hand. The Four

Applied their Four Trumpets & them sounded to the Four winds

And then, in one of the justly famous moments in the poem, the poet returns to his immediate surroundings:

Terror struck in the Vale I stood at that immortal sound
My bones trembled. I fell outstretched upon the path
A moment, & my Soul returnd into its mortal state
To Resurrection & Judgment in the Vegetable Body
And my sweet Shadow of Delight stood trembling by my side

Immediately the Lark mounted with a loud trill from Felphams Vale
And the Wild Thyme from Wimbletons green & impurpled Hills
And Los & Enitharmon rose over the Hills of Surrey

Here, as in the first lines I quoted, we have an effective and touching
bringing together of the familiar and the mythical. The poet outstretched
on the path, his wife trembling by his side, the lark mounting with a loud
trill, the wild thyme, the green and impurpled hills – these things can be
clearly seen and heard, and their meaning in the context felt, if not fully
defined. And when Los and Enitharmon appear, they have been given
sufficiently distinct characters earlier in the poem for their significance here
to be intelligible. In a sense William and Catherine Blake *are* Los and
Enitharmon, Milton and Ololon. The familiar and the myth reverberate
against each other, reinforce each other. But when Oothoon appears in the
following line so little has been done in the two passing references to her
earlier in the poem to give her any distinct meaning that within the
context of this poem alone the reader cannot be expected to make much of:

soft Oothoon
Pants in the Vales of Lambeth weeping oer her Human Harvest

Is Blake entitled to expect the reader to bring forward his memories of the
Oothoon of *Visions of the Daughters of Albion*? And is the remembering
reader confident in doing so, in view of the shifts of meaning which
Blake's mythical personages undergo? Blake would probably dismiss these
questions as idiotic, saying that he is simply recording his visions. He *saw*
Oothoon weeping over the harvest, and that is that. But the literary critic
is still entitled to ask the questions, and to feel that Blake's method of
composition was the cause of some of the defects of the prophetic books.
This line and a half exemplify in the wording the way in which Blake too
often leaves the reader without firm ground under his feet. Stevenson
glosses 'soft' as 'softly',[5] and Bloom says that Oothoon is weaping with

[5] *Poems*, ed. Stevenson, p. 565.

joy over the Human Harvest she was denied in *Visions* (E843). Probably they are both right; but there is no reason in the words on the page why one should not take soft as an adjective, nor why one should not say that Oothoon is weeping in the more usual sense over the thinness of the harvest which humanity actually reaps in the fallen condition. The case for this latter reading is strengthened by the following line, in which 'Los listens to the Cry of the Poor Man'. The Apocalypse is only being prepared; it has not yet come. The cry of the poor still rises from London to Los, who hangs over it as a cloud in anger. So if Oothoon is weeping with joy – which the illustration probably confirms, though it is not a very impressive one – she is anticipating events – which, of course, is quite possible. For, as we are periodically reminded, we are not really seeing a sequence of events in time, but visions taking place within a pulsation of an artery. The images in 42.21–4 take us back to 39.3–9, and mention of the lark and the wild thyme to Plates 35 and 36. All the things we have been seeing have been aspects of a single happening.

The change of tense at 42.32 is expressive. A series of past tenses – 'I fell', 'my Soul returnd', 'the lark mounted', 'Los and Enitharmon rose' – has seemed to be leading us, as in an ordinary narrative, through a series of events towards. . . . But then there is a change to the present tense – 'Oothoon pants', 'Los listens', 'the Ovens are prepar'd'. Blake turns aside from saying that the Last Judgement has happened, or is about to happen. There is still a sense of a tremendous event being possibly imminent; the imagery of harvest and vintage leads the imagination through time to a conclusion. But the present tenses confront us with the thought that eternity is not at the end of time, but now. Every moment has its judgement, its harvest. So the last lines can be understood as referring both to some possible final judgement and to the way we stand always on the brink; perhaps also, on the historical level, to the resumption of war with France in 1803. The note of menace is combined with that of triumph:

> Rintrah & Palamabron view the Human Harvest beneath
> Their Wine-presses & Barns stand open; the Ovens are prepar'd
> The Waggons ready: terrific Lions & Tygers sport & play
> All Animals upon the Earth, are prepard in all their strength
>
> To go forth to the Great Harvest & Vintage of the Nations

The imagery reminds us of the equivocal endings of some of the Lambeth books, especially of *Europe*, where also the vineyards ('of red France'), lions and tigers appear as Los calls his sons to the 'strife of blood'. Did Blake still retain some lingering hope that the strife of blood, however terrible in itself, might usher in the Apocalypse? If so, this seems rather out of key with his new stress on self-annihilation and forgiveness.

The ending can be understood in more than one way. So perhaps we could have accepted both the possible senses of Oothoon's weeping? The reader of Blake constantly finds that what at first seemed to him obscure or confused in the end comes to seem clear or meaningfully ambiguous. With more understanding I shall probably come to withdraw some of the criticisms in this essay. But I still think that Blake in the prophetic books is an uneven writer, who at his best conveys by rhythm and image far more than spectrous explicators can hope to define, but who elsewhere is sometimes too much the spectrous explicator himself, and more often one whose command of language is not equal to the reach of his imagination.

CHAPTER 7

PREFACES TO *JERUSALEM*

JAMES FERGUSON

The purpose of this essay is twofold. Taking each of the prose prefaces of *Jerusalem* in turn, it is, first, to highlight what I see as the crucial aspect of each, and to follow its development in that particular chapter in a way which will illuminate our path through the poem. Second, it is to focus attention on the poetry of *Jerusalem*, which still needs to be set free from lingering doubts about its positive achievement.

Increasing recognition of the coherence of Blake's design in *Jerusalem* has come with the realization that its contexts are the traditions of the English epic and of Biblical prophecy. At the beginning of *Jerusalem* the poet takes to himself the prophetic mantle of Ezekiel, whose symbolic actions, as he told Blake, were with 'the desire of raising other men into a perception of the infinite':[1]

> I rest not from my great task!
> To open the Eternal Worlds, to open the immortal Eyes
> Of Man inwards into the Worlds of Thought: into Eternity
> Ever expanding in the Bosom of God. the Human Imagination
>
> (*J* 5.17–20, E146/K623)

The warning of the impending collapse of national identity in a situation of growing assimilation of a people into their environment leads in *Jerusalem* to the same 'head-on collision between the divine reality and the empirical world' which Eichrodt sees as the inevitable result of the prophet's role in Biblical times.[2] At the same time, *Jerusalem* has many affinities with the classical epics of Homer and Virgil, and with *Piers Plowman* and *The Faerie Queene*, not least in Blake's desire for a similar fullness of scope and universality of range in the design of his poem. *Jerusalem*, as the mature expression of Blake's understanding of art and life, reveals the same concern with disclosing the direction of historical pro-

---

[1] *The Marriage of Heaven and Hell* 13, E38/K154.
[2] W. Eichrodt, *Theology of the Old Testament*, trans. J. A. Baker (2 vols, London, 1961), p. 345.

gression, reshaping it in human terms, and thereby laying the foundation for cultural renewal; a concern which is, in C. S. Lewis's words, 'The explicitly religious subject for any future epic . . . dictated by Virgil.'[3]

In the 'Author's Preface' to the 1656 edition of his poems, Abraham Cowley is the Baptist to Milton's Messiah in his assertion that the most fitting subjects for epic poetry are Biblical. He asks whether 'the friendship of David and Jonathan' does not afford 'more worthy celebration than that of Theseus and Perithous' for 'All the books of the Bible are either already most admirable and exalted pieces of poesy, or are the best materials in the world for it.'[4] The merging of the traditions of epic and of prophecy only becomes a reality, however, with *Paradise Lost*, where Milton achieves that imaginative transformation of his Biblical material which Cowley failed to reach in his *Davideis*. Milton fuses Biblical and Western themes in his poem's uniting of the Genesis story of the fall of man, and its lament for the present state of humanity, with the Renaissance spirit of 'glorification of the physical world and heroic achievement'[5] and its heroic endurance of reality, so reconciling the themes of man's lamentable rebellion and his heroic struggle. In bringing together Biblical and English history, and as interpreter of both, Milton seeks to create an image of the fall, redemption, and recreation of the earth for his own age and society. It is this concept of a national religious epic which Blake adopts from Milton and strives for in *Jerusalem*.[6]

Central to the concept of a national epic in Blake's time was the idea of sublimity, in which the question of obscurity played an important part. In his *Enquiry* Burke writes of finding 'reasons in nature why the obscure idea, when properly conveyed, should be more affecting than the clear'.[7] The role of obscurity was an equally important question in discussions of Biblical prophecy. Robert Lowth's emphasis on the sublime in prophecy is echoed in assertions of the need for obscurity, such as that expressed by

---

[3] C. S. Lewis, *A Preface to Paradise Lost* (London, 1942), p. 39.

[4] *Select Works in Verse and Prose of Mr. A. Cowley*, ed. Richard Hurd (2 vols, London, 1772), vol. I, p. 88.

[5] Eric Smith, *Some Versions of The Fall* (London, 1973), p. 7.

[6] For discussion of Milton's aims in relation to Blake, see J. A. Wittreich Jr, 'Opening the Seals: Blake's Epics and the Milton Tradition', in S. Curran and J. A. Wittreich Jr (eds), *Blake's Sublime Allegory* (Madison, 1972), pp. 23–58.

[7] Edmund Burke, *A Philosophical Enquiry into the Origin of our Ideas of the Sublime and Beautiful* (London, 1757), part 2, section IV.

East Apthorp in his *Discourses on Prophecy*: 'From the very nature of Prophecy, as flowing from the Divine Prescience, Obscurity is essential to it. A prophecy, divested of its mystic and recondite character, would be a direction rather than a presage.'[8] In uniting his epic and prophetic aspirations, Blake first rejected the whole attitude to prophecy which Apthorp represents. This traditional view saw prophecy as prediction or 'presage', and was thoroughly rational in its dependence on revealed knowledge.[9] Blake's rejection of such a rational view of prophecy was in favour of an understanding of it as the warning of the honest man to avert impending disaster. Secondly, Blake necessarily rejected the suggestion that obscurity had any part to play either in his radical view of prophecy or in the concept of sublimity. His response to Sir Joshua Reynolds's suggestion that 'obscurity . . . is one source of the sublime' is well known: 'Obscurity is Neither the Source of the Sublime nor of any Thing Else.'[10] Rather, Blake's warning that 'What is Grand is necessarily obscure to Weak men',[11] is directly related to Böhme's warning to those who would impose abstract speculation on his work: 'As to the children of God, they shall perceive and comprehend this my Writing, what it is, for it is a very convincing Testimony . . . But it continues hidden and obscure to the Children of Malignity and Iniquity, and there is a fast Seal before it.'[12] Far from deliberately concealing meaning, it is part of Blake's epic intention in *Jerusalem* that he should invite his reader to participate in the action of the poem, in its movement from fall to the establishment of the New Jerusalem. As Lewis writes of Milton, it is 'Precisely because the poet appears not as a private person, but as a Hierophant or Choregus', that 'we are summoned not to hear what one particular man thought and felt about the Fall, but to take part, under his leadership, in a great mimetic dance of all Christendom, ourselves soaring and ruining from heaven, ourselves enacting Hell and Paradise, the Fall and the repentance'.[13]

---

[8] E. Apthorp, *Discourses on Prophecy* (London, 1786), discourse II, p. 53.

[9] This view of prophecy is closely allied to what Rudolf Otto has called 'the traditional theory of the miraculous as the occasional breach in the causal nexus in nature by a Being who himself instituted and must therefore be master of it – this theory is itself as massively "rational" as it is possible to be'. *The Idea of the Holy*, trans. J. W. Harvey (London, 1923), p. 3.

[10] Annotations to the works of Sir Joshua Reynolds, *Discourse* VII, p. 194, E647/K473.

[11] Letter to Dr Trusler, 23 August 1799, E676/K793.

[12] 'Author's Preface' to Jacob Behmen, *The Three Principles of the Divine Essence*, *The Works of Jacob Behmen*, with figures by W. Law (4 vols, London, 1764–81), vol. I, p. 8.

[13] Lewis, *Preface*, p. 60.

Originally, the ironic inscription above the archway on the first plate of the poem, an inscription which Blake later deleted together with all the text of the first plate, most probably for visual artistic reasons, presented the reader with Albion's situation, and called upon him to share the poet's vision:

> His Sublime & Pathos became Two Rocks fixd in the Earth
> His Reason, his Spectrous Power, covers them above.
> Jerusalem his Emanation is a Stone laying beneath.
> O [Albion behold Pitying] behold the Vision of Albion[14]
>
> (J 1, E143/K620)

Having deleted this from his text, it is the prose prefaces, which introduce each chapter, which remain as the poet's direct communication to the reader, elucidating the basic dialectical structures of the poem.

I

The first prose preface, on Plate 3, is addressed 'To the Public', a public inevitably comprising both sheep and goats, for the coming of the light inevitably brings with it such a separation. This is the reality of division with which the poem begins, but *Jerusalem* is to be an integrating work:

> Therefore I print; nor vain my types shall be:
> Heaven, Earth & Hell, henceforth shall live in harmony
>
> (J 3, E144/K621)

The first chapter is prefaced by an address to the public because it is to reveal the basic forces at work for integration or disintegration in human life. The deletions which Blake made from this plate reveal a growing sense of determination, and perhaps also of isolation, similar to that experienced by Ezekiel at the beginning of his prophetic work: 'Behold, I have made thy face strong against their faces, and thy forehead strong against their foreheads. As an adamant harder than flint have I made thy forehead.'[15] So, Blake deletes any apologies for his poem, clearly demonstrating a new awareness of prophetic calling, and exhibiting a much tougher attitude to his reader. Yet the theme remains the same. 'Piety &

---

[14] Erdman suggests in his textual notes that the reading 'Albion behold Pitying' is 'somewhat conjectural'. E731.

[15] Ezekiel iii.8–9.

Virtue is Seneca', whereas 'The Spirit of Jesus is continual forgiveness of Sin'.[16] *Jerusalem* is to be a 'more consolidated & extended Work', to meet the consolidation of Albion's situation, a situation which Blake sees as metaphorically eschatological, in that it confronts a people with the ultimate issues of life and death, with the fulfilment or rejection of their national calling.

It is Blake's claims for the measure of his poem which I want to examine more closely, for they are claims which have seldom been taken seriously by those who have found *Jerusalem* to be lacking in coherence and proportion. Modelled on Milton's defence of the verse of *Paradise Lost*, Blake's claim is a similar assertion of 'ancient liberty recovered', in his case from the bondage of predictability, just as Milton desired to be free from the restrictions of rhyme which so hampered Cowley in his *Davideis*, and just as Spenser affirmed the primacy of the artist above the rules of the grammarians. In defence of the measure, then, Blake writes:

I therefore have produced a variety in every line, both of cadences & number of syllables. Every word and every letter is studied and put into its fit place: the terrific numbers are reserved for the terrific parts – the mild & gentle, for the mild & gentle parts, and the prosaic, for inferior parts: all are necessary to each other. (*J* 3, E144/K621)

While much has been done to dispel the mists of which Swinburne complained in finding *Jerusalem* to be a 'noisy and misty land',[17] the poem remains to many a remarkably noisy place, dominated, according to Alicia Ostriker in her study of Blake's verse, by 'the horrid clang of the Blake–Los hammer'.[18] Yeats's characterization of the Blake of *Jerusalem* as 'a too literal realist of imagination' who 'hated every grace of style',[19] has tended to persist in different guises, notably in claims that *Jerusalem* is harsh and ugly, but necessarily so, if it is to incarnate the reality of an ugly fallen world. Frye defends the poem on the grounds that it is governed by 'a grim resolve to portray experience as it is regardless of its horror'. Thus, 'the fundamental difference in approach between *Jerusalem*

---

16 Annotations to R. Watson's *An Apology for the Bible*, letter v, p. 48, E608/K394; and *J* 3, E144/K621.

17 A. C. Swinburne, *William Blake: A Critical Essay* (London, 1868), p. 276.

18 Alicia Ostriker, *Vision and Verse in William Blake* (Madison, 1965), p. 190.

19 W. B. Yeats, 'William Blake and his Illustrations to the Divine Comedy', *The Savoy*, 3-5 (1896), 41-57, 25-41, 31-6.

and *The Four Zoas*, which latter has much more of the rococo spirit, and much loveliness', is that '*Jerusalem* is harsh . . . continually muttering or howling sinister spells to compel the devil to appear in his true shape';[20] a view which has continued largely unchallenged.

It is not my intention to claim that *Jerusalem* is never rugged, but to suggest that ruggedness is by no means the most important of the diverse poetic styles to which Blake refers in his defence. In reading *Jerusalem* we are aware, on the one hand, of the vigour of the language of the prophet, seeking to call a remnant from their group situation, to belong to the true people of God, few in numbers and isolated from the rest of society; and on the other hand, of the calmness and objectivity with which the poet seeks to delineate his vision.

Jerusalem begins with the Saviour's 'mild song', a song which is calm and controlled, gently attempting to awaken Albion to reality; a song of love and friendship, wholly without anger, which establishes the tone and serves as a model for the poet whose task it is to rescue Albion. It is the very expression of the Saviour whose love, like morning sunlight, greets the newly awakened sleeper, and as such it is a reversal of the early part of St Mark's Gospel, which records growing opposition to Jesus until his brothers and mother attempt to take him away forcibly. Here Albion's brethren, together with his whole family, weep at the disease which has caused him to hide his emanation, fearing, like Adam, 'a God afar off', rather than accepting a God of forgiveness.[21]

The contrast between the controlled song of the Saviour and the panic-stricken protest of Albion which immediately follows it could scarcely be more complete, nor more significantly placed than at the very beginning of the poem. Albion's accusing and self-justifying language is the language of fear, driving him, as Blake's skilful juxtaposition of adjectives conveys, along the steeply descending path to self-destruction:

> So spoke Albion in jealous fears, hiding his Emanation
> Upon the Thames and Medway, rivers of Beulah: dissembling

---

[20] Northrop Frye, *Fearful Symmetry* (Princeton, 1947), pp. 358–9.

[21] J 4.11–13, E145/K622 and Mark iii. 31–5. Blake identifies Albion with Jesus in this allusion in a more subtle way than later in the same speech when Jesus claims that 'Within your bosoms I reside, and you reside in me: / Lo! we are One'. The attribution of madness to Jesus by his family is now transferred to Albion, who is seen to be the one who is really mad, 'the perturbed Man' who 'away turns down the valleys dark'.

His jealousy before the throne divine, darkening, cold!

(J 4.33–5, E145/K622)

Faced with this situation, the poet recognizes that it is only the spirit of the Saviour's mild song which can enable him to accomplish his task of open- ing the Eternal Worlds, and so he calls upon the Saviour to 'pour upon me thy Spirit of meekness & love'.[22] This is because he knows that Albion's separated parts

> have divided themselves by Wrath. they must be united by
> Pity: let us therefore take example & warning O my Spectre,
> O that I could abstain from wrath! O that the Lamb
> Of God would look upon me and pity me in my fury.

(J 7.57–60, E149/K626)

It is one of Los's problems throughout the poem to be able to restrain anger and join the Divine Family 'following merciful' by continually relearning compassion and pity.

It is important to distinguish true pity and mildness from its uncreative and selfish form in *Jerusalem*, just as it is necessary to distinguish true from false wrath. It is possible to curse mildly, as Satan does in *Milton*,[23] just as it is possible for pity to take the form of self-pity, as it does with Albion:

> He felt that Love and Pity are the same; a soft repose!
> Inward complacency of Soul: a Self-annihilation!

(J 23.14–15, E166/K646)

The typical form of female pity in the poem is a possessiveness which constricts and strangles. This false pity is closely allied with uncreative and unproductive remorse, such as Albion's, on seeing Jerusalem,

> My soul is melted away, inwoven within the Veil

(J 23.4, E166/K645)

in contrast to the selfless remorse of Britannia on Plate 94. Albion's pity is uncreative because he never sees beyond himself, and so it never becomes action. It sinks into brooding introspection which, as Jerusalem perceives, leads only to despair:

> The Infant Joy is beautiful, but its anatomy

22 *J* 5.18–21, E146/K623.
23 *M* 7.36, E100/K487.

Horrible ghast & deadly! nought shalt thou find in it
But dark despair & everlasting brooding melancholy!

(J 22.22–4, E166/K645)

The Biblical prophets similarly refuse to acknowledge remorse which is
unaccompanied by action, and which remains as ridiculous as Albion's
protestations of worthlessness 'before the watry Shadow'.[24]

True pity, on the contrary, recognizes the reality of sacrifice, as do the
cities, though they turn away from it:

If we are wrathful Albion will destroy Jerusalem with rooty Groves
If we are merciful, ourselves must suffer destruction on his Oaks!

(J 38[43].8–9, E182/K672)

Los must learn the same truth in his search of the interiors of Albion,
knowing that 'he who takes vengeance alone is the criminal', leaving him
only with the force of pity, for:

O whom
Should I pity if I pity not the sinner who is gone astray!

(J 45[31].34–5, E192/K657)

This is the theme of Blake's retelling of the story of Mary and Joseph on
Plate 61, just as it becomes clear that it is the theme of Ezekiel's retelling of
Israel's history: 'Like as I pleaded with your fathers in the wilderness of
the land of Egypt, so will I plead with you, saith the Lord God.'[25] Los
must learn to reserve his wrath only for himself in the form of his Spectre,
just as Albion, when he eventually rises, rises 'In anger', using his anger on
himself to reorganize his Zoas.[26] It is a constant theme of *Jerusalem* that the
only way to deal with others is in pity, while wrath is reserved for dealing
with oneself. It is whenever a poetic form characterized by the same
mildness as the Saviour's mild song is achieved that we have a progression
in the narrative of the poem. This happens with the mild song of the
Regions of Beulah on Plate 25, whose call to the Lamb of God to deliver
individuals by the creation of states is answered on Plate 31. This pattern
is repeated with the call to the Lamb to 'take away the remembrance of
Sin' in the mild song of the Daughters of Beulah on Plate 50; a call

[24] J 43[29].41, E190/K654.
[25] Ezekiel xx. 36.
[26] J 95.5–6, E252/K742.

answered, as Kiralis points out, in Joseph's awakening to 'the Continual Forgiveness of Sins' on Plate 61.[27]

The contrast between the serenity of the Eternals and Los's attempts to control his anger and inner conflicts, remains central until the turning-point of the poem. Los's spiritual sword is a work of 'sighs & tears' as well as 'bitter groans', and his city of art, Golgonooza, is built only of those qualities which characterized the Saviour's song; pity, compassion, and forgiveness, the 'labour of merciful hands'. In contrast, Blake writes of Los's Spectre, his 'Reasoning Power . . . that Negatives every thing':

> Shuddring the Spectre howls. his howlings terrify the night
> He stamps around the Anvil, beating blows of stern despair
>
> (*J* 10.23–4, E152/K629)

while later, in his panic, Albion is described 'Hoarse from his rocks', and his twelve sons' 'thunders hoarse appall the Dead'. 'Storms & fire' have replaced 'the sweet sound of his harp' in Albion's land. Over against this Blake sets the mild songs of the fellow labourers of Los and of the Regions of Beulah.

The turning-point of *Jerusalem* occurs when, in the Song of Los, Los achieves the same mildness, serenity and beauty which characterized the Saviour's mild song:[28]

> And thus Los replies upon his Watch: the Valleys listen silent:
> The Stars stand still to hear: Jerusalem & Vala cease to mourn:
>
> . . .
>
> O lovely mild Jerusalem! O Shiloh of Mount Ephraim!
> I see thy Gates of precious stones: thy Walls of gold & silver:
> Thou art the soft reflected Image of the Sleeping Man
>
> (*J* 85.14–15, 22–4, E241–2/K730)

The whole creation, which has been groaning under its heavy burden of being subjected to vanity, grows silent in expectancy, awaiting Los's song, a song which begins the second main movement of the poem, with its acceleration towards Albion's awakening and the reintegration of the whole of human activity in the life of imaginative perception. The tone of the song signifies that Los has begun to become one with Jesus in the

---

[27] Karl Kiralis, 'The Theme and Structure of William Blake's *Jerusalem*', *English Literary History*, 23 (1956), 127–43.

[28] *J* 85. 22–86. 32, E242/K730–1.

saving and uniting power of pity, providing pity with the opportunity to 'join together those whom wrath has torn in sunder'. Essentially it is a song in praise of Jerusalem, drawing from the visions of Isaiah in Isaiah vi and St John in Revelation xxi and xxii, and from the description of the garments of the priests in Exodus xxviii. To underline that Los's uniting with Jesus has begun, the descent of the dove, which is the song of Los, is followed immediately by a time of great testing, in the form of Los's most painful temptation. Enitharmon, in refusal of Los's dominion, appears 'like a faint rainbow', in mockery of the appearance of Jerusalem earlier in the song of Los, 'clear as the rainbow'.[29] She separates from him and instead of offering her love in self-giving, provokes him with her beauty, tempting him to envy. Los overcomes the temptation by sternly opposing the pattern of relationship which is based on self-giving to that of female domination, proposed by Enitharmon, and the way towards the resolution of the poem is open.

The triumph of Los bears fruit in the new confidence and wisdom which he reveals in his speech on Plate 91. This again clearly demonstrates the diversity of Blake's poetic achievement in *Jerusalem*, for following the beauty of Los's song, here his poetry is stripped down until it has all of the 'stark, bare, rocky directness of statement' which Lawrence was to seek a hundred years later. Los's triumph also signifies the end of his struggles with the Spectre:

> Thus Los alters his Spectre & every Ratio of his Reason
> He alterd time after time, with dire pain & many tears
> Till he had completely divided him into a separate space.
>
> (*J* 91.50–2, E249/K739)

J. Middleton Murry wrote perceptively of Blake's poetry in *Jerusalem* when he suggested that 'it almost satisfies Wordsworth's condition of poetry – emotion recollected in tranquillity'.[30] The speech of the Living Creatures on 55.36–46 may well serve to show in microcosm, in its gradual movement from loudness to peace and serenity, the movement which takes place in *Jerusalem* as a whole, following the Saviour's mild song. The poetic variety which Blake has incorporated within the general movement of the poem is immense. The way in which he has sought to

[29] *J* 86.50, 21, E242–3/K731–2.
[30] J. M. Murry, *William Blake* (London, 1933), p. 257.

put 'Every word and every letter . . . into its fit place' remains a source for inexhaustible elucidation.

II

Blake addresses his second preface 'To the Jews', because of their central position and intimate involvement in the quest to transform history into vision. Yet the truths about life perceived by the Jews are the common possession of all mankind: 'Ye are united O ye Inhabitants of Earth in One Religion. The Religion of Jesus: the most Ancient, the Eternal: & the Everlasting Gospel' (*J* 27, E169/K649). The basis for Blake's imaginative identification of Israel and Britain is the former wholeness of man's apprehension of life:

> Her Little-ones ran on the fields
> The Lamb of God among them seen
> And fair Jerusalem his Bride:
> Among the little meadows green. (*J* 27.5–8)

The work of Satan, separated from Albion's loins in the form of his Spectre, signifying the basically sexual origins of war and hatred, is summed up in terms which describe much of the action of the first chapter of the poem:

> He witherd up the Human Form,
> By laws of sacrifice for sin:
> Till it became a Mortal Worm:
> But O! translucent all within. (*J* 27.53–6)

The Biblical concept of community, which Blake so perceptively grasped, underlies his attack on the degeneration of the idea of the family, which he sees as having become merely an extension of a false individualism; an isolated unit set over against other family units, in the process destroying the openness of brotherhood and community which is behind the Saviour's appeals to Albion, and which is the goal of Blake's vision, when

> In my Exchanges every Land
> Shall walk, & mine in every Land,
> Mutual shall build Jerusalem:
> Both heart in heart & hand in hand. (*J* 27.85–8)

174

The second prose preface, then, is addressed to the Jews because the chapter is concerned to present a reworking of Hebrew history from the beginning in the Garden of Eden to the moment when the Daughters of Beulah can call upon the Lamb of God with confidence to 'take away the remembrance of Sin'. The aim is to provide a bridge for the redemption of a people from the inevitable consequences of their actions, and 'in all the terrors of friendship', to rescue them from the dominion of the law.

The contrast between the former wholeness of man's apprehension of life, when it was that 'every English Child is seen, / Children of Jesus & his Bride', and the present withered state of 'Jerusalem's Gates', is clearly expressed in the incidents involving Reuben in the second chapter. Apart from Karl Kiralis's essay, 'A Guide to the Intellectual Symbolism of William Blake's Later Prophetic Writings',[31] Reuben has not received a great deal of critical attention, whereas an examination of his symbolic function in *Jerusalem* underlines the depth of the coherence of Blake's design in the poem.

The situations which involve Reuben in the second chapter are not the isolated incidents they have often been taken to be, and as Kiralis seems to see them when he writes that 'many seemingly disconnected things occur to him'.[32] The introduction of Reuben on Plate 30 is directly related to Los's attacks on Hand and the other sons of Albion. Hand, who is described earlier as condensing his thoughts into bars, to be forged into 'the sword of war',[33] is under the dominion of Vala, who was herself fed and nourished in childhood with 'the flesh of multitudes', and Los's purpose is to recount how this present situation of Hand's being completely unmanned has come about.

Hand is a doubly representative figure. His name testifies to his normality, and he is the eldest son of Israel, as Jacob came to be called. However, by enrooting into Bashan, land of cruel giants, he eventually becomes merely 'a vaporous Shadow in a Void', and just as his father's name was changed to Israel to signify his change of character, so Reuben's is changed to Hand to signify his corruption into a vicious accuser, in his role as

31 Karl Kiralis, 'A Guide to the Intellectual Symbolism of William Blake's Later Prophetic Writings', *Criticism*, 1 (1959), 190–210. Repr. in John E. Grant (ed.), *Discussions of William Blake* (Boston, 1961).
32 Kiralis, 'Intellectual Symbolism', p. 197.
33 *J* 9.4–5, E150/K628.

representative of the Hunt brothers, editors of the *Examiner*. As David Erdman has shown in his study, *Blake: Prophet against Empire*, Blake focusses his attention on 'the Cerberus of the press, the triple editorial person of the *Examiner* collectively called Hand because of the accusing "indicator" or printer's fist of Leigh Hunt's editorial signature'.[34] Reuben's enrooting into Bashan, the kingdom of Og, speaks of the freedom of man to choose the state in which he dwells, which may be a state of humanity, or as in this case, of inhumanity, for of Og it is written: 'For only Og king of Bashan remained of the remnant of giants; behold, his bedstead was a bedstead of iron; is it not in Rabbath of the children of Ammon?'[35] As the representative of the tribe which settled with Gad and half of Manasseh east of the Jordan, outside of the promised land, Reuben is the very incarnation of Albion's problem of being enslaved and corrupted by his passive nature:

> Reuben slept in Bashan like one dead in the valley
> Cut off from Albions mounts & from all the Earths summits
>
> (*J* 30[34].43–4, E175/K661)

Los's work of sending Reuben over the Jordan has been variously understood. Kiralis surmises that

What Blake must have had in mind here was the fact that Reuben as a 'Vegetative Man' (36.23–4) was not ready for the Promised Land and so Blake interprets the Biblical Reuben's decision to remain on the east side of the Jordan. Los therefore was trying to force the hand of Providence, since Reuben was eventually to settle on the east bank and his descendants preferred to live there.[36]

This is very close to the truth. Los's work becomes more comprehensible, however, if it is understood as Blake's refashioning of the events of Joshua xxii, where the Reubenites build their altar over against the Promised Land. In this chapter, Joshua calls the Reubenites, together with the Gaddites and the half tribe of Manasseh, to come from their home east of the Jordan to receive his blessing. This they do, and return home again to the other side of the Jordan. On the way home they build a great altar, which the Israelites assume to be a claim by the Reubenites of their own separate identity over against the rest of the people, so that they prepare to

---

[34] D. V. Erdman, *Blake: Prophet against Empire* (Princeton, 1954, revised edn 1969), pp. 458–9.
[35] Deuteronomy iii. 11.
[36] Kiralis, 'Intellectual Symbolism', pp. 199–200.

go to war with the Reubenites. Peace is restored when it is made clear that the opposite was in fact the intention, for the Reubenites wished the altar, built at the Jordan, to be a symbol of solidarity with Israel, lest it should ever be said that the Jordan formed a frontier between Israel and Reuben. Blake's reworking of the story is to say, in effect, that the building of the altar was indeed an inhuman act, and that in accepting the explanation of the Reubenites, the Israelites were becoming what they beheld, seeing evil as good. Los begins, then, by organizing and giving distinct form to Reuben's weaknesses in contracting his senses, and presents him to the people of earth that they may see the reality of their situation:

> Los rolled his Eyes into two narrow circles, then sent him
> Over Jordan; all terrified fled: they became what they beheld.
>
> (J 30[34].53-4, E175/K661)

Although those living in delusion and the 'pleasant shadow of repose' cannot face the reality when they see it, the artist knows that there is a principle at work whereby, though individuals may flee the reality, the community is gradually changed, in the process of time, into what it beholds.

The story of Reuben in *Jerusalem* is an expansion of Blake's words earlier in the poem, when Los says that he labours in order

> That he who will not defend Truth, may be compelld to defend
> A Lie: that he may be snared and caught and snared and taken
>
> (J 9.29-30, E151/K628)

Although it may appear that Los's work is rejected, in that the people flee from the revelation of themselves which he sets before them, the description of his situation, 'standing on Mam-Tor, looking over Europe & Asia', emphasizes the vantage-point of the artist. The reference of this to Blake's own situation, and the reason he addresses himself to Hand, as the representative of the fiercest attacks on his work, is clear. At the beginning of the poem, in calling upon the Saviour for the 'Spirit of meekness & love', the work of the poet is seen to be not only writing of the building of Golgonooza, but also:

> of the terrors of Entuthon:
> Of Hand & Hyle & Coban, of Kwantok, Peachey, Brereton, Slayd & Hutton:
> Of the terrible sons & daughters of Albion. and their Generations.
>
> (J 5.24-6, E146/K623)

Blake's confidence is that the results of his epic will be analogous to the results of Los's giving distinct form to Reuben's weaknesses, as a necessary stage on the path to reintegration:

> every-one that saw him
> Fled! they fled at his horrible Form: they hid in caves
> And dens, they looked on one-another & became what they beheld
>
> (*J* 30[34].48–50, E175/K661)

The horror from which the people flee is the truth which the poet reveals about them, as is borne out by the warnings which Los draws from his refashioning of the events of Joshua xxii:

> If Perceptive Organs vary: Objects of Perception seem to vary:
> If the Perceptive Organs close: their Objects seem to close also:
>
> (*J* 30[34].55–6, E175/K661)

Los's work for Reuben is paralleled by a similar act of the Saviour for Albion, giving two limits and outlines to his fallen condition, called Satan and Adam. The Saviour's voice is the voice of the universal man, of 'multitudes without number'. Again he enters the furnace in the appearance of a man to save the law-breakers from the punishment of their judges, as in the Book of Daniel, when a fourth man was seen in Nebuchadnezzar's fiery furnace, and 'the form of the fourth . . . like the Son of God'.[37] Here, the Saviour appears out of pity for the punisher as well as the victim, for at the beginning of the second chapter Albion had become 'punisher & judge' as well as sufferer. The Saviour's pity, and his counsels which once again are described as mild, are a reinforcement to Los at this time of the lessons he needs to learn if his work is to be accomplished and man set free from a state of self-condemnation for not having kept the laws of moral virtue and natural religion, which are death 'to every energy of man, and forbid the springs of life':

> Albion goes to Eternal Death: In Me all Eternity.
> Must pass thro' condemnation, and awake beyond the Grave!
>
> (*J* 31[35].9–10, E176/K662)

Reuben, as we see from Plate 32, is still in the process of being conformed to the fallen world, but has not yet reached the state of confining

---

[37] Daniel iii. 25.

all his desires to the attainable. When fully conformed, he will find and accept physical and aesthetic satisfaction as beyond his reach:

> Reuben return'd to his place, in vain he sought beautiful Tirzah
> For his Eyelids were narrowd, & his Nostrils scented the ground
> (*J* 32[36].1–2, E176/K662)

Reference to the continual work of Los, raging 'in the Divisions of Reuben, / Building the Moon of Ulro plank by plank & rib by rib',[38] labouring to give form to the material world in order that its delusions may become evident and be rejected, reminds us at this stage that these plates are a retrospective summary, called forth to explain the nature of Hand and how he came to be in the state in which we find him in *Jerusalem*. Hand is a Reuben who has turned towards the reasonings which character-ize Heshbon, whose springs issue into the Dead Sea, and who finds only frustration and doubt in daily life, for 'In the love of Tirzah he said: Doubt is my food day & night.'[39]

With four of Reuben's senses turned outward and limited, Blake explains precisely the relationship between his symbolic figures:

> Hand stood between Reuben & Merlin, as the Reasoning Spectre
> Stands between the Vegetative Man & his Immortal Imagination
> (*J* 32[36].23–4, E176/K663)

Just as Reuben's father became an Israel, so Reuben may become a Hand or a Merlin, the very incarnation of Albion's fall into destruction or of his potential. As the flood of limited sense perception and materiality pours in upon Albion, Blake reminds us of the state from which Reuben has fallen, and of the potential which he still retains:

> The Atlantic Continent sunk round Albions cliffy shore
> And the Sea poured in amain upon the Giants of Albion
> As Los bended the Senses of Reuben Reuben is Merlin
> Exploring the Three States of Ulro; Creation; Redemption. & Judgment
> (*J* 32[36].38–41, E177/K663)

These lines have been made much more difficult than they really are. Kiralis writes that 'If the quotation read "Reuben *could be* Merlin" rather

---

[38] *J* 32[36].3–4, E176/K662.
[39] *J* 32[36].7, E176/K662.

than "Reuben *is* Merlin", then Northrop Frye's explanation of these lines ("Reuben purified of his selfhood would become a prophetic imagination") would be highly acceptable and desirable.'[40] In fact, the Reuben whom we see exploring Ulro, and whose senses have been contracted, *is* Merlin, the 'Immortal Imagination'. Blake is concerned to emphasize that Reuben's only true identity is Merlin, for as the poem constantly affirms:

> There is an Outside spread Without, & an Outside spread Within
> Beyond the Outline of Identity both ways, which meet in One:
> An orbed Void of doubt, despair, hunger & thirst & sorrow.
>
> (*J* 18.2–4, E161/K640)

This reminder of man's true identity is set over against the war which is taking place within Albion himself, where the 'Four Eternal Senses of Man' gradually become 'Four Elements separating from the Limbs of Albion' until they change into 'Four ravening deathlike Forms'.[41]

III

At the root of Blake's indictment of Deism in the third prose preface on Plate 52 is his insistence that the individual must be seen apart from the state in which he may be at any given moment. The state of Rahab which must be put off is a state of Deistic folly, characterized by the twin enemies of natural morality and natural philosophy, which teach that 'Man is Righteous in his Vegetated Spectre'. Natural morality is the religion of Satan, the marks of which are the taking of vengeance for sin, and the waging of war in the name of God. In summing up these elements of Deism, Blake castigates self-righteousness as being just as great if not a greater evil than the destructive power of self-condemnation, which latter continually robs Albion of his resources for positive action: 'Deism, is the Worship of the God of this World by the means of what you call Natural Religion and Natural Philosophy, and of Natural Morality or Self-Righteousness, the Selfish Virtues of the Natural Heart. This was the Religion of the Pharisees who murderd Jesus' (*J* 52, E199/K682). It is their freedom from such self-righteous hypocrisy which absolves both Monk and Methodist from Blake's scorn, and their gospel of forgiveness which

---

[40] Kiralis, 'Intellectual Symbolism', p. 201.
[41] *J* 32[36].31–5, E177/K663.

unites them in the religion of Jesus. The stanzas which conclude the preface show that real power resides not in the weapons of corporeal warfare, but in the only forces which can redeem Albion, the power of pity and forgiveness:

> For a Tear is an Intellectual thing;
> And a Sigh is the Sword of an Angel King
> And the bitter groan of a Martyrs woe
> Is an Arrow from the Almighties Bow!   (*J* 52.25–8)

In many ways, the dominating figure of the third chapter of *Jerusalem* is Rahab, particularly in that all the forces of evil are drawn together into one in this symbolic figure. However, before examining the function of Rahab in this chapter, it is important to understand the place of the

7. *Jerusalem*, **Plate 51**

frontispiece, Plate 51 (see fig. 7), in the structure of the poem. It shows, as Wicksteed writes, 'the Nadir of Creation, the dark and cavernous chamber underlying the materialist's Universe',[42] with its three despairing figures:

[42] J. Wicksteed, *William Blake's 'Jerusalem'* (London, 1954), p. 205.

Vala, ironically seated as queen of this realm of death on her throne of stone; Hyle, the image of materialistic blindness; and Scofield, the image of hopelessness. In her essay, 'The Human Form Divine', Anne K. Mellor is no doubt right to point out that this plate 'exposes the unholy trinity of the Deist faith',[43] but she misses the main point of the plate. It is not so much the unholiness of the three figures which is presented, as the fact that they are pitiable, and the design is a vital part of the structure of the poem in expressing the despair of their situation as Los must see it if he is to succeed in his own struggle to 'abstain from wrath' and unite Albion through pity. It has been pointed out that the recently discovered original pencil drawing for this plate (see fig. 8) would add weight to this reading,

8. Original pencil drawing for *Jerusalem*, Plate 51

in that the drawing shows a fourth figure, fierce and crouching, on the left, whom Blake may well have excluded, after experimenting by folding the paper, because of the need to show figures expressing the pitiable nature of despair.[44]

Bearing this in mind, we can go on to look at the way in which the enemies of Albion gradually take on a single monstrous form which Blake characterizes as Rahab, the expression of warring arrogance in the books of Job and Isaiah.[45] On Plate 64 Vala, at her most vindictive, becomes the embodiment of all the Daughters of Albion in their hatred of Los:

[43] *Studies in English Literature*, 11 (Autumn 1971), 595–620 (p. 606).
[44] I owe this point to Michael Phillips.
[45] Job xxvi.12 and Isaiah li.9.

And she put forth her hand upon the Looms in dreadful howlings
Till she vegetated into a hungry Stomach & a devouring Tongue.
Her hand is a Court of Justice, her Feet: two Armies in Battle
Storms & Pestilence: in her Locks: & in her Loins Earthquake.
And Fire. & the Ruin of Cities & Nations & Families & Tongues

(J 64.7–11, E213/K698)

She becomes the embodiment of the web woven by the Daughters of
Albion to hide the light of eternity from man, a web which exists both
within the mind of man, in 'the Indefinite Spectre, who is the Rational
Power', and also in the universe of his perception, in 'the Earths sum-
mits'.[46] Los manifests a divine restraint and forgiveness in his response to
Vala's hysterical accusations that he will cause man to become a worm and
a shadow compared to the substance of manhood under the dominion of
woman, urged on to power and to war.

It is very clear at this stage of the poem that there is a gradual movement
taking place towards the summing up of all the forces of evil in one, just as
the powers for good, since the beginning, have been as 'One Man all the
Universal Family: and that One Man / We call Jesus the Christ'.[47] This
Satanic imitation of the unity of the Divine Family has already been
suggested in the assimilation of Luvah with the Spectre of Albion, and is
confirmed by the appearance of all the Daughters of Albion in the form of
Vala; with Vala, in her turn, bringing the assimilation full circle by being
drawn into the bosom of Albion's Spectre, thus uniting Luvah, the
Daughters of Albion, and herself with the Spectre of Albion in one
hermaphroditic form:

magnificent terrific

Glittering with precious stones & gold, with Garments of blood & fire.

(J 64.25–6, E213/K699)

The outcome of this Satanic assimilation is inevitably self-defeating, in
that the forces of evil themselves become the victims of their torture.
Desiring two imposed worlds of an elect to mercy and a non-elect to
punishment, in place of the distinction between the sheep and the goats,
Ragan and Gwendolen sentence Luvah, as France, to die nailed 'to
Albions Tree'. The intoxicating madness of such delight in cruelty has its

---

[46] J 64.4–5, E213/K698.
[47] J 38.19–20, E178/K664–5.

self-defeating outcome as 'they become what they behold', and suffer themselves the deadly pain which they inflict upon Luvah:

> Spasms smite their features, sinews & limbs: pale they look on one another.
> They turn, contorted: their iron necks bend unwilling towards
> Luvah: their lips tremble: their muscular fibres are crampd & smitten
>
> (*J* 65.76–8, E215/K701)

The greater the assimilation of the enemies of Albion, the greater their physical and mental bondage to one another, the more they suffer at the hands of each other, and the more distinct and undisguised becomes that which must be cast off for a return to a true humanity to be realized.

Blake's introduction of new characters at this point, in the Sons of Urizen, has often puzzled commentators, and it appears to be purely to increase this sense of growing assimilation that Blake includes them at this point. They are encouraged to join in the cruel work of forging weapons for warfare, destroying all that is associated with innocence, 'blind to all the simple rules of life', part of their armoury being the increasingly sophisticated mechanization of daily work:

> that they might spend the days of wisdom
> In sorrowful drudgery, to obtain a scanty pittance of bread
>
> (*J* 65.25–6, E214/K700)

Their address to Vala as goddess of war is in the tradition of Lamech's Sword-song in Genesis iv:

> Now smile among thy bitter tears: now put on all thy beauty
> Is not the wound of the sword sweet! & the broken bone delightful
>
> (*J* 65.30–1, E214/K700)

It is a song in praise of cruelty, for the Sons of Urizen, in their turn, have been assimilated into the Spectre and become 'the Spectre Sons of Albion', demonstrating again that whatever is spectrous can only live by devouring, by 'what he imbibes from deceiving / A Victim!'.

The spectrous imitation of the unity of mankind in the 'One Man' who is Jesus is continued on Plate 69, where 'all the Males combined into One Male', forming 'A Polypus of Roots of Reasoning Doubt Despair & Death'. The difference between the reality of the unity of the 'One Man', and the unity of the 'One Male', reveals the extent to which the Satanic imitation exists in shadow only, and not in substance:

> Envying stood the enormous Form, at variance with Itself
> In all its Members, in eternal torment of love & jealousy
>
> (J 69.6–7, E221/K707)

The Satanic uniting of male and female reproduces, in opposition to the image of God, 'the Images of various Species of Contention / And Jealousy & Abhorrence & Revenge & deadly Murder'. In contrast, Blake creates an image of relationship in the Eden of humanity where the male and female create living room for one another in self-giving, the male creating time and the female space.

The coming together of the Sons of Albion on Plate 70 into 'One Male' emphasizes again that it is in outward appearance only that there is any unity, and even then it is monstrous in the form it takes:

> Three strong Necks & Three awful & terrible Heads
> Three Brains in contradictory council brooding incessantly.
>
> (J 70.4–5, E222/K708)

This grotesque three-headed monster, drawing its inspiration from the three editors Hunt of the *Examiner*, Blake's personal accusers and obstacles to the social realization of his vision, is revealed to be an amalgam of Bacon, Newton and Locke. The link between such diverse figures, according to Blake, is the presence within each of Rahab, their 'Feminine Power unreveal'd', in the form of an abstracting philosophy 'Imputing Sin & Righteousness to Individuals'.

So long as the Antichrist appears in such diverse forms, his concealment within society is not difficult. It is axiomatic in *Jerusalem* that all consolidation of evil is self-defeating and suicidal, as is seen in the ultimate confrontation with the vision of Jesus at the end of the third chapter, where:

> Jesus breaking thro' the Central Zones of Death & Hell
> Opens Eternity in Time & Space; triumphant in Mercy
>
> (J 75.21–2, E229/K716)

IV

The fourth prose preface on Plate 77 is, as Harold Bloom suggests, a statement 'definitive of Blake's Christianity',[48] and the central position of the

---

[48] Harold Bloom, *Blake's Apocalypse* (New York, 1963), p. 416.

stanza which introduces the plate emphasizes its importance as what might be called Blake's 'Motto' for the fourth chapter of *Jerusalem*, and also provides an insight into his poetic intentions in the poem:

> I give you the end of a golden string,
>   Only wind it into a ball:
> It will lead you in at Heavens gate,
>   Built in Jerusalems wall.   (*J* 77, E229/K716)

By way of contrast, the lines alongside this stanza direct our attention to the persecution of the vision of Jesus which takes place in all forms of false religion. The stanzas which conclude the plate contain a call to England, as persecutor and crucifier of Jesus, to embrace Jerusalem once again. In the Pauline polemics of the prose passage which precedes this, Blake sets out what this embracing of Jerusalem involves. Jerusalem is 'the liberty both of body & mind to exercise the Divine Arts of Imagination. Imagination the real & eternal World of which this Vegetable Universe is but a faint shadow'. To achieve this demands a directed and world-facing rather than abstract search for knowledge, for 'to Labour in Knowledge. is to Build up Jerusalem: and to Despise Knowledge, is to Despise Jerusalem & her Builders'. Continual building is necessary to offset the continual decaying caused by the devouring and reductive effect of the 'Wheel of fire', the wheel on which Lear was bound in his self-imprisonment,[49] and which is a parody of the whirlwind of fire in Ezekiel's vision,[50] the wheel of natural religion.

Despite the polemical nature of the preface, it concludes with a confidence which prepares for the resolution of the poem, and a reminder that power resides in pity and not in wrath:

> But to the Publicans & Harlots go!
> Teach them True Happiness, but let no curse
> Go forth out of thy mouth to blight their peace
> For Hell is opend to Heaven . . .   (*J* 77.31–4)

This confidence is reinforced by the explicit identification of Albion and Jesus at the beginning of the chapter where Albion is described as 'The Sleeping Humanity', and in the new fearless assurance of Los in his destroying of self-righteousnesses.

---

49 *King Lear* IV. vii. 46–7.
50 Ezekiel i.4.

In discussing the resolution of *Jerusalem*, it will be helpful to bear in mind W. H. Stevenson's claim in his essay, 'Blake's *Jerusalem*', that in *Jerusalem* 'we have a number of incidents, but no real purpose: the round is endless, and a *deus ex machina* is required to stop it',[51] highlighting the need for an understanding of the motivating force behind Blake's view of historical progression in the poem. Taking up Stevenson's claim of a *deus ex machina*, we might formulate the question in terms of what motivates Albion to cast himself into the 'Furnaces of affliction', and lose his selfhood, so soon after we have seen that 'Albion cold lays on his Rock: storms & snows beat round him'.

Harold Fisch, in his essay, 'Blake's Miltonic Moment',[52] rightly points to the dialectical apparatus for understanding history which Blake adapted from his readings in Paracelsus and Böhme, but as Michael Phillips points out in his essay 'Blake's Early Poetry',[53] the parallelistic organization of Blake's later poetry has a much more basic source in the similar use of contrasted images in Biblical writings, especially in Ezekiel and the Johannine writings. The Biblical antitheses of life and death, light and darkness, and freedom and slavery, are concrete and vivid expressions of the existential possibilities in their concept of man, and the reader is confronted with images of man in living situations, rather than as an object within the natural order.

The direction which Blake's concern took, in reaction to the wearying cycle of 'The Mental Traveller', was towards the challenge of creating an image of the movement of time from fall to redemption, to such an extent that the question of historical progression became the major concern of the later books, and played an important part in determining their form. The prominence of Los in the action of *Jerusalem*, as the director of history, bringing together ideas of time and of poetic activity, is clear evidence of these concerns.

Blake's perspective on history in *Jerusalem* has much in common with the Biblical prophetic sense of the coming apocalypse. The prophets had this eschatological concern because, as G. B. Caird suggests, 'they saw in the historic crisis with which they were immediately concerned the point

[51] *Essays in Criticism*, 9 (1959), 254–64 (p. 259).
[52] A. H. Rosenfeld (ed.), *William Blake: Essays for S. Foster Damon* (Providence, 1969), pp. 36–56.
[53] Morton D. Paley and Michael Phillips (eds), *William Blake: Essays in Honour of Sir Geoffrey Keynes* (Oxford, 1973), pp. 1–28.

at which the circle of eternity touched the line of time, the moment when Israel was confronted with the ultimate issues of life and death'.[54] Their prophetic awareness brings together the present and the future in a single composite image. Blake's historical perspective is concerned with the same reaction against abstract, linear and measured time, as is Böhme in his motto:

> Wem Zeit ist wie Ewigkeit,
> Und Ewigkeit wie Zeit,
> Der ist befreit von allem Zeit.

Awareness of apocalypse is a release from Newtonian categories of time and space, as Blake makes clear in *Milton*:

> And every Moment has a Couch of gold for soft repose
> (A Moment equals a pulsation of the artery)
> And between every two Moments stands a Daughter of Beulah
> To feed the Sleepers on their Couches with maternal care.
>
> (M 28.46–9, E125/K516)

Visionary history then, as Blake and the Jews understand it, is the locus of such moments, the locus of revelation, from which the lineaments of universal human life may be synthesized by the imaginative mind, as in Blake's reading of the *Canterbury Tales*: 'The Characters themselves for ever remain unaltered and consequently they are the Physiognomies or Lineaments of Universal Human Life.'[55] Such organization of history provides the nourishment of mythology for the poet's imagination, the cultivating and vivifying power which Blake found in the integration of spirit, mind and body in Hebraic culture.

Jerusalem draws largely on Ezekiel in theme, imagery and structure, and in Ezekiel's book the radical nature of the prophet's vision, though taking its form from the movement from Paradise, through fall, to the New Jerusalem, rules out any optimism over natural progress towards a new social order. Instead, we find the elements of apocalypse in Ezekiel's rich and vivid description of the intervention of God in history, establishing his kingdom centred around Jerusalem. This involves the destruction of Israel's illusory protective wall, just as in *Jerusalem* the human form of

[54] G. B. Caird, *The Gospel of St Luke*, The Pelican Gospel Commentaries (London, 1963), p. 199.
[55] 'Blake's Chaucer – Second Prospectus', E558/K590.

Albion's mountains, a social force which is by no means illusory, is destroyed, Albion's possessiveness making them barren and opaque:[56] 'There shall be an overflowing shower, and ye, O great hail stones, shall fall, and a stormy wind shall rend it.'[57] Böhme develops Ezekiel's imagery in his Epistle no. 41, where he warns that 'The tribulation and collapse of Babel fast approaches; the thunderstorm arises in all places; it will rage violently; vain hope deceives, for the tree's destruction is near . . . Babel's tower has become without foundation; one hopes to keep it up with props, but a wind from the Lord will collapse it.' In *Jerusalem*, only the completeness of fourfold vision, vision which sees all sides, can bring about such an apocalypse, for the restoration of the community of man in the new kingdom is a restoration of what finally constitutes reality, for 'the Last Judgment is not Fable or Allegory but Vision'.[58] Blake sees approaching the day of the Lord 'to whom the Ancients look'd and saw his day afar off, with trembling and amazement',[59] a day which will reveal the centrality of the human form of the 'One Man' who is Jesus. Blake mythologizes Ezekiel's apocalyptic concerns in adapting them to his own vision, identifying Jerusalem with the God of Ezekiel's book. False religion, which caused the glory of God to depart eastwards and rest on the mountains outside of Jerusalem in Ezekiel's vision, drives Jerusalem herself eastward in Blake's poem until she rests on the mountains as a parody of God's glory, 'howling in pain, redounding from the arms of Beulahs Daughters'.[60] She is driven by the starry wheels, associated with the mechanical revolutions of the law, which may well derive from Böhme's description of 'The outward life . . . fallen quite under the power of the Stars', a 'fall into Wrath, Murder, Whoredom, Theft, Poisoning and Death'.[61]

The integration achieved in the final plates of *Jerusalem* is similar to that which the symbol of Byzantium signified for Yeats: a society not content with mere worldly splendour, but one in which the hope of a new Jerusalem brings all human activities together to share a common goal.

[56] *J* 4.29, E145/K622 and *J* 45[31].2–28, E192/K656–7.
[57] Ezekiel xiii.11.
[58] 'A Vision of the Last Judgment', E544/K604.
[59] *J* 3, E144/K621.
[60] Ezekiel xi.23 and *J* 5.46–9, E147/K624.
[61] Behmen, *The Threefold Life of Man*, vol. 2, p. 116.

Such an integration is brought about in *Jerusalem* through Albion's willingness to cast himself into the 'Furnaces of affliction', when:

> Self was lost in the contemplation of faith
> And in wonder at the Divine Mercy & at Los's sublime honour
>
> (*J* 96.31–2, E253/K743)

Blake's preparation for Albion's resurrection is thorough. I have already suggested that the Song of Los on Plates 85 and 86 is the turning-point of the poem and begins its second movement, for in it Los, as the artist working in time, achieves a poetic form characterized by the serenity and confidence of tone of the Saviour, which is effective to bridge the gulf between himself and Albion, and which leads directly to his growing unity with Jesus in action. Earlier, Jerusalem's lament on Plate 79 had revealed on the one hand the clarity with which she recognized her former innocence and joy and her present fallen state, but on the other hand, her complete helplessness in terms of effective action to release herself from her captivity. Instead of the life-giving power which Ezekiel possessed in the Valley of Bones, where Ezekiel writes that 'I prophesied as he commanded me, and the breath came into them, and they lived, and stood up upon their feet',[62] Jerusalem is reduced to counting the bones, and to a helpless appeal to Vala:

> I walk & count the bones of my beloveds
> Along the Valley of Destruction, among the Druid Temples
> Which overspread all the Earth in patriarchal pomp & cruel pride
> Tell me O Vala thy purposes
>
> (*J* 79.65–8, E233/K721)

Once he has achieved the tone and poetic form of the Saviour, Los's words take on a similar life-giving power to Ezekiel's, and have their effect on both Albion and Jerusalem, until Albion, like Los, is able to be united fully with Jesus.

I have already mentioned, too, the suicidal effect of the consolidation of Albion's enemies, a consolidation which reaches its fullness in the appearance of the 'Covering Cherub' on Plate 89. Blake again turns to Ezekiel and St John for his imagery, the figure being inspired by Ezekiel's description of the Prince of Tyre, where Tyre is spoken of as 'the anointed

---

[62] Ezekiel xxxvii.10.

cherub that covereth'.[63] The 'Covering Cherub' shares with Tyre the threefold deceit of arrogance in beauty, beauty disguising evil, and evil claiming divinity. He is in every way a parody of the Divine Humanity, living and thriving on death, for 'In three nights he devourd the rejected corse of death', while absorbing and devouring all who put their trust in war. He is thus the ultimate consolidation of the forces of Antichrist, and in the light of our discussion of the third chapter, the ultimate incarnation of all that is self-defeating.

The motivating power behind Albion's revival is the progression not so much in self-knowledge, the theme of *Milton*, as in the realization of this self-knowledge in action. This takes place in Los, as we have already seen, in his achievement of a poetic form worthy of the Saviour, and also in the reader whom Blake has called upon to participate in his epic. All human growth is thus a movement towards Albion's liberation. Conceiving of his poem as a record of the activity of the poetic mind, in the figure of Los, and of the prophetic mind of 'every honest man',[64] *Jerusalem* adapts the imagery of eschatology to signify the establishment of a community of the imagination in 'Friendship and Brotherhood', without which 'Man is Not'. This integration is realized in *Jerusalem* in the complete oneness of Los and Jesus, as is clear even to Albion:

> Albion replyd. Cannot Man exist without Mysterious
> Offering of Self for Another, is this Friendship & Brotherhood
> I see thee in the likeness & similitude of Los my Friend
>
> (*J* 96.20–2, E253/K743)

Albion's recognition of the oneness of Los and Jesus leads to his own achievement of unity with them. The integration with which *Jerusalem* ends is identical to the goal of the prophecies of Isaiah and Ezekiel, as Ernst Cassirer describes it in *An Essay on Man* (1944), where he writes of the Biblical prophets that:

Their ideal future signifies the negation of the empirical world, the 'end of all days'; but it contains at the same time the hope and the assurance of 'a new heaven and a new earth.' Here too man's symbolic power ventures beyond all the limits of his finite existence. But this negation implies a new and great act of integration: it marks a decisive phase in man's ethical and religious life.[65]

---

[63] Ezekiel xxviii.14.
[64] Annotations to R. Watson's *An Apology for the Bible*, letter II, p. 14, E607/K392.
[65] E. Cassirer, *An Essay on Man* (N.Y., 1970), p. 60.

The final plate of *Jerusalem* bears witness to the fact that the central images of the poem are images of work and of action. Man's salvation is achieved through creative work, as the central figure of the plate testifies, with his instruments of labour, his hammer and tongs, to break down all that becomes inhumanly hard and opaque, and to forge forms of brotherhood. His fellow labourers are both male and female, working in spite of the coiling embraces of the serpent temple, the male carrying the sun of time, the female 'Weaving the Web of life', the three figures uniting in a trinity of human creativity. Here again Blake adapts the prophetic approach to action as a receptivity and response to a divine initiative, in a purely metaphorical sense. The Albion with which the poem begins is firmly entrapped in a Heideggerian state of *Verfallenheit*, a state of passivity in which he is no longer master of his own circumstances, but rather drawn into the anonymous life of the void, a 'pleasant Shadow of Repose', which leaves him only with a perversion of action:

> Every ornament of perfection, and every labour of love,
> In all the Garden of Eden, & in all the golden mountains
> Was become an envied horror, and a remembrance of jealousy:
> And every Act a Crime, and Albion the punisher & judge.
>
> (*J* 28.1–4, E172/K652)

This leaves Albion continually open to the Spectre's play on stock responses:

> But the Spectre like a hoar frost & a Mildew rose over Albion
> Saying, I am God O Sons of Men! I am your Rational Power!
> Am I not Bacon & Newton & Locke who teach Humility to Man!
>
> (*J* 54.15–17, E201/K685)

In contrast, the image of the truly human in *Jerusalem* is an image of man in action, 'creating exemplars of Memory and of Intellect / Creating Space, Creating Time'.[66] *Jerusalem* has no *deus ex machina*. It is creative action which brings about the realization of potential from the struggle of contraries.

The furnaces of affliction into which Albion casts himself become 'fountains of living waters', part of the transformation involved in the renewal of nature in human form. The waters which flow from the

---

[66] *J* 98.30–1, E255/K746.

sanctuary in Ezekiel's vision of the temple, also bring life and health wherever they pass: 'There shall be a very great multitude of fish, because these waters shall come hither: for they shall be healed; and everything shall live whither the river cometh.'[67] In *Jerusalem*, the black water of the 'dark Atlantic vale', associated with the flood of time and space, sweeping away all but the eternal arts, and the 'waters of death' become 'living waters flowing from the Humanity Divine', linked once more with the rivers of Eden, bringing fertility and blessing wherever they flow. The furnaces which become fountains used to stand on Udan-Adan, a lake of death, until

The Four Living Creatures Chariots of Humanity Divine Incomprehensible
In beautiful Paradise expand These are the Four Rivers of Paradise

(*J* 98.24–5, E255/K745)

just as in Ezekiel the waters of chaos which would engulf Tyre, 'when I shall bring up the deep upon thee, and great waters shall cover thee',[68] become in the renewed city, waters of healing and life. In returning so often to Ezekiel for its basic structure and imagery, *Jerusalem* seeks finally to affirm the same fusion of social and cultural aspirations in a common religious and national life which the final chapters of Ezekiel envisage for Israel.[69]

V

Jerusalem has proved to be particularly resistant to attempts to impose a formal structural principle upon it, whether in the form of 'the Three Regions immense / Of Childhood, Manhood, and Old Age' of Karl Kiralis's essay,[70] the particular Zoas of E. J. Rose,[71] or the apocalyptic animals of Joanne Witke.[72] In this essay I have concentrated on four aspects of the prose prefaces which are crucial for an understanding of the poem's structure, if the structure is to be seen as an integral part of its central concerns.

[67] Ezekiel xlvii.9.
[68] Ezekiel xxvi.19.
[69] For discussion of the relationship between *Jerusalem* and the Book of Ezekiel, see Harold Bloom's essay, 'Blake's *Jerusalem*: The Bard of Sensibility and the Form of Prophecy', *Eighteenth Century Studies*, 4 (1970–1), 6–20.
[70] Karl Kiralis, 'The Theme and Structure of William Blake's *Jerusalem*', *English Literary History*, 23 (1956), 127–43.
[71] E. J. Rose, 'The Structure of Blake's *Jerusalem*', *Bucknell Review*, 11 (1963), 35–54.
[72] Joanne Witke, '*Jerusalem*: A Synoptic Poem', *Comparative Literature*, 22 (1970), 265–78.

From the first preface I concentrated on Blake's defence of his poetic styles, particularly in relation to the supposed harshness of the poem. The Saviour's 'mild song' at the beginning of the first chapter sets the tone for the poem, and is permeated with the 'Spirit of meekness & love' which Los seeks from the Saviour, and which he needs if he is to fulfil his task of abstaining from wrath and learning pity in its place. The contrast between the serenity of the language of the Eternals and the conflicts of Los continues until the turning-point of the poem, the Song of Los (85.22–86.32). In this song Los achieves the mildness of the Saviour, a potential which he has possessed from the beginning of the poem, and goes on to exhibit a new confidence and wisdom which reveals itself in the ending of his inner struggles and in the redemption of Albion.

The central point of the second preface on Plate 27 is Blake's insistence on the task of the poet as the refashioning of history in human terms, a work analogous to that of the Hebrew prophet. To illustrate this, I traced in detail the symbolic function of the figure of Reuben through the second chapter, a figure who proved suitable for a number of reasons. Firstly, Reuben has not received a great deal of critical attention, whereas a detailed examination of his function in the poem reveals the remarkable coherence of Blake's design. In addition, just as Reuben's father had his name changed from Jacob to Israel to signify his changed character and new commission, so Reuben is capable of becoming a Hand or a Merlin, the very incarnation either of Albion's problem or of his potential.

The third preface, Plate 52, is concerned with what Blake calls the 'State named Rahab', a Deistic state characterized by the self-righteousness which is the inevitable product of Natural Religion and natural morality. Here I took the figure of Rahab and traced through the third chapter the way in which she becomes the symbolic figure in which all the forces of evil are drawn together. The gradual movement towards this summing-up of all the forces of evil in one is a Satanic imitation of the unity of the Divine Family, who appear from the beginning of the poem as 'One Man . . . and that One Man / We call Jesus the Christ'. The assimilation is seen to be self-defeating, however, in that the greater the assimilation, the greater the shared mental bondage, and the easier identification and rejection become.

The fourth preface leads us straight into the resolution of the poem and the establishment of a new community which takes place in the fourth chapter. Here my main purpose was to trace what motivates the integration brought about through Albion's self-sacrifice, showing that Blake prepares carefully for the establishment of an imaginative community of 'Friendship and Brotherhood', which the poem finally affirms.

The assumptions which this essay challenges are both persistent and widespread. The poetry of *Jerusalem* is often held to be necessarily harsh and ugly, and the design of the poem lacking both in coherence and sustained control. On the contrary, Blake employs a great variety of poetic styles, and the action of the poem is most frequently forwarded by a poetry exemplifying the creative power of pity rather than wrath. I have tried to demonstrate the structural coherence of *Jerusalem* by seeing it as an integral part of the poem's recurring themes and parallelistic organization. Blake's control over the minute particulars of his material has been all too easily and frequently underestimated. He warns us at the outset that 'every word and every letter is studied', and we should not be blinded by the fertility of his mental powers to the control and organization which he enforces on his most 'consolidated & extended Work'.

CHAPTER 8

INFLUENCE AND INDEPENDENCE
IN BLAKE

JOHN BEER

Recent critical work has brought about a new interest in the concept of influence. A welcome feature of this development is that it brings together the varying concerns of scholars and critics. Traditionally, the question of influence has been thought of primarily as a matter for scholars and associated with the useful kind of article that one finds in the pages of *Notes and Queries*, where close parallels, observed between passages in two writers of different periods, are adduced to suggest that the earlier one 'influenced' the later. The underlying paradigm, if there is one, would seem to be that of an apprentice learning from his master. Just as one looks in a painter's predecessors to discover, say, where he learned to draw hands, so we look at particular expressions in a design or turns of phrase in a piece of writing, discover that they have occurred somewhere previously, infer the existence of a connection and draw attention to it as a fact of artistic history.

In the early part of the twentieth century, such discussion as took place concerning the larger theoretical issues involved was dominated by T. S. Eliot's essay, 'Tradition and the Individual Talent'. Eliot, as is well known, sees the question of the artist's relationship to works created by his predecessors as that of a man aware of an achieved body of work and turning it to his own uses. Not for him the apprentice analogy; if we can divest ourselves of prejudiced assumption that a poet's best work will also be his most original, he maintains, 'we shall often find that not only the best, but the most individual parts of his work may be those in which the dead poets, his ancestors, assert their immortality most vigorously. And I do not mean the impressionable period of adolescence, but the period of full maturity.'[1] Such statements form part of a view of art which directs our attention towards the objective, presented structures rather than to the artist who

[1] T. S. Eliot, *Selected Essays* (London, 1932), p. 14.

created them. Though exercising an impersonal priesthood before the altar of his art, however, such a man is not without his reward, according to Eliot; for if he succeeds in creating a work of art which is 'really new' the whole body of previous art will simultaneously be seen in a slightly different light. As the present is directed by the past, so the past can be altered by the present.

Eliot's approach has the merit that it releases the artist from some of the oppressive personal concerns which might otherwise mar his work or even inhibit him altogether from creating. By escaping from his personality, by escaping from his emotion, he may actually achieve the liberty to create.[2]

The idea of 'influence' as such does not occur explicitly in Eliot's essay; it appears only in the imagery. 'The poet must be very conscious of the main current, which does not at all flow invariably through the most distinguished reputations.'[3] We cannot tell from this whether the poet is to be thought of as a navigator on the current, a swimmer within it, or simply as an engineer who looks down at it from a god-like height and organizes a diversion into the channel where it will be of most use. Eliot turns away from his metaphor too quickly to allow such questions to be asked. The view which he expresses in the remainder of his essay, nevertheless, has proved of great worth to those looking for some sure standard in judging literature. It conveys a sense (however chimerical it might turn out to be) that we are being offered the materials from which to create a large, almost scientific view of literature.

The point of view from which Eliot approaches the question of influence is, it will be noted, opposite to that involved in traditional scholarship. The learning apprentice has been quietly replaced as focus of discussion by the practising master. 'Immature poets imitate; mature poets steal.'[4] The good poet takes from his predecessors things which are recognizably theirs, yet grafts them so successfully on to his own work that they can never be reclaimed. In relation to the past, the good poet works eclectically and always knows what he is doing.

These central statements serve as a valuable introduction to Eliot's dealings with the past in his own work; yet the renewed interest to which

[2] Eliot insists, of course, that he must *have* a personality and emotion to escape from. *Ibid.*, p. 21.
[3] *Ibid.*, p. 16.
[4] *Ibid.*, p. 206.

I have referred suggests that the original problem, neatly sidestepped by Eliot's tactical device, has by no means been removed. Returning to the records of actual practising poets we find that for them tradition has often worked not as a main current but in a more complicated manner. They see the writing of the past not as elements in a malleable tradition, but as a completed citadel which they are powerless to enter; or they experience the past in the form of an overwhelming seizure by some powerful predecessor, less to be detected by us in single lines and passages than sensed as a daemonic presence within the creative powers themselves.

Among writers of the romantic tradition this last factor has long been acknowledged. Coleridge, for instance, declared in 1796 that Collins's 'Ode on the Poetical Character' had 'inspired' and 'whirled' him along with 'greater agitations of enthusiasm than any the most *impassioned* Scene in Schiller or Shakspere . . .'; the effects are apparent in the last stanza of *Kubla Khan*.[5] In the *Biographia* he records how, soon afterwards, Kant's writings took possession of him 'as with a giant's hand'.[6] Middleton Murry, Eliot's chief antagonist during the 1920s, wrote a study of Keats which was organized round the idea that he had written during various phases under an immediate devotion to Milton or Shakespeare which involved a tutelary submission of his creative powers.[7] W. H. Auden may be seen at one stage of his career to have succumbed to the controlling music of Yeats, while Eliot himself described his own early devotion to Laforgue as 'a sort of possession by a stronger personality'.[8]

Such areas of relationship between the poet and previous tradition are opened up afresh in W. J. Bate's *The Burden of the Past and the English Poet* and Harold Bloom's *The Anxiety of Influence*. Bate indicates and documents the growing despair of neoclassical poets, faced by achievements in the past which they could not hope to emulate, while Bloom discusses the topic of 'possession' in connection with certain romantic and post-romantic writers. For them, he argues, the dominant and characteristic emotion was (and remains) an anxiety, provoked by precisely the situation

[5] S. T. Coleridge, *Collected Letters*, ed. E. L. Griggs (6 vols, Oxford, 1956–71), vol. 1, p. 279; and my *Coleridge the Visionary* (London, 1959), pp. 257–9ff.

[6] S. T. Coleridge, *Biographia Literaria*, ed. J. Shawcross (2 vols, Oxford, 1907), vol. 1, p. 99.

[7] J. M. Murry, *Keats and Shakespeare* (London, 1925).

[8] See Auden's '1st September 1939' and T. S. Eliot, letter to E. J. H. Greene, *Revue de Littérature Comparée* (July–September 1948), p. 365, quoted in Warren Ramsey, *Jules Laforgue and the Ironic Tradition* (N.Y., 1953), p. 199.

suggested in Eliot's essay. Each is afraid that the dead poets, his forbears, may not simply be 'asserting their immortality vigorously' but speaking through him so powerfully as to extinguish his own sense of originality. Modern literature, according to Bloom, should therefore be seen as a series of ingenious attempts to deal with this situation.

Eliot and Bloom point us to important aspects of the artist's function. In Eliot's account he is seen as a kind of god-like figure who must yet humble himself before the tradition in order to be able to contribute to it; in Bloom's he is more like a fallen angel who lives in perpetual dread and must therefore be roused by us from the brimstone lake, ministered to and shown that in his descent he has in fact made a creative 'swerve' (to use Bloom's expression), which has endowed him, in spite of everything, with an identity of his own.

Suggestive as such views are, however, neither does justice to the degree of originality and independence which is sometimes aimed at by artists and poets. While some may be content to descry, like Eliot, a tradition into which their own contributions are felt to fit naturally, others have felt that some wholly new departure was required. (We may also mention the special case of those who, like the young Blake, or Ezra Pound, or Eliot himself for that matter, thought they could find the tradition they were looking for but only at an earlier time, separated from the present by some important discontinuity.)

The more extreme assertion is characteristic of many romantic poets and artists. They appraise the tradition only to conclude that it has taken a wrong turning and that little less than total renovation is needed to meet the case. Such artists may exhibit, in their more intoxicated moments, an unusual arrogance, while at other times they plunge into depths of despair. They may also feel themselves obliged to deal with their predecessors in a way which lacks the calm, reassessing creativity suggested by Eliot's account, at times seizing on elements which can be incorporated into their own new way of seeing things with a quickness of absorption which leaves bewildered successors groping for clues to their meaning.

The extreme romantic individualist of this type stands to his predecessors in a relationship which almost defies generalization. Sometimes a mode of delineation, or a phrase, will be endowed by his power with a distinctiveness that makes reference to the past seem irrelevant; in many cases that distinctiveness will be associated with a context of response to contemporary needs. It may spring from a straightforwardly hostile reaction to a given depiction ('I will *not* paint like that!'), or from the sense of a meaning that has escaped the original artist ('He did not know what he was doing, but I will now proceed to show you'); or from a more friendly version of the same ('There are some living elements here: I am going to concentrate on what is alive, to the exclusion of what is dead').

This kind of relationship with sources, which presupposes a decisive intervention on the artist's part, provides the scholar with some knotty problems. Such gestures, if left unrecorded by the artist, can only be inferred; yet they are central to the matter. In default of direct evidence, the scholar may be forced to return to traditional methods of influence-study, using them as a source of possible inference concerning the larger interventions.

Two questions come to the fore at this point, so far as Blake is concerned. The first, 'What is the likelihood of his knowing the proposed source?', is often difficult to answer. We know surprisingly little about Blake's reading habits or his knowledge of available visual materials. The number of authors cited in his Notebook suggests that he may have undertaken a strenuous course of reading at some point in the 1780s, excited, perhaps, by the existence of many works which dealt with 'imaginative metaphysics' in one form or another, from Plato and Paracelsus to Böhme and Milton. He probably had a small working library of books of his own. But there were libraries and bookshops everywhere in London, and he knew various people who might have lent him volumes: theoretically he had access to almost any given book. The nearest one can get to any kind of working presupposition, perhaps, is to say that as a practising engraver he was most likely to have been drawn to books which contained illustrations; that he must have had an unusually wide knowledge of separate engraved prints; and that (as a matter of simple probability) he is more likely to have known books published in England than those published abroad and more likely to have read in English than in other languages. Yet such rules can never be more than very rough guides, which may at least serve to suggest sometimes when we are on the right scent; they can never in themselves be used as direct evidence.

The second question to be asked in examining apparent parallels is whether there is any distinctive element which raises probability above the level where mere coincidence provides a more likely explanation. Such elements may take the form either of *intensive effects* (some unusual feature of the proposed source, for example, or something markedly distinctive in the author's usage) or *extensive effects* (as where two or more noteworthy parallels between the proposed source and the later work may be found). In all such cases, obviously, uniqueness is at a premium.

At the same time, consideration of such evidence, coupled with further enquiry into the full nature of the supposed debt, will often, in its turn, lead the investigator back to the larger questions. If the source is transformed in some way, for example, it will be natural to enquire into the nature of the human being who effected the transformation. And if we once ask ourselves, *why* did this particular piece strike him or her so forcefully? to what in his current concerns did it connect? it will be hard to press the investigation without beginning to infer, however shadowily or tentatively, the nature of the artist's controlling sensibility. We are forced (as in all normal human relationships) to suppose a central, organizing personality which is, in some respects at least, self-consistent.

What kind of personality is it, then, that we descry at the centre of Blake's multifarious works? An account of his personal identity should certainly take account of several factors, such as the strength and stubbornness of his individual stance; the very clear eyes with which he looked at society and at other human beings (a kind of 'Emperor's new clothes' clarity of vision); his indignation at the existence of social evils; and, behind all, the powerful imagination which sometimes filled him with an irradiating vision, yet would occasionally drive him into a semi-paranoid attitude, especially so far as certain other people were concerned.

But I believe that at the heart of his work something less personal is involved, something which I have discussed elsewhere and to which Morton Paley has devoted a whole book;[9] a belief, that is, in the importance of both energy and imagination, coupled with a conviction that neither can operate properly unless interinvolved with the other. Children, in Blake's view, are born into a world of imagination, but must grow up to confront incursions of energy in many different forms. The Mental Traveller must enter continually into a new vortex of energy, but when

[9] M. D. Paley, *Energy and the Imagination* (Oxford, 1970).

the vortex is passed his imagination comes into play, giving form to the experience and enabling him to see it as englobed. If energy fights the wars of eternity, there is also a place (Blake's 'Beulah') for rest and renewal of vision. If imagination is lost, on the other hand, energy simply riots in destruction; if energy is lost, similarly, imagination continues to create an endless series of limiting circles and mathematical globes without ever breaking out of them. The energetic movement of the serpent, which naturally expresses itself in coils and spirals, is, by this kind of loss, petrified into the rocky Druid serpent temple, where the coil of the serpent remains forever hardened into a single round.

One could elaborate on this much more fully: of all the keys to an understanding of Blake's symbolism, in fact, I believe it to be the most central. My purpose here, however, is simply to reiterate the assertion that when Blake confronted possible sources, he confronted them primarily not as a potential disciple or adept, but as a man whose response was dominated above all by his own obsessive concerns.

One other suggestion may be made in this connection. The earlier the confrontation, the more powerful the impact may be expected to have been. I think of the young Blake, in other words, as an impulsive figure, passionately concerned with certain issues, subject to horror or ecstasy from his imaginative and artistic experiences. The effects of these might well survive through many later reflections and changes of attitude, so that the nature of the influence might itself change over the years.

Above all, I would take a passion for human liberty to be the single most persistent element in his continuous thought. The question, 'What is it that makes men free?' overshadows most of his other concerns, running as a single link of significance through them. And by the same token, he has from the first an almost morbid concern with anything that restrains liberty; prisons, cages, bonds, bands, chains, nets, locks and so on.

With this briefest of introductions, then, we may move to the study of particular instances, asking what kind of probability we are justified in assigning to each as a possible source for his art and seeking for further clues to the nature of the transforming agency at the centre of the process.

VISUAL INFLUENCES

The study of visual influences is always more difficult to discipline than that of verbal influences, since no resemblances of line and tone can have the same precise articulation as identical repetition of words, or of combinations of words. Nevertheless, there are times when the resemblances of visual pattern may be so many and so striking as to constitute a strong *prima facie* case for the existence of an influence. A classic example is provided by Anthony Blunt, who reproduces an engraving 'The Prodigal Son' by Martin de Vos side by side with Plate 99 of Jerusalem.[10] The resemblance between the postures of the son rushing to be embraced by his father on the one hand, and Jerusalem rushing into the arms of fading Albion on the other, are so striking that one is justified in asking whether Blake did not actually have de Vos's design before him as he worked.

The drawing of such an inference, however, immediately invites discussion of the relationship between the plates at a different level. The fact that Blake found an engraving of the Prodigal Son's return relevant to a design which describes the crucial moment when humanity attains final reintegration suggests that the symbolism of the parable may long have been reverberating in his mind; and this in turn reminds us of a recurrent preoccupation of his with a more general theme: that of 'the Father and the Sons'. The father and his serpent-entwined sons in the *Laocoön* design provide one version, the various designs representing Ugolino and his sons in the Tower of Famine another. In that pre-Darwinian age the ultimate instance of the paradigm was of course that of Adam and his two sons; there was also, however, in a world where the Swedenborgian interpreters of the Bible concentrated on finding the symbolic sense of each particular incident, direct encouragement to make connection with other examples of the paradigm in the Bible. In the case of Cain and Abel, the story is one of unpremeditated violence against an innocent brother; later, however, in the story of Isaac and his two sons Esau and Jacob, the balance of blame shifts. Though Jacob is ostensibly the hero, he is less attractive by reason of his clever deceits against his rough, obtuse but essentially energetic brother. Blake's words in *The Marriage of Heaven and Hell*, 'Now is the dominion of Edom, & the return of Adam into Paradise',[11] indicate his

---

[10] A. Blunt, *The Art of William Blake* (London, 1959), plates 49a and 49b.
[11] E34/K149. For Edom see Genesis xxv.30, xxvii.39–40, etc.

belief that in a world dominated by smooth deceivers it is time for the Esaus to have their day. The story of the Prodigal, equally, might act in his mind as a powerful support for the argument that a rough exertion of energy, if that exertion also involved an active learning, was preferable to a career of blameless virtue. The father finally responds to his returning son with an exuberant gesture that he has never been disposed to offer to his more upright elder son.

The first of my visual examples for discussion in detail belongs as it happens to this paradigm; it is the motif of Count Ugolino and his sons, which occurs, for example, in the Notebook, in the *Gates of Paradise* series and, much later, in the Dante designs and in a tempera painting (see figs 9–11).[12] In this case, none of the material to be discussed is new; the aim is

9. *The Gates of Paradise*, Plate 12, 'Does thy God O Priest'

rather to re-examine some opinions expressed about it in the past and to view this favoured theme of Blake's both in its historical context and in terms of his own development.

If we apply the criterion of looking for the unusual, our first instinct

[12] See e.g. *The Notebook of William Blake*, ed. D. V. Erdman and D. K. Moore (Oxford, 1973), plate N 59; E263/K768; *The Marriage of Heaven and Hell*, plate 16; A. S. Roe, *Blake's Illustrations to the Divine Comedy* (Princeton, 1953), plates 67 and 68, and *The Tempera Paintings of William Blake* (Arts Council of Great Britain, London, 1951), plate xi. Roe (pp. 132–4) gives a more complete list of Blake's designs on this theme.

10. Pencil sketch for illustration to Dante's *Inferno* XXXIII, 'Count Ugolino and his sons'

11. Tempera painting, 'Ugolino and his sons in prison' (1827)

will no doubt be to fasten on the fact that Blake should have chosen this incident, of all the possible incidents in the *Divine Comedy*, to illustrate at this early date; whereas he did not get to the rest of Dante until the last years of his life.

Although this is a natural question, however, it turns out to be the wrong one. Some years ago Dr Frances Yates published an excellent article entitled 'Transformations of Dante's Ugolino'.[13] In this she pointed out that a concentration on the Ugolino incident had in fact been characteristic of most translations or illustrations of Dante in England before Blake's time. That incident, along with the Paola and Francesca episode, was seized upon time and again. And the reason, she suggested, was that English writers and artists, brought up in the Protestant tradition, and basically unsympathetic towards (perhaps even uncomprehending of) Dante's dominant theology, seized on those episodes in the poem which stood out strikingly by their dramatic force and human appeal. She also pointed out that, because of this situation, the English writers and illustrators concerned concentrated on the story of Ugolino in isolation from its context in Dante, and lost sight of any sense that Ugolino too had been consigned to hell for his treacherous dealings or of his one consolation there, which was to spend eternity gnawing away at his oppressor's skull. As soon as he has finished his account of Ugolino's speech, Dante continues:[14]

> Quand' ebbe detto ciò, con gli occhi torti
> Riprese il teschio misero coi denti,
> Che furo all'osso, come d'un can, forti.　　　　(xxxiii.76–8)

> Thus having spoke,
> Once more upon the wretched skull his teeth
> He fasten'd like a mastiff's 'gainst the bone,
> Firm and unyielding.

Dr Yates quotes Ruskin's satirical comment on this propensity of his fellow-countrymen, which survived, apparently, well into the nineteenth century:[15]

---

[13] Frances Yates, 'Transformations of Dante's Ugolino', *Journal of the Warburg Institute*, XIV (1951), 92–117.

[14] *Ibid.*, p. 92.

[15] *Ibid.*, p. 101, quoting Ruskin, *Complete Works*, ed. E. T. Cook and A. Wedderburn (1908), vol. XXXV, p. 637.

The only bit of Dante that English people have ever read, or have heard of (after their favourite piece of the adultery of Francesca) is . . . the starving of Count Ugolino . . . They are content to enjoy the description of his starvation, when they might see any number of Ugolinos, not counts, starved to death in their own villages. Also, they never inquire what the Count had done to deserve starving; nor what sort of feasting he had in hell after he was starved.

The existence of the tradition helps to explain why, when Blake included the motif in *The Gates of Paradise*, he captioned it with the words,

> Does thy God O Priest take such vengeance as this?

And of course it could be argued that there was no reason why anyone *should* need to take cognizance of Ugolino's being in hell, since after all it was Dante, not God, who put him there. It was entirely in the English tradition, with its love of the empirical fact, that one should simply isolate the historical incident and illustrate that. At all events, Blake's 1793 caption aligns him firmly with those at that time who saw in the Ugolino story evidence for use against the tyranny of the priesthood.

The story does not end there, however, since this theme belongs not merely to the social history of the eighteenth and nineteenth centuries but to the history of taste. The Ugolino story was calculated to appeal to those who had begun to appreciate the projected horrors of Gothic art or who had learned to melt in pity over a tale of sorrow. Boswell, for instance (as Frank Parisi has pointed out to me), referred to the incident in an essay of 1778 where he described the situation of Ugolino and his sons (one of 'mere corporeal privation . . .') as a 'subject of very affecting horror', even if Aphra Behn's Oronooko and Imoinda, or Rousseau's St Preux and Eloise touched 'the finer springs of feeling in the heart in a more exquisite manner'.[16]

This further sidelight is relevant when we ask what visual sources Blake might have had for his design. Here, it seems to me, there is only one serious contender – and that a controversial one. Joshua Reynolds's painting of Ugolino was exhibited at the Royal Academy in 1773, when Blake was fifteen. It was also reproduced as a mezzotint (fig. 12).[17] It must, I think, have had a very dramatic effect on an audience which came to it

---

[16] James Boswell, *The Hypochondriack*, ed. M. Bailey (Stanford, 1928), vol. I, p. 176.

[17] By John Dixon in 1774; and engraved again later by S. W. Reynolds and H. Raimbach. Yates, 'Dante's Ugolino', p. 115. Dr Yates reproduces the original painting, facing p. 105.

with a more genteel eighteenth-century taste; during the following years it certainly became very famous.[18]

At the same time it has not been taken seriously as a source for Blake. A. S. Roe describes it as 'very theatrical and stilted';[19] certainly there is little in the way of obvious detail to suggest a direct visual influence, and Blake's later antipathy to Reynolds is too well known to need illustrating. Dr Yates cites as evidence of this some comments made in 1806. In that year Fuseli had illustrated the subject, in a fashion which his biographer later described as showing him petrified by the effects of his own emotion: 'bereft of tears his heart is turned to stone'.[20] In *Bell's Weekly Messenger* the reviewer had been less kindly: he ridiculed the postures of Ugolino's

12. John Dixon: mezzotint after Reynolds, 'Count Ugolino and his sons' (1774)

18 William Hazlitt (*Works*, ed. P. P. Howe (1930–4), vol. XVIII, p. 59) records the approval of Warton, Burke and Goldsmith; he himself felt that the design did little justice to the subject.
19 A. S. Roe, *Blake's Illustrations to the Divine Comedy* (Princeton, 1953), p. 133.
20 John Knowles, *Life and Writings of Henry Fuseli* (1831), vol. I, pp. 358ff; cited by Yates, 'Dante's Ugolino', p. 111, who also includes an 1811 engraving after Fuseli's untraced illustration.

children, who were shown as turning away from him, and the melo-dramatic rendering of his facial expression.[21] Blake indignantly reached for his pen and wrote to the editors a letter which included the following remarks:

Under pretence of fair criticism and candour, the most wretched taste ever produced has been upheld for many, very many years: but now, I say, now its end is come. Such an artist as Fuseli is invulnerable, he needs not my defence; but I should be ashamed not to set my hand and shoulder, and whole strength, against those wretches who, under pretence of criticism, use the dagger and the poison.

My criticism on this picture is as follows:

Mr. Fuseli's Count Ugolino is the father of sons of feeling and dignity, who would not sit looking in their parent's face in the moment of his agony, but would rather retire and die in secret, while they suffer him to indulge his passionate and innocent grief, his innocent and venerable madness, and insanity, and fury, and whatever paltry cold hearted critics cannot, because they dare not, look upon. Fuseli's Count Ugolino is a man of wonder and admiration, of resentment against man and devil, and of humiliation before God; prayer and parental affection fills the figure from head to foot. The child in his arms, whether boy or girl signifies not, (but the critic must be a fool who has not read Dante, and who does not know a boy from a girl); I say, the child is as beauti-fully drawn as it is coloured – in both, inimitable! and the effect of the whole is truly sublime, on account of that very colouring which our critic calls black and heavy. (E705/K863–4)

Dr Yates justifiably argues that Blake's reference to children who would not sit looking at their parent's face in the time of agony is a covert blow at Reynolds's design, where they are doing just that, and goes on to dismiss Reynolds as a direct source. We must also acknowledge that Ugolino's expression in the *Gates of Paradise* design, though not in detail like that given him by Fuseli, is still closer to the latter than to his calmness in the Reynolds version.

If an artist's version of a motif differs significantly from that made by a predecessor, however, there is still a possibility that his initial reaction to that predecessor might have been very powerful, so acting – at least at that time – as an important stimulus. I suspect that the youthful Blake,

---

[21] 'Criticism upon the Royal Academy Exhibition', *Bell's Weekly Messenger* (25 May 1806). Cited by Yates, 'Dante's Ugolino', p. 112.

confronted by Reynolds's picture in the Royal Academy, or looking at the corresponding etching in his own shop, would have responded very immediately to so powerful a rendering of human imprisonment and to the implied nobility of Ugolino's endurance.

There are also indications that Blake's own sense of the theme changed as he used it in different contexts. In the *Gates of Paradise* design, for instance, where Ugolino's expression is one of intense suffering, by comparison with the crazed staring eyes given him by Fuseli, one of the children *is* looking at him, as in the Reynolds design. And 'The Keys of the Gates', a poetic commentary written twenty years later, displays a view of Ugolino which has shifted from the social emphasis of 'Does thy God O Priest take such vengeance as this?' to the more personally oriented

> Holy & cold I clipd the Wings
> Of all Sublunary Things
> And in depths of my Dungeons
> Closed the Father & the Sons   (E266/K771)

This is not simply a shift of attitude over a period of years, moreover. Though his emphasis might shift, the indications are that Blake always found it difficult to dissociate external social abuses from internal human failure. He believed, for instance, that we build dark Satanic mills in our cities because we have dark Satanic mills in our mind. And the sense that this association was natural to him throughout his career is strengthened when we turn to *The Marriage of Heaven and Hell* and discover another version of the Ugolino motif illustrating the plate which begins 'The Giants who formed this world into its sensual existence and now seem to live in it in chains, are in truth, the causes of its life & the sources of all activity . . .' (E39/K155). What might at first have seemed a simple protest against the actions of an established and tyrannical priesthood is now seen to involve a larger statement, concerning the ways in which human liberty is forfeited. The chains, Blake continues, are 'the cunning of weak and tame minds, which have power to resist energy'. We need not look far to find such a priesthood, evidently: there creeps one in the human mind.

If there is a change in Blake's attitude over the years, it seems rather to have been caused by a growing sense that this self-imprisoning of human beings was perhaps inevitable in important respects, so that its effects were to be endured rather than fought. Certainly it is noticeable that when Blake returned to the Ugolino theme for his Dante illustrations nearly twenty years later, he did not invest him with fierce passion of any kind. Instead, he gave him a calm, clear-eyed expression more like that associated with Blake's Job. There is a quality of steadfast endurance in the midst of his sufferings (further elaborated in the tempera painting on the subject) which for me at least aligns the design now with Reynolds rather than Fuseli, and suggests that, in the more visionary radicalism of his later years, Blake may have been returning, at least partially, to a reaction experienced many years before, when he first looked at Reynolds's version.

The shift here – from indignation at the actions of an established priesthood, combined with an assertion that they correspond to an imprisoning of the body which every human being permits his senses to undertake, to a more stoical, Job-like, acceptance of the situation, now regarded as inseparable from human existence – aligns itself with other examples of a similar development in Blake; and the changing relevance of Reynolds's design during that development suggests the diverse ways in which a single 'influence' may work as a poet or artist considers, and reconsiders, a favourite theme over a long period.

My next example is new, and very different – so much so that I am willing to predict an initial half-second in which anyone looking at the first of the two designs, engravings on the subject of Perseus and Andromeda executed in 1789 by Bartolozzi after Cipriani (fig. 13), will regard the idea that Blake could possibly have been influenced by them as utterly preposterous. What, he will immediately ask, can these two simpering and coy figures, executed by an engraver whom Blake later attacked,[22] possibly have to do with any figures in Blake's designs?

Yet I want to suggest that these designs may after all have had an

22 See, for example, his scathing references in the annotations to Reynolds (E663/K455) and in the *Public Address* (E561, 563, 570/K592, 594, 600). It must be remembered that Andromeda chained to the rock was a familiar subject in previous art, particularly as a detail in illustrations to Ovid's *Metamorphoses*. Professor E. J. Kenney has kindly shown me several examples from his collection, including Picart *ap*. Banier (Amsterdam, 1732), Zocchi *ap*. Fontanelle (Lille, 1767) and Eisen *ap*. Le Mire and Basan (Paris, 1767–9). None, however, is as close to the 'rocky seat' design as the present one, which is also much the closest to Blake in time and place of production.

The second engraving (not reproduced here) shows the head of the Medusa, which Perseus is holding away from Andromeda while telling her about its transforming powers.

important, if subterranean, effect on Blake's work at the time. To begin with, the landscape of the first one corresponds interestingly with that of a scene to which Blake returns several times in the 1790s. The maiden sitting on a ledge by the shore, chained to the rock, with a view of the sea on the left beyond, has a good deal in common with the landscape of the frontispiece to *Visions of the Daughters of Albion* (see fig. 14), where Bromion

13. F. Bartolozzi: stipple engraving after Cipriani,
'Perseus having rescued Andromeda . . .'

14. *Visions of the Daughters of Albion*, frontispiece. Colour print

and Oothoon sit shackled back to back on the shore, and to that of the design known as 'The Jealousy of Los', in which a male, his foot shackled to the earth, rises up against a woman who snatches her child away from him in fear and apprehension.[23]

In this case, however, it is hard to see why Blake should have acquired a positive stimulus from the engravings simply as designs. The clue to an answer must, I think, be looked for rather at the level of myth and symbol. It was the legend of Perseus, surely, that fascinated Blake in the first place: the story of the young man with winged shoes and magic helmet who was able to set free the bound maiden, but could do so only after defeating the Medusa who turned to stone all those who looked at her. This 'freezing' of vision would fall in naturally with Blake's ideas about the nature of perception; it is the same legend, in fact, which seems to haunt the imagery of 'Earth's Answer' in *Songs of Experience*:

> Earth rais'd up her head,
> From the darkness dread & drear.
> Her light fled:
> Stony dread!
> And her locks cover'd with grey despair.
>
> Prison'd on watry shore
> Starry Jealousy does keep my den
> Cold and hoar
> Weeping o'er
> I hear the Father of the ancient men   (E18/K210–11)

There is a further point to be taken into account. The original painting by Cipriani (which may well have been a more attractive version) was exhibited at the Royal Academy in 1774. It is almost certain that Blake would have seen it there in his late adolescence, at a time when he was in the first flush of his visionary enthusiasms. What I am suggesting, therefore, is a complicated relationship, first with the picture and then with the engraved design. Blake's original interest in the symbolic significance of the story of Perseus and Andromeda, as emblematic of the freezing and petrifying power of contemporary reason and its distorting imprisoning effect on human energies, was on this reading newly stimulated by his

[23] The two versions are reproduced together in my *Blake's Humanism* (Manchester, 1968), fig. 30.

sight of this clear but insipid depiction of an actual girl shackled to the shore and of the distorted features of the Medusa head, to use a similar landscape and seascape for the scene of bondage at the opening of *Visions of the Daughters of Albion*, where the young man is shutting himself off from vision, and to produce a vestigial version of it in other designs where related themes are present. (One might also reflect on the possible influence of the story upon the winged figure hovering above the Bard at the beginning of *Songs of Innocence*, who seems to have for him something of the same function as did the winged shoes and helmet for Perseus.)[24] The nexus of imagery here relates, in fact, to a larger skein of imagery involving sun, serpent and wings which takes the investigator far into the contemporary study of mythology.[25] Here we need only register the central point that concerns Blake and which seems to dictate his response to many versions of the theme: that human liberty is ultimately dependent upon the achievement of an *inner* freedom which reconciles the individual's energies and perceptions.

SOME VERBAL SOURCES

(i) *Intensive Influences*

Turning to Blake's verbal structures we find a medium which is in some respects easier to handle. The nature of language is such that discussion of influence can be more easily controlled and influence-study may sometimes be a direct assistant to exegesis.

In his illuminations to the Prophetic Books, Blake sometimes introduces the image of a net. It is used, for example, in connection with Urizen, where the various contexts suggest that it symbolizes the effects of a quantifying, mathematical approach which organizes the world and the heavens by a set of intercrossing lines until it can see nothing but the reticulations themselves.[26] Yet although the interpretation is persuasive as one inspects the various contexts in which the image is used, it receives a

---

[24] Frontispiece to *Songs of Innocence*.

[25] Cf. my *Coleridge the Visionary*, pp. 69–71 and *Blake's Visionary Universe* (Manchester, 1969), pp. 18–23.

[26] See particularly his illustrations to 'The Human Abstract' in *Songs of Experience* and to Plates 40, 47 and 56 of *Jerusalem*; and cf. *Urizen* 25.22, 30; 28.13; *The Four Zoas* ii.158 and viii.181.

new access of confirmatory power when we discover that Donne (whom Blake quotes elsewhere) had written these lines about the mathematical activities of his time:

> For of Meridians, and Parallels,
> Man hath weav'd out a net, and this net throwne,
> Upon the Heavens, and now they are his owne.[27]

This kind of pursuit, attempting to render the universe into final mathematical definition, was evidently felt by Blake to be damaging to the psyche of the human being who undertook it – and who could not, he thought, cast such a net around the heavens without himself becoming caught in the meshes. So Blake takes over and extends Donne's image, in order to make the further point that such an organizer has 'become what he beheld'.[28]

Now let us take a more complicated problem and see whether awareness of influence offers any assistance. In the course of a recent article, David Erdman draws attention to the fact that the closing line of 'Africa' in *The Song of Los*, 'The Guardian Prince of Albion burns in his nightly tent', is identical with the opening line of *America*, and he identifies the Prince with George III, seeing Blake's line as a straightforward characterization of tyranny.[29] The interpretation receives strong support from his earlier book, *Blake: Prophet against Empire*, where he both pointed out that Joel Barlow, author of *The Vision of Columbus*, had described George as 'Prince of Albion', and drew attention to other usages of the words 'guardians' and 'Prince' in *America* to describe supporters of the existing system in England.[30] Yet I believe that the naïf reader, coming to the line in isolation, might well read it as a more optimistic, prophetic statement, and that Erdman's interpretation gains credence mainly from Blake's use of the same words later in the poem. If one takes the line by itself, it has a positive ring, an energetic imagery which reminds one of the equivalently placed 'Rintrah roars & shakes his fires in the burdend air' of the prelude to

27 John Donne, 'An Anatomie of the World: the first Anniversary', lines 278–80, *Poems*, ed. H. J. C. Grierson (Oxford, 1912), p. 239.
28 Cf. *The Four Zoas* iv.203, 285–6; *Jerusalem* 30[34] and 32[36] *passim* (E329, 331, 174–7/K302, 305, 661–3).
29 D. V. Erdman, 'The Symmetries of *The Song of Los*', *Studies in Romanticism*, XVI (1977), 179–88. This article is based on a paper given to the 1974 Edinburgh Blake Symposium.
30 D. V. Erdman, *Blake: Prophet against Empire* (Princeton, 1954), pp. 21, 54–5, 58, 138 etc.

The Marriage of Heaven and Hell; if one resists the weight of the later usages, in other words, it becomes possible to argue that here, at least, Blake is using the imagery of his poem more purely. The Prince of Albion and the ancient guardians may go about trying to rescue their civilization; but meanwhile the *real* guardian prince of England, hidden from their sight by his tent, continues to burn with inspiration – communicating covertly, in fact, with the Americans who are inspired by a similar (if misguided) energy to kindle the flames of their own violent revolution.

No firm guidance towards either reading is offered by Blake's other usages, since all the major words involved are used in good or bad senses, according to the context (though it may be remarked that 'tent' more often has good connotations than bad). Nor is there any clear or decisive analogue for the line in previous literature. On the other hand, we may remember Blake's fondness for the Exodus story, and his apparent distinction between the pillar of cloud by day and the fire by night as alternating bad and good elements respectively in the march through the wilderness.[31] It is possible, too, that Blake knew Herbert's poem, 'The Bunch of Grapes', a poem full of Exodus imagery which includes the line 'Then have we too our guardian fires and clouds'.[32] It should also be noticed that the locution 'nightly tent' is reminiscent of Milton, who uses the word 'nightly' to describe the faithfulness of his muse in a phrase ('thou visit'st my slumbers nightly . . .') which Blake himself echoes in *Jerusalem* – 'This theme calls me in sleep night after night'.[33] The collocation of 'burns' and 'nightly', also, is found in *Paradise Lost*, where we read how, when Satan's followers began their revolt, the 'eternal eye' of God

> whose sight discerns
> Abstrusest thoughts, from forth his holy mount
> And from within the golden lamps that burn
> Nightly before him, saw without their light
> Rebellion rising[34]

This, last passage, in particular, if we allow it force, creates an imaginative context in which the first line of *America* and the last of *The Song of Los*

[31] See my *Blake's Humanism*, pp. 107, 113, 115, 137, 227.
[32] George Herbert, *Works*, ed. F. E. Hutchinson (Oxford, 1941), p. 128.
[33] *Paradise Lost* VII.29; *Jerusalem* 4.3.
[34] *Paradise Lost* V. 711–15.

appear as statements, not of a pessimistic and persistent state in the monarchy but of a flame which continues to burn in inspiration beyond all the sorry political events in England, keeping the idea of liberty alive, as the poet himself ('William Blake a Mental Prince')[35] keeps alive the flame of such inspiration in his art and poetry. The reading has the further virtue that it links the line directly to the corresponding design in *The Song of Los*, which shows a crowned figure and a woman sleeping on a giant leaf under the stars.[36] (If they are aligned with Oberon and Titania, it is, as Erdman suggests in his article, as guardians of the night – not in their state of jealousy.) An interpretation which links the sense of Blake's text to the sense of its accompanying illumination is always attractive.

Let us take another example, one that has already been discussed by two contributors to this collection: Blake's use of the word 'marks' in 'London'. In chapter 2 above, Edward Thompson relates Blake's use of the word to radical documents of the time, where there is much talk of the 'mark of the beast' as described in Revelation.[37] According to his interpretation the word is the lynch-pin of the poem, bringing into the foreground a chain of imagery involving identification of London with Babylon, and denunciation of current political and commercial tyrannies.

That this run of images and thoughts was in Blake's mind can hardly be doubted; among other things such an interpretation is, as Mr Thompson points out, authorized by the brilliant use of 'charter'd' in the first two lines. But the question remains: is this the *dominant* meaning of 'marks' at the point in question? And here a doubt may legitimately be registered. In the Bible it is always emphatically singular – 'the mark' – whereas Blake uses the plural 'marks'. This in itself suggests that he is not very concerned to direct the reader's attention toward the biblical context. And there are other influences that may be pursued – less dramatic and striking, perhaps, but also closer to Blake's own usage.

Blake was, after all, steeped in the writings of the Elizabethan poets, and particularly of Shakespeare. The ironic use of 'chartered' is itself relevant. When he described Liberty as 'the chartered right of Englishmen' in 'King Edward the Third',[38] Blake was no doubt thinking not only of Jaques'

[35] *Public Address*, E569/K599.
[36] Plate 5, repr. in D. V. Erdman (ed.), *The Illuminated Blake* (London, 1975), p. 178.
[37] See above, pp. 12–14.
[38] E415/K18.

demand 'I must have liberty / Withal, as large a charter as the wind, / To blow on whom I please . . .', but also of the description of the king in *Henry V*:[39]

> when he speaks,
> The air, a charter'd libertine, is still.

In the same way, Shakespeare often uses the word 'marks' in connection with the human face. 'She's a fair lady', says Benedick, seeing Beatrice, 'I do spy some marks of love in her.'[40] Shakespeare also uses 'mark' as a verb in the same connection:

> And mark the fleers, the gibes, and notable scorns,
> That dwell in every region of his face

says Iago to Othello.[41] Sometimes the two usages may be found close together. In *Richard III*, Queen Margaret says of Richard,

> Sin, death, and hell have set their marks on him,
> And all their ministers attend on him.[42]

while Richard himself says, fifty lines later,

> Clarence is well-spoken, and perhaps
> May move your hearts to pity, if you mark him.

We may even find the two forms of the word 'mark' as a conscious play of words in *Love's Labours Lost*.[43] Maria says

> A mark marvellous well shot, for they both did hit it

to which Boyet replies

> A mark! O, mark but that mark! A mark, says my lady!

and relapses into bawdy.

When contemplated in the midst of these varying usages, Blake's use of 'marks' seems less distinctive, less evocative of *any* single external reference; the effect of the last quotations, moreover, is to remind one of Blake's deep and abiding interest in the actual human face and its lineaments.

[39] *As You Like It* II.vii.48–50; *Henry V* I.i.48–9.
[40] *Much Ado About Nothing* II.iii.255–6.
[41] *Othello* IV.i.83.
[42] *Richard III* I.iii.293–4.
[43] *Love's Labours Lost* IV.i.132–3.

This is no barren argument about the provenance of a single word; it is germane to one's sense of the poem. For if we read 'mark' in Edward Thompson's primary, biblical sense, it is hard not to hear a strong apocalyptic note in the whole poem; messengers go about the streets of the great city, as it were, and pronounce its doom. In such an atmosphere, the 'hapless Soldier's sigh', running in blood down palace walls, sounds like a prophecy of forthcoming revolution, and even the harlot of the last stanza can become that favourite figure of late eighteenth-century apocalyptists, the Great Whore of Babylon, and so a sign of the city's approaching fall.

Read in the Shakespearean context, on the other hand, the word focusses our attention on the individual faces themselves: we are more aware of a poet who walks about those same streets, looking intently into every face that he sees for signs of weakness or strength, joy or woe. In this context, the business of charters, trade and law becomes subordinate to the plight of the individual. The individual is the subject of the abstract tyranny, but the tyranny is there because of all the inadequate individuals who make up the city. The 'mark of the beast', if present, is itself reinterpreted by such a reading to become a mark of human energies when unpenetrated by imaginative vision, and the harlot is a human harlot, herself victim as well as agent, rather than the majestic woman of Revelation.

One's judgement in so delicately balanced a matter is likely to be swayed by one's sense of Blake's work as a whole at this time; it is from my own sense of it, certainly, that I question whether 'London' is *primarily* an 'apocalyptic' poem – at least in the common sense of the word. Edward Thompson argues it to be a virtue of such an interpretation that in making all the final images ones of commerce and of forthcoming doom it allows the poem to 'shut like a box'. With most eighteenth-century poets this would indeed be a virtue, but I am not sure that the same applies to Blake. For his poems have a habit (irritating when first encountered) of springing open again just when one thinks one has closed them – almost as if they were the work of a man who believed that a poem which shut like a box might also be a prison. Despite my own strong interest in the structures of ideas in Blake's poems, and the undoubted existence of an apocalyptic note in them, I also feel that the interpretations which are most faithful to their total effect are those which (like Dr Glen's) preserve an antinomian quality in the very meanings of the poems themselves.

There is on the other hand a price to be paid for such openness; for there will be times when we simply do not have the means to decide between possible interpretations. To take up one of Dr Glen's own claims, it is hard to see how we can be sure that the observer in 'London' who 'marks' the marks in the faces that he sees is thereby demonstrating an abstracting and mechanical mental narrowness of his own. The obsessive focussing of his gaze on those of others might be a sign of extreme and generous humanity rather than its opposite.

One answer to such problems, of course, is to regard them as demonstrating the hermeneutic versatility of Blake's poetry and adding to their richness; but that will not quite do either. There is something about the very intensity of his writing in such places which urges the reader to interpret it directly. On any particular occasion, therefore, it is likely that the reader will make up his or her mind one way or the other. What our discussion seems to demonstrate is that in certain cases the reading of a single word may be decisive in fixing the balance of interpretation: in so short a poem as 'London' the leading significance assigned to 'mark' is enough to swing the dominant tone of the whole.

Investigation of a single word in Blake can prove equally fruitful elsewhere – and especially so if it turns out to unravel a concise shorthand for some complicated train of thought and imagery. Another word which repays study is 'intellectual', as in the line 'A tear is an intellectual thing'. Although that line no doubt makes gratifying reading to sentimental theoreticians, it stands out strangely in Blake – particularly since the specific use of 'intellectual' as we have come to know it belongs to a later period. At this point, however, we can turn to Kathleen Raine, who points out that 'intellect' is a term which appears in Thomas Taylor's translations from the Platonists. She quotes, for example, a passage which begins as follows: 'Intellect indeed is beautiful, and the most beautiful of all things, being situated in a pure light and in a pure splendor, and comprehending in itself the nature of beings, of which indeed this our beautiful material world is but the shadow and image . . .'[44] A passage such as this

---

[44] Kathleen Raine, *Blake and Tradition* (2 vols, London, 1969), vol. II, p. 195, citing T. Taylor, *Five Books of Plotinus* (1794), pp. 243–4.

certainly seems to be echoed by Blake, who, after speaking in *Jerusalem* of Imagination as 'the real & eternal World of which this Vegetable Universe is but a faint shadow',[45] goes on to inquire whether the Holy Ghost is 'any other than an Intellectual Fountain'.[46] Shortly afterwards he describes God as 'the intellectual fountain of Humanity'.[47] The coupling of the two favourite neo-Platonist concepts of 'intellect' and 'fountain' as attributes of the divine provides strong evidence for the existence of a direct influence.

Although these are comparatively late statements, moreover, they seem to reflect an earlier formulation of Blake's, for his earlier uses of 'intellect' also carry a charge which suggests that he thinks of it in dynamic terms, as an in-dwelling power – directly linked, as in Plotinus, to a realm of intellect which transcends the world of generation and death.

And in the case of the line with which we began, the point may be pursued further, since in the preface to one of his very first translations (the short *Concerning the Beautiful*, published in 1787), Taylor draws a specific distinction between the 'corporeal eye' and the 'intellectual eye', which looks forward to Blake's distinction between the 'Corporeal or Vegetative Eye' and the visionary act which involves looking 'thro it & not with it'.[48]

For Blake, as for Plotinus, the eye may serve either as a simple mirror to reflect the natural world, or as a medium of transforming perception. But it may be that Blake goes further: for just as the vortices of experience, once passed, englobe themselves,[49] so the natural complement to the

---

[45] *Jerusalem* 77 (Raine, *Tradition*).

[46] *Jerusalem* 77 (not in Raine).

[47] *Jerusalem* 91.11 (not in Raine).

[48] T. Taylor, *Concerning the Beautiful* (1787), pp. xiii and xvi (cf. E555/K617, quoted below, p. 249). I suspect that Taylor's little book, coming at an important stage in Blake's career. may have had a disproportionately large influence on his individual vocabulary, by comparison with Taylor's later works. Other points in it to which Blake may have reacted strongly (favourably or otherwise) are Taylor's argument (p. vii) that 'the science of universals, permanent & fixt, must be superior to the knowledge of particulars, fleeting and frail' (cf. Blake's contrary insistence that 'Art & Science cannot exist but in minutely organized Particulars', *Jerusalem* 55.62 *et passim*); Taylor's question (p. ix) 'Where . . . is the microscope which can discern what is smallest in nature? Where the telescope, which can see at what point in the universe wisdom first began?' (cf. Bromion's gloomy and uncomprehending questions in *Visions of the Daughters of Albion* 4.13–24); and Plotinus's point (p. 11) that 'Since matter . . . is neither soul nor intellect, nor life, nor form, nor reason nor bound, but a certain indefiniteness . . . it . . . is deservedly called non-entity' with Blake's frequent and idiosyncratic use of the word 'non-entity' in a similar frame of reference, from *Visions of the Daughters of Albion* 7.15 onwards and his associated use of 'indefinite' – especially in *The Four Zoas* and *Jerusalem*.

[49] See *Milton* 15.21–35.

illuminated eye might be said to be the globing tear which it drops in the reflexive moment of pity – a globe which in the moment of falling reflects everything about it in miniature, momentarily enabling the observer (as, more actively, in the experience of illuminated vision) to see all things in one. In this sense the tear may be said to be, very exactly, 'an intellectual thing'; and awareness of that further possible sense not only enriches the line in question but may throw light on other uses of the tear image in Blake.[50]

This is not the only case where a single word, lifted from some particular context, still seems to carry some overtones from the passage or passages in which it was originally found. When, for example, Blake writes of the five senses as the 'chief inlets of Soul in this age' (*The Marriage of Heaven and Hell*, Plate 4), the word 'inlets' stands out. Morton Paley has pointed out that the whole discussion at this point is almost certainly a covert advance on a passage in Priestley's *Disquisitions relating to Matter and Spirit*, first published in 1777. Where Priestley writes, 'I had always taken it for granted, that man had a soul distinct from his body . . .', Blake writes firmly, 'Man has no Body distinct from his Soul for that calld Body is a portion of Soul discernd by the five Senses, the chief inlets of Soul in this age'.[51] Priestley, moreover (though Paley does not mention this), actually uses the word 'inlet' in Blake's sense[52] – which is not recorded by the Oxford English Dictionary at all.

Further investigation, however, suggests that the position is less simple than it might appear at first sight. For the word 'inlet' had also appeared in the same sense in Berkeley,[53] and then again in Berkeley's opponent,

50 E.g., 'Urizen dropt a tear' (*The Four Zoas* ix.200) and similar references; and Blake might have gained something from Donne's ingenious use of the tear image in 'A Valediction: Of Weeping'. This is simply exploratory and tentative, however.

51 Joseph Priestley, *Disquisitions relating to Matter and Spirit* (1777), p. xi (quoted by Paley, *Energy and the Imagination*, p. 9); E34/K149.

52 Priestley, *Disquisitions*, p. 34. Priestley uses the word in connection with 'Dr Clarke's *Demonstration*' but I have not found it in Samuel Clarke's *Demonstration of the Being and Attributes of God* (1705). It may be noted, however, that this book, too, might conceivably have been read by Blake, since Clarke argues (p. 90) that God has 'no Divisibility . . . any such Separation or Removing of Parts, is *really* or *mentally* a setting Bounds; either of which, destroys Infinity' – which might have assisted the conception of the false God, Urizen, who *does* set 'Bounds'. Clarke also (pp. 162–71) precedes Baxter in the argument that man's five senses do not necessarily constitute a necessary and ultimate limit to the possibilities of perception (see below).

53 *Principles of Human Knowledge* (1710), section 81 (cited by Raine, *Tradition*, vol. II, p. 127). I owe this reference to E. P. Thompson.

Andrew Baxter, who writes in his *Enquiry into the Nature of the Human Soul* (1733):

The last disadvantage the soul labours under, from the present constitution of the body, is that it perceives external things but *a few ways*, and by a few inlets, or passages of the body . . . It is no better argument against the possibility of more ways of perceiving external objects than *five*, because there are but five, than it would have been against the possibility of more than *one* or *two*, if there had been but one or two; or because some creatures may have but one or two.[54]

At this point, of course, we immediately think of Blake's *There is No Natural Religion* (1788): 'From a perception of only 3 senses or 3 elements none could deduce a fourth or fifth' (E1/K97). On his next page Baxter begins a long note with the reflection that

It may perhaps be the more easily conceived, that the body may be all over one common sensory to the soul, if we consider that the body, in its present constitution, *limits* and *confines* the perceptions of the soul, but no way effects them. The fabrick of the eye is indeed wonderful, and by it this mechanical (or rather optical) problem is performed, that a living percipient *Being* confined to a *dark* and *close* place, is apprized of what exists, and is done without, and at a distance.

It would be rash to conclude that either Baxter or Priestley is Blake's ultimate source, nevertheless, since (as Kathleen Raine has pointed out)[55] several of the points in question can be found in Locke. Locke, too, uses (and indeed probably originates) the use of 'inlet' in this connection, describing Perception as 'the first Operation of all our intellectual Faculties, and the inlet of all Knowledge into our Minds'.[56] His *Essay* is also the source of the observation that if man had been made with less than five senses he would not have been able to imagine the existence of others.[57] (He goes on to argue that there may actually be other faculties in man which are shut up 'as a worm in one drawer of a Cabinet' for want of an organ by which they can assist in perception.) It is Locke, finally, who likens the understanding to 'a closet, wholly shut from light, with only some little opening left, to let in external visible resemblance, or *ideas* of

---

54 Andrew Baxter, *An Enquiry into the Nature of the Human Soul*, 2nd edn (2 vols, 1737), vol. I, p. 295.

55 Raine, *Tradition*, vol. II, pp. 105–6.

56 John Locke, *An Essay concerning Human Understanding* II.9.15 (1788, vol. I, p. 135). Cf. also II.7.10; II.21.52; IV.3.23, etc.

57 *Ibid.*, I.2.3 (1788, vol. I, pp. 102–3). Raine, *Tradition*, vol. II, pp. 105–6.

things without . . .'.[58] So, we are forced to acknowledge, Blake's statements in *There is No Natural Religion* may be no more than a direct reaction to the impact on him of Locke's philosophy, which we know he read as a young man with 'Contempt and Abhorrence'.[59] The inference that Baxter, also, intervened rests upon the close compactness of his statements, but still more on the implication in them that the body is a prison. Locke thinks of it as no more than a closet or 'dark room', thus preserving a sense of civilization. Baxter's reflections correspond more closely to Blake's celebration, elsewhere in the *Marriage*, of the energy which he believes to be imprisoned in every living thing; and when we discover that in the observation right after his reference to the 'chief Inlets of Soul in this age', Blake describes reason as 'the bound or outward circumference of Energy', the presumption gains ground that Blake's observations, though written no doubt as an answer to Locke and others, may also have derived some of their force from Baxter's more dramatic presentation of the body as a dark, confined place which '*limits* and *confines* the perceptions of the soul'.

In investigating Blake's sources, it will be observed, the pursuit of particular words and ideas necessarily and continually goes hand in hand with attempted reconstruction of Blake's state of mind as he approached such sources in their original contexts. Part of one's suspicion that Blake was responding to Baxter as well as to Locke and Priestley derives from Baxter's depiction of that very horror of imprisoning force which we assumed to have been dominant in Blake's personality, particularly in youth. Confronting Reynolds's 'Ugolino', we contended, his direct response to a vivid depiction of that force had been strong enough to outweigh any other feelings he might have had, then or later, about Reynolds's work and attitudes as a whole. In the same way, the 'influence' of an earlier writer might be exercised upon him by way of a response to his work that was either positive or negative. Sometimes, indeed, it seems almost as if Blake were actually reading his predecessors with an eye to the *contrary* currents in their work. We know, for instance, that he read Burke's treatise on *The Sublime and Beautiful* as a young man and disliked it.[60] He is also very likely to have read Hume's *Treatise on Human Nature*.

---

[58] *Ibid.*, II.11.17 (1788, vol. I, p. 150–1).
[59] See his annotation to Reynolds (E650/K476–7), quoted by Harald Kittel above, p. 111. Kittel's whole discussion is, of course, germane to our central theme.
[60] Annotation to Reynolds (E650/K476–7).

In the first of these he would have found a discussion of the relation between smoothness and pleasure on the one hand and of that between roughness and painfulness on the other. Towards the end, Burke comments,

Before we quit this article, we must observe; that as smooth things are, as such, agreeable to the taste, and are found of a relaxing quality; so on the other hand, things which are found by experience to be of a strengthening quality, and fit to brace the fibres, are almost universally rough and pungent to the taste, and in many cases rough even to the touch.[61]

There is the germ here of a possible counter-aesthetic, which might find a beauty in things rough and pungent, but Burke is too much a child of his century to develop it. Hume, similarly, could undertake a long discussion of the passions, in which he argued that the sensations created by pride and love were always agreeable, while those set up by humility and hatred were always painful. This was in itself somewhat unconventional (if also in conformity with the larger spirit of the age); but he went further, to make a reservation about the difference between pride and love: 'Let us remember, that pride and hatred invigorate the soul; and love and humility enfeeble it.'[62] In a single aphorism in *The Marriage of Heaven and Hell* Blake skims the cream of both comments, producing a statement which draws upon and extends each, by running together Burke's aesthetic 'relax versus brace' formula with Hume's psychological observation of the effects of pride and hatred on the one hand and love and humility on the other. What he produces, very simply, is

> Damn. braces: Bless relaxes.

Blake may here be said to be lighting on opportunities which are latent in the text – and to some degree supported by it. This may also be the case (and if so, more directly) with another philosopher, George Berkeley, whom Blake is likely to have read during his period of interest in Locke's philosophy.[63] In the *Principles of Human Knowledge*, Berkeley turns Locke's philosophy of human limitation back upon itself by declaring his convic-

---

[61] Burke, *A Philosophical Enquiry into the Origin of our Ideas of the Sublime and Beautiful* IV.xxii (2nd edn 1759, p. 298).

[62] Hume, *Treatise on Human Nature* (1739) II.x (ed. L. A. Selby-Bigge, 1896, p. 391).

[63] Blake annotated *Siris* later in life (E652–4/K773–5), but it seems unlikely that this marked his first acquaintance with him. Kathleen Raine's arguments for an earlier knowledge (*Tradition*, vol. II, pp. 101–50, etc.), are, if not finally conclusive, highly persuasive.

tion that there are 'a great variety of spirits of different orders and capacities, whose faculties, both in number and extent, are far exceeding those the Author of my being has bestowed on me . . .'. He continues, 'And for me to pretend to determine by my own few, stinted, narrow inlets of perception, what ideas the inexhaustible power of the Supreme Spirit may imprint upon them, were certainly the utmost folly and presumption.'[64]

To see Locke's 'inlets' so neatly turned to the service of his own side would have delighted Blake; the notion that he read and enjoyed the treatise may be supported by the fact that in developing his thesis Berkeley goes on to attack the assertion, which he ascribes to the sceptics, that we are 'under an invincible blindness as to the *true* and *real* nature of things':

We are miserably bantered, say they, by our senses, and amused only with the outside and shew of things. The real essence, the internal qualities, and constitution of every the meanest object, is hid from our view; something there is in every drop of water, every grain of sand, which it is beyond the power of human understanding to fathom or comprehend. But it is evident from what has been shewn, that all this complaint is groundless, and that we are influenced by false principles to that degree as to mistrust our senses, and think we know nothing of those things which we perfectly comprehend.[65]

Perhaps it was Blake's meditation on this reported objection (and Berkeley's not altogether convincing reply to it) which led him to write the lines in which he affirms it to be the visionary's triumph that he can actually see in the apparently unfathomable and incomprehensible inner nature of such things qualities which are at once infinite and revelatory of eternity:

> To see a World in a Grain of Sand
> And a Heaven in a Wild Flower
> Hold Infinity in the palm of your hand
> And Eternity in an hour   (E481/K431)

For him the fact became a prime weapon against sceptics later than those whom Berkeley had attacked:

> Mock on Mock on Voltaire Rousseau
> Mock on Mock on tis all in vain

---

[64] George Berkeley, *Principles of Human Knowledge*, section 81.
[65] *Ibid.*, section 101.

You throw the sand against the wind
And the wind blows it back again

And every sand becomes a Gem
Reflected in the beams divine
Blown back they blind the mocking Eye
But still in Israels paths they shine

The Atoms of Democritus
And Newtons Particles of light
Are sands upon the Red sea shore
Where Israels tents do shine so bright   (E468–9/K418)

Nor does the chain of possibilities stop there, even. The reference to Newton's 'Particles of light' in the last stanza may be read in conjunction with an interesting passage in Locke's *Essay*, where he comments on the deceptiveness of the appearances of things, by comparison with what they reveal under the microscope: 'Had we senses acute enough to discern the minute particles of bodies and the real constitution on which their sensible qualities depend, I doubt not but they would produce quite different *ideas* in us . . .' One of the examples he gives relates directly to our discussion:

Thus sand, or pounded glass, which is opake, and white to the naked eye, is pellucid in a microscope; and a hair seen this way, loses its former colour, and is in a great measure pellucid, with a mixture of some bright sparkling colours, such as appear from the refraction of diamonds, and other pellucid bodies.[66]

The fact which Locke is recording is clearly relevant to the whole matter of 'seeing the world in a grain of sand'; it is also possible that his use of the term 'minute particles' bears upon one of Blake's more unusual terms. There is for many readers something puzzling about the repetitive use of the term 'minute particulars' in *Jerusalem*. At one level, its meaning seems clear enough. 'He who would do good to another, must do it in Minute Particulars': that is straightforwardly good advice. Elsewhere, however, the 'minute particulars' themselves have a more concrete existence. The speaker in the poem complains that he sees them 'in slavery . . . among the brick-kilns': Los sees 'every Minute Particular of Albion degraded & murderd'; in London, likewise, he sees

[66] *Essay concerning Human Understanding* II.23.11 (1788, vol. I, p. 313).

> every minute particular, the jewels of Albion, running down
> The kennels of the streets & lanes as if they were abhorrd[67]

The puzzle here is that such repetitive concern for 'minute particulars' might savour of the close and anxious attention to the details of nature which one would associate with a follower of Urizen rather than with the kind of care expected of a visionary painter. If, on the other hand, Blake in coining the phrase had in mind not only (say) Thomas Taylor's 'particulars',[68] but also the special significance of Locke's minute particles, which open out a source of light that would otherwise be invisible to the eye, his use of it is more comprehensible: it makes cultivation of the minute particular not a blind care for exact representation of what the eye sees but an interpretative process, bringing out the visionary nature of every detail while remaining faithful to their own nature. Such a reading of the phrase may be supported by another line in *Jerusalem*, where Los sees to his dismay that

> Every Universal Form, was become barren mountains of Moral
> Virtue: and every Minute Particular hardend into grains of sand
>
> (*J* 45[31].19–20)

It is also consonant with the assertion elsewhere that benevolence

> protects minute particulars, every one in their own identity
>
> (*J* 38[43].23)

and with the Blakean use of the word 'organized' in the lines

> he who wishes to see a Vision; a perfect Whole
> Must see it in its Minute Particulars; Organized   (*J* 91.21–2)

In the cases just discussed, the verbal resemblances are strong enough to support a skein of interpretations, the acceptability of which is likely to be in proportion to their success in actually illuminating the text for any given reader. Something of the same kind is true of the various 'intensive' influences which go to make up the sequence of plates entitled *The Gates of Paradise*. As one traces the winnowings and reorderings by which Blake reduced his original sequence of drawings to the few finally selected, studying en route the various developments from the earlier inscriptions to

---

[67] *J* 55.60; 89.17; 45[31].7; 45[31].17.
[68] See above, p. 222, note 48.

the later ones,[69] it becomes possible to glimpse the weight of reading which lay behind the view of life propounded in them. I have discussed elsewhere some of the verbal influences, and the assistance which they offer to our interpretation of the series;[70] Frank Parisi, in his contribution to this collection, has conducted a searching analysis of further sources, especially the visual ones. I should like now to add three more possible sources which, taken with my earlier discussion of Ugolino, help to suggest the catholicity of Blake's sources in this early period and to bring out still further the underlying pattern of ideas in the series.

In his *Characteristics*, Shaftesbury includes a discussion concerning the role of man in nature. His character Theocles draws attention to the fact that man must 'submit to the elements of Nature, and not the elements to him': 'Few of these are at all fitted to him; and none perfectly. If he be left in *Air*, he falls headlong; for Wings were not assign'd him. In *Water* he soon sinks. In *Fire* he consumes. Within *Earth* he suffocates.——'[71] A few pages later, Theocles goes on to imagine the lowest kind of process by which man might be supposed to have come into the world: 'For instance, let us suppose he sprang, as the old Poets feign'd, from a *big-belly'd Oak*: and then belike he might resemble more a Man-Drake than a MAN.'[72] In this case, the parallels between the first passage and Plates 3 to 5, the 'Water Earth Air Fire' sequence in *The Gates of Paradise*, on the one hand, and those between the second passage and Plate 2, showing a woman gathering human beings from under a tree, on the other, suggest that a reading of Shaftesbury may have assisted the development of the series. Yet the parallels are not exact in all details, and the plates seem to have been in a different sequence when they were first drawn in the Notebook. Shaftesbury's passages, on this account of the matter, provided further material for the enquiry into the role of man in the natural order against which Blake undertook the successive reorderings of the plates for his book, helping him to give it its final shape.

It is fairly clear, similarly, that in using various stages from birth to

---

[69] This study has been made much easier by the isolation of the various stages in David Erdman's edition, *The Notebook of William Blake: a Photographic and Typographic Facsimile* (Oxford, 1973).

[70] In appendix 1 of my *Blake's Humanism*, pp. 231–43.

[71] Shaftesbury, 'The Moralists: a Philosophical Rhapsody' II.iv, in *Characteristics of Men, Manners, Opinions, Times*, 6th edn (1738), vol. II, p. 302.

[72] *Ibid.*, Sect. II.xv.

death to form the sequential patterns of his series, Blake had in mind the old model of life as a journey from the cradle to the grave which figures in many allegories. And in this connection it is worth pointing out that on 14 July 1790, during the period when Blake was beginning to evolve his sequence, there appeared in London a game entitled 'The New Game of Human Life'.[73] Intended as a board game, this had eighty-four stages, beginning with the infant, the child and the boy, proceeding through various forms of boyhood, youth and manhood, showing various forms under which human life may be lived ('The Negligent Boy', 'The Assiduous Boy', 'The Traveller' and so on) until it reached 'The quiet Man', 'The Thoughtful Man' and, finally, 'The Immortal Man'. *The Gates of Paradise* was published in 1793. When, years later, Blake produced a poetic gloss for his series, it included towards the end the lines:

> But when once I did descry
> The Immortal Man that cannot Die
> Thro evening shades I haste away
> To close the Labours of my Day   (E266/K771)

As usual, Blake's conception of 'the Immortal Man' is very different from that which concludes the game (fig. 15); his own is shown in his series in the plates (figs. 16 and 17) where the spirit of man is seen as an essential living form within, surviving at the moment of death, and immanent in Blake's own version of 'The Traveller'. Yet the appearance of this phrase, coupled with the general shape of his series, suggests an influence from yet another quarter; if valid it would further emphasize the fact that his interpretation of human life, in this series and elsewhere, comments upon – and protests against – the conventional view of life as a simple progress, imprisoned by time, with immortality conceived as a linear process which starts, as it were, only at the moment of death.

And it is possible, finally, that the caption itself was conceived, in the same spirit, as a reply to the arguments in favour of accepting one's fate with resignation in Johnson's 'The Vanity of Human Wishes'. The concluding passage of that poem begins,

> Where then shall Hope and Fear their objects find?
> Must dull suspense corrupt the stagnant mind?

[73] Published 14 July 1790, by John Wallis, no. 16 Ludgate Street and E. Newbery, the corner of St Paul's Church Yard.

15. Detail from 'The Game of Life' (1790)

> Must helpless man, in ignorance sedate,
> Roll darkling down the torrent of his fate?

Blake's caption answers the question by undermining its very terms, asserting:

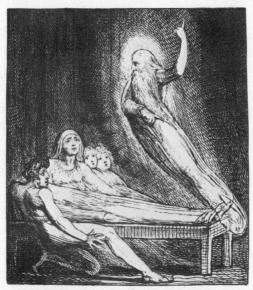

16. *The Gates of Paradise*, Plate 13, 'Fear & Hope are – Vision'

17. *The Gates of Paradise*, Plate 14, 'The Traveller hasteth in the Evening'

Fear & Hope are – Vision

Though not immediately relevant to our central theme, since she is not primarily concerned with influences as such (whether historical or literary), Heather Glen's essay in the present collection raises some important issues at this more general level also, where the critic is concerned with the mind behind the work of art. Her approach, which involves attending primarily to the poem itself, both looking at Blake's illumination and listening to the exact words and tonal quality of his text, and searching for the precise meaning there, is valuable, even if it directs attention away from the kind of enlarged response which is available when, for example, one learns from Kathleen Raine's investigations that Swedenborg at one point made the chimney-sweeper a symbol of the 'Seminal Vessel'[74] – an identification which suggests the existence of a sexual symbolism in the poem, an implicit critique of current attitudes to sex as 'dirty', in addition to its strong element of direct social criticism. What is more important, for our purpose, is the kind of issue concerning interpretation that is raised by the method being employed; for the probing delicacy of Dr Glen's investigation of poems such as 'London' and the first 'Holy Thursday' confronts us with an important question concerning the *Songs of Innocence and of Experience*, involving Blake's use of the dramatic voice. What sort of identity do we believe Blake himself to have had, and is there a justification for seeing the various narrating persons of the *Songs* as being distinct from the personality of the poet himself? On the one hand, *An Island in the Moon* provides ample evidence of his skill at allowing different characters to speak in their own voice; it is a fact that a version of the lines

> Pity would be no more,
> If we did not make somebody Poor   (E27/K217)

which are presented directly in the finished poem, was originally, in the manuscript draft, assigned to a 'Devil'; Blake also continued to produce good dramatic writing in his later poetry. On the other hand, the intensity of affirmation which is a keynote of his work from the late 1780s onwards makes it natural for one to read his poetry as direct and personal statement. The problem is as before: it is perfectly possible for the reader to draw his

---

[74] Raine, *Tradition*, vol. I, p. 25, quoting from *Concerning the Earths in Our Solar System*, section 79 (1787, pp. 87–8).

own conclusions, but Blake has not always given him the means to validate those conclusions. And in this case there is not even the possibility of recognizing and interpreting influences as a guide; one is left to decide for oneself whether Blake's love of freedom expresses itself here in enhanced self-projection or in a decision to let the speaker of each song have an identity of his or her own.

Peter Butter's essay (chapter 6 above) takes us still more directly to the central critical question raised by Blake's independent stance. Is it in fact possible to define a broad critical position from which it might be agreed, as between one reader and another, that one passage in Blake is *better* than another? And does awareness of influences help? A point at which he takes issue with my own interpretation[75] provides a convenient illustration of the problems involved. The lines in question describe how the Virgin divides away from Ololon:

> Away from Ololon she divided & fled into the depths
> Of Miltons Shadow as a Dove upon the stormy Sea.

> Then as a Moony Ark Ololon descended to Felphams Vale
> (*M* 42.5–7, E142/K534)

In my book I describe the dove as a 'negative symbol of inspiration', followed by the 'positive' one of the 'moony ark'. Professor Butter finds this hard to accept, preferring (even if he disagrees with it in other respects) Harold Bloom's interpretation, which links the first image to the dove who was sent out from the ark in the Old Testament narrative; this, he argues, 'does not ask one to fight against the natural associations of the images'. But it must be pointed out that when the dove appears it has no such natural association, since the ark has not yet been mentioned; and in any case the dove was sent out of the ark not when the sea was stormy, but after the waters were 'assuaged'. For me the 'natural associations' of the image, in a poem entitled *Milton*, are not with Noah's dove but with Milton's Holy Spirit which, as described in *Paradise Lost*,

> with mighty wings outspread
> Dove-like sat'st brooding on the vast abyss
> And madest it pregnant[76]

[75] In *Blake's Humanism*; see above, p. 158.
[76] *Paradise Lost* I.20–2.

Such an association links it naturally with 'Milton's shadow' and with what has just been said in Blake's poem concerning

> the Void Outside of Existence, which if enter'd into
> Becomes a Womb.   (*M* 41.37–42.1)

It is for that reason, and because the image sets up for me an image not of birth but of dark potency, that I called it a 'negative symbol' of inspiration, while the 'moony ark', which is no more physically effective, perhaps, but which, appearing 'in clouds of blood, in streams of gore', offers a glimpse of what revelation would actually be like, is for me a 'positive symbol' of inspiration.

The question remains: is it better to read the passage with loose reference to the more publicly available associations of the images, so achieving a smooth-flowing, if vague, reading, or to tease out the allusive intricacies of Blake's thought about inspiration – at the risk of losing the flow of the passage as a piece of verse writing?

Professor Butter's discussion, for all its trenchancy, does not offer a firm answer to the basic question one way or the other, for, as we read it, we become aware that even his most open evaluations involve something more than a direct reading of the text: that this critic is still being driven to ask himself questions about, for example, the significance of certain characters in the Prophetic Books, and that the force of his criticisms is often strengthened by the use of, and inference from, information which might not be available to a reader coming to the text for the first time.

It is no part of my purpose to pursue the critical issue at a theoretical level, simply to point out that if the kind of enterprise to which Professor Butter addresses himself must also at some point involve asking how much information the 'common reader' might reasonably be expected to acquire before reaching his critical judgements concerning the poetry, that question must in turn presuppose another kind of enterprise, in which one tries to acquire *all* the relevant information. An investigation which seems at first sight recondite may turn out to be less so if it culminates in the discovery of information which helps bring diverse elements of Blake's own work into some simpler pattern of coherent and readily accessible interpretation. And since such a pattern will in some sense change the reader's imaginative response to what is being presented, his critical attitude to what he is reading or looking at will accordingly be affected.[77]

The kind of critical activity to which Professor Butter and Dr Glen direct the reader must always, in fact (as they themselves acknowledge) stand in a complementary relationship to the scholarly investigation of sources, sometimes protesting against its more recondite concerns, but sometimes learning from it. In practice, however – as is evident from the present investigation itself – the separation is never so absolute in practice; and it is still less so when larger influences are involved, as we shall see.

(ii) *Extensive influence*

So far we have moved back from some unusual individual words in Blake to possible sources for them in previous literature. Now we may turn to a different kind of case, where three successive pages of an eighteenth-century book seem to have generated various echoes in Blake over a long period of time. Whichcote's *Aphorisms*, first published in 1703,[78] was a popular volume; there is no difficulty in believing that Blake had access to it. The striking feature of the pages in question is that Blake seems to have returned to them at different times for verbal formulations, in each of which he expressed a modified, or contrary sentiment. Thus Whichcote writes,

272. Reason and Virtue are Things that have *Bounds* and Limits: but Vice and Passion have *none*.

In *The Book of Los* (Plate 4), Blake writes, of Los falling, 'Truth has bounds. Error none'.[79] He himself would hardly have identified 'Truth' with 'Reason and Virtue', of course; his own formulation seems rather to involve a distinction between 'limits' (which he would associate with Reason and regard as irksome restraints) and 'bounds', which, though sometimes synonymous with limits in his writings, can also be associated

---

[77] A good example is Blake's line 'Truly My Satan thou art but a Dunce', the meaning of which is illuminated as one learns not only that it refers to a line in Young's *Night Thoughts* but that Blake illustrated that line with a very relevant design (see H. M. Margoliouth's article in V. de Sola Pinto (ed.), *The Divine Vision* (London, 1957), p. 198 and my *Blake's Humanism*, p. 18).

[78] Benjamin Whichcote, *Moral and Religious Aphorisms* (1703, new edn 1753). My quotations are all taken from the later, expanded, edition, but most appear in the earlier one also.

[79] E91/K258.

with that 'bounding line' of form, with its 'infinite inflexions and movements',[80] which he regards as necessary to all art. It is in this second sense,
that 'truth has bounds'.

There are one or two other usages in these pages that remind one of
Blake. In Whichcote's 'He that gives way to Self-will, hinders Self-
Enjoyment' (no. 278), the word 'hinders' has the flavour of the usage by
which Blake describes the negative actions he hates (e.g. 'Accident is the
omission of act in self & the hindering of act in another, This is Vice . . .'
etc.).[81] Again, Whichcote's 'The Traveller means to go directly; but hath
lost his way, and is bewildered: is any so cruel, as not to shew him the
right way?' (no. 287), anticipates Blake's favourite image of the Traveller
who, for example, 'hasteth in the evening' and who may dream 'The lost
Travellers Dream under the Hill'.[82] Whichcote's reflections on 'holiness',
beginning 'Holiness, in Angels and Men, is their Dei-formity' (no. 262),
might have prompted Blake's more radical conviction that 'every thing
that lives is holy'. These might be no more than chance resemblances,
however, and are worth mentioning only because of their proximity to
some more striking parallels between ideas and phrases in these pages and
certain equivalents to be found in the sequence entitled 'The Everlasting
Gospel'. Michael Tolley has drawn attention to the large number of
biblical phrases in the latter poem – many more than might be noticed at a
first reading[83] – and his account may now be supplemented by reference to
Whichcote; indeed it looks as if Blake was sometimes deliberately
commenting on the *Aphorisms* as he hammered out the opinions in his
poem. Thus Whichcote writes,

270. It is altogether as worthy of God, and as much becoming Him; to *Pardon*
and shew Mercy, in case of Repentance and Submission and Reformation: as to
Punish, in case of Impenitency and Obstinacy.

and continues the point for several paragraphs. Blake, arguing that
humility is to be exercised only towards God and not towards man
('Thou art a Man God is no more / Thine own humanity learn to adore')

[80] *Descriptive Catalogue*, E540/K585.
[81] Annotations to Lavater, E590/K88. It is also a favourite pejorative word of Blake's in his *Public
Address, Descriptive Catalogue* and 'A Vision of the Last Judgment'.
[82] *The Gates of Paradise*, E264, 266/K769, 771.
[83] Michael Tolley, 'William Blake's Use of the Bible in . . . "The Everlasting Gospel" ' and 'Blake's
"Eden's Flood" Again', *Notes and Queries* CCVII (1962), 171–6; CCXIII (1968), 11–19.

produces his own ironic version of the sentiment, assigned apparently to
Satan:

> Gods Mercy & Long Suffering
> Is but the Sinner to Judgment to bring
> Thou on the Cross for them shalt pray
> And take Revenge at the Last Day. ((c) 41–2; 45–9, K750–1)

This parallel, again, is no more than conjectural, but ten aphorisms later
one is startled to find in Whichcote an actual verbal formula which is also
to be found in Blake's poem. Whichcote writes:

281. . . . Sinners are made-up of Contradictions: contradictions to Truth and
Reason, to God, to themselves, and to one another. *Virtue* is uniform, regular,
constant and certain.

Blake (who would surely have disagreed with the last sentiment) takes the
point a stage further back in the next lines of his poem:

> Do what you will this Lifes a Fiction
> And is made up of Contradiction.   ((c) 50–1, K751)

He elaborates on his meaning in a later version:

> Reasoning upon its own dark Fiction,
> In doubt which is Self Contradiction.   ((d) 97–8, K753)

At this point Blake has returned to a favourite image (paralleled, as we have
seen, in Baxter and others): the 'dark Fiction' is caused by failure to realize
that, as physical tool, the eye is an 'inlet' only of sense-perception, not of
total revelation:

> This Lifes dim Windows of the Soul
> Distorts the Heavens from Pole to Pole
> And leads you to Believe a Lie
> When you see with not thro the Eye   ((d) 103–6, K753)

Two further possible parallels may be mentioned. Whichcote wrote

273. Some things must be *good in themselves*: else there could be no Measure,
whereby to lay-out Good and Evil.

Blake (who satirized a similar mode of reasoning in his verses beginning
'Pity would be no more, / If we did not make somebody Poor') writes in
'The Everlasting Gospel',

> Good & Evil are no more
> Sinais trumpets cease to roar
>
> . . .
>
> To be Good only is to be
> A God or else a Pharisee   ((e) 21–2; 27–8, K754)

A little earlier, Whichcote had written:

267. *Joy* is the Life of man's Life. *Joy* and *Grief* are things of great hazard and Danger, in the life of man: The one *breaks* the Heart; the other *intoxicates* the Head. An Eye to God, in both, doth poise and balance.

While Blake might have agreed that joy and grief could be things of 'great hazard and Danger', he would have regarded any attempts to 'poise and balance' them as based upon a total misunderstanding of the relationship involved. Indeed, his well-known lines, this time in 'Auguries of Innocence', read rather like a vigorous retort to Whichcote's prudential sentiments:

> Man was made for Joy & Woe
> And when this we rightly know
> Thro the World we safely go
> Joy & Woe are woven fine
> A Clothing for the Soul divine
> Under every grief & pine
> Runs a joy with silken twine   (E482/K432)

One very interesting feature of Blake's dealings with Whichcote is the fact that although there are some other suggestive formulations among the *Aphorisms* (e.g. 'There ought to be a Subordination of the transactions of Time to the subsistencies of Eternity' (no. 992); cf. Blake's 'Eternity is in love with the Productions of Time'),[84] most of the striking examples are concentrated in a sequence of less than fifty out of a total of twelve hundred; yet the echoes in Blake (assuming, of course, that they are so) extend over a wide range of his writings. One is drawn to suppose either that this sequence had a powerful effect upon him when he read it, or that he had a copy of Whichcote which he turned to from time to time – partly to prime the pump of his own writing, perhaps, partly to argue with the underlying presuppositions which he encountered there.

[84] E35/K151.

Another such cluster of words and expressions, where again some of the similarities with Blake are striking enough to encourage the supposition of a direct relationship, is to be found in a very different place: Pope's 'Eloisa to Abelard'.[85] In this case it is possible to speculate further about the dates of such an influence. Blake must have known the poem from boyhood and no doubt responded then to its emotive power; but it would also seem likely that he re-read it in a more allegorical sense at a later point. This re-emergence, moreover, would seem to belong to a specific period: the years of his work on *Vala*, during which he also produced some manuscript poems about love relationships where the concepts of his larger poem are applied to more immediate human encounters.

Pope was far from congenial to Blake, whose general comments (such as the one on his 'Metaphysical Jargon of Rhyming')[86] are invariably disparaging. Yet 'Eloisa to Abelard', with its uncharacteristic intensity of emotional utterance has always had a place of its own in Pope's work (Fuseli, for example, characterized it as 'hot ice').[87] Blake depicted it as one of the two background scenes for the 'Head of Pope' which he painted for Hayley.[88] From what we know of his intellectual development, moreover, it might be expected that in later years he would have read the poem as an allegory of the deprived human spirit, craving to be reunited with its 'emanation' – indeed, the very formulation of that word might well have been partly prompted by Eloisa's own words to Abelard:

> My fancy form'd thee of Angelick kind,
> Some emanation of th' all-beauteous Mind. (61–2)

A further general correspondence may be noted between Eloisa's comment on love,

> Love, free as air, at sight of human ties,
> Spreads his light wings, and in a moment flies (75–6)

(a sentiment which, as Pope himself pointed out, is also to be found in Chaucer's *Franklin's Tale*),[89] and Blake's lines beginning:

---

[85] *The Poems of Alexander Pope*, ed. John Butt (London, 1963), pp. 252–61.
[86] *Public Address*, E565/K596.
[87] John Knowles, *Life of Fuseli* (1831), vol. 1, p. 359.
[88] See *William Blake's 'Heads of the Poets'* (Manchester City Art Gallery, Manchester, 1969), pp. 25 and 37. The other illustration is to the 'Elegy to the Memory of an Unfortunate Lady'.
[89] 'Franklin's Tale', lines 36ff (Pope's note).

He who binds to himself a joy
Doth the winged life destroy
But he who kisses the joy as it flies
Lives in Eternitys sun rise   (E465/K184)

The most striking resemblances, however, are to be found in the landscape of desolation which Pope creates around Eloisa, which corresponds, in particular features, to certain landscapes in Blake. Eloisa's reference to

The darksom pines that o'er yon' rocks reclin'd
Wave high, and murmur to the hollow wind[90]

may be echoed both in Blake's spectre's laugh as he pours molten iron on the limbs, first of Enitharmon then of Urizen – a laugh described as 'Hollow upon the hollow wind' – and in the final state of the lover in 'The Crystal Cabinet' after he ruins his state of threefold love by trying to seize its essential fire, and becomes

A weeping Babe upon the wild
And Weeping Woman pale reclind
And in the outward air again
I filld with woes the passing Wind   (E480/K430)

In Pope's poem the happy state 'When love is liberty, and nature, law' is contrasted with its opposite in the phrase

No craving Void left aking in the breast   (94)

This unusual use of 'craving' as an adjective to 'void' might well have prompted both a striking image in 'The French Revolution':

to plant beauty in the desart craving abyss   (E285/K136)

and that of the 'craving Hungry Cavern' which is created in Urizen's ribs in Blake's creation myth.[91] The same word reappears in a stanza of 'My Spectre around me . . .', preceded by another possible echo from Pope's poem. Eloisa says:

we wandring go
Thro' dreary wastes, and weep each other's woe   (241-2)

---

[90] 155–6; cf. *The Four Zoas* iv.197. Blake's use of 'darksom' several times in *The Four Zoas* may owe something to Pope's use of the word, though his prime source is, no doubt, Milton (*Paradise Lost* II.973; IV.232; V.225; XII.185 and – most interesting for our larger discussion – the reference to Christ as having chosen 'with us a darksom home of mortal clay' (Nativity Ode, line 14)).
[91] *The Book of Urizen* 13.6 (*The Four Zoas* iv.240).

Blake writes

> A Fathomless & boundless deep
> There we wander there we weep
> On the hungry craving wind
> My Spectre follows thee behind   (E467/K415)

Finally, a more complicated parallel may be noted. At an important moment in *The Four Zoas* Urizen rounds on his emanation, Ahania, declaring

> once thou wast in my breast
> A sluggish current of dim waters. on whose verdant margin
> A cavern shaggd with horrid shades. dark cool & deadly. where
> I laid my head in the hot noon   (iii.120–3, E322/K295)

As Blake's recent editor points out,[92] the third line follows almost exactly a line in Milton's *Comus* concerning the Lady:

> By grots, and caverns shagged with horrid shades,
> She may pass on with unblenched majesty

Since the reference is to the power of the Lady's chastity, however, the relevance of the Miltonic source to Blake's poem, where it is the delusions of purity that have brought about the present state of the Zoas, is not immediately clear. When we turn to 'Eloisa to Abelard', on the other hand, we discover that Pope, also, adapted Milton's line to describe the places where a religiously enforced chastity finds itself confined:

> Ye rugged rocks! which holy knees have worn;
> Ye grots and caverns shagg'd with horrid thorn!
> Shrines! where their vigils pale-ey'd virgins keep   (19–21)

Bearing in mind the 'pale virgins shrouded in snow' of 'Ah Sunflower!' we can see that Pope's portrayal of chastity is more relevant to Blake's concerns than that in Milton's *Comus*. Although the verbal detail of Blake's line in *The Four Zoas* corresponds more closely to Milton's, therefore, it seems unlikely that it would have returned to him at this moment had he not also been aware of Pope's bitter adaptation of the same line, which would have suggested for him the imprisoning power of an enforced chastity, by comparison with the liberating power of the Lady's freely elected virtue in *Comus*.

[92] *The Poems of William Blake*, ed. W. H. Stevenson (London, 1971), p. 335n.

This critique may be extending itself in further echoes. When Eloisa has to witness the terrible effects of Abelard's punishment,

> what sudden horrors rise!
> A naked Lover bound and bleeding lies!   (99–100)

she and her lover, together victims under the law, seem close to the pair who appear at one point in 'The Mental Traveller':

> Till he becomes a bleeding youth
> And she becomes a Virgin bright   (E475/K425)

Echoes and evidence are equally compelling and elusive elsewhere. When Eloisa says, of Abelard's monastery, raised in the wilderness,

> the desert smil'd,
> And Paradise was open'd in the Wild   (133–4)

both 'smil'd' and 'open'd' have a Blakean ring; but the nearest to a direct echo is a muted one, occurring in the couplet in 'The Little Girl Lost' that describes how the earth shall seek her maker

> And the desart wild
> Become a garden mild.   (E20/K112)

In Blake's companion poem ('The Little Girl Found'), on the other hand, where Lyca's parents search for her 'While the desarts weep', it would seem likely that the unusual image is to be traced directly to Pope's contrary image, 'the desert smil'd'.

Reading 'My Spectre around me . . .' as a whole, we may take into account the possibility that one of its controlling ideas was also directly prompted by a contemporary text. As we find Blake using the terms 'spectre' and 'emanation' to suggest the two forces between which the visionary individual must necessarily work, we may legitimately ask whether he had not read, in the *Morning Post* for 4 December 1801, Coleridge's 'Ode to Tranquillity', with its lines,

> Idle Hope
> And dire Remembrance interlope,
> To vex the feverish slumbers of the mind:
> The bubble floats before, the spectre stalks behind.[93]

[93] S. T. Coleridge, *Poetical Works*, ed. E. H. Coleridge (Oxford, 1912), vol. I, p. 361.

Blake addresses his own emanation as

> Poor pale pitiable form
> That I follow in a Storm   (E468/K417)

and says of the spectre:

> On the hungry craving wind
> My Spectre follows thee behind   (E467/K415)

If so, it may be the case that Coleridge's striking psychological symbolism prompted in Blake's mind a revival of Pope's emotive lines. I also suspect, however, that (rather as was suggested in the use of the Ugolino painting), Pope's language may have sprung up so readily because his poem had formerly been one to which Blake turned for an expression of his own unhappy love-yearnings in youth.

Now let me turn to a much more difficult case, which I mention because it meets the criterion mentioned earlier for 'extensive' influence – that there should be at least *two* possible links. Here, in fact, we are dealing less with unusual words than with unusual ideas. Some of the more striking features of *The Marriage of Heaven and Hell* occur in the account of Milton's Satan, the new emphasis on Genius (Plates 6–7) and the account of the ancient poets who 'animated all sensible objects with Gods or Geniuses'; none, apart from the general interest in Genius, has any obvious precedent in his previous work. Now, as it happens, all three occur together in a work published in the 1790s: John Ogilvie's *The Theology of Plato, compared with the Principles of Oriental and Grecian Philosophers.* This book, which finds a natural place in a sequence of books on Platonism which appeared in the late eighteenth century, was not altogether typical of its author. Ogilvie's claim to fame lies in quite another quarter: he was the gentleman who defended Scotland to Dr Johnson on the ground that it had many noble prospects, only to receive a devastating reply. In his own day he was well known as a minor poet; but it was primarily in his capacity as divine that he wrote his last book, seeking to vindicate the cause of theism by exploring the pagan philosophers. In the process, however, the poet in him evidently became more than half enamoured of the Greek religion he was describing. He was led to write a long chapter on the 'Daemons or Genii' who 'figure in the theology of the ancients', the final section of which includes the following passage:

we may consider as a fourth class of terrestrial Genii, inferior in rank to the former; the Dryads, Hamadryades, Satyrs, Wood-nymphs, and in general, the whole race of beings who have the charge of rivers, forests, fields and fountains; the subjects of many beautiful poetical fables.

Upon the whole therefore we may venture to pronounce, that a review of the scenes which the philosophers of ancient Greece have presented as the theme of the preceding remarks, afford a lively representation of the character of its inhabitants. The busy ingenuity of this happy race imparted life to all objects indiscriminately; nature teemed around them with universal animation; the fields, the groves, the fountains, the forests, the very air of this delightful region, were prolific, and the face of the country displaying alternately, villas and statues, lawns and altars; the harvests of Ceres, the shades of Diana, the haunts of the Naiads, and the gardens of Pomona, presented testimonies in every quarter of genius, elegance, and superstitious observance.[94]

This passage may be compared with Blake's development of the same theme in the *Marriage*:

The ancient Poets animated all sensible objects with Gods or Geniuses, calling them by the names and adorning them with the properties of woods, rivers, mountains, lakes, cities, nations, and whatever their enlarged & numerous senses could percieve.

And particularly they studied the genius of each city & country. placing it under its mental deity.

Till a system was formed, which some took advantage of & enslav'd the vulgar by attempting to realize or abstract the mental deities from their objects; thus began Priesthood.

Choosing forms of worship from poetic tales.

And at length they pronouncd that the Gods had orderd such things.

Thus men forgot that All deities reside in the human breast.   (E37/K153)

The fact that Ogilvie's passage comes at the end of a long discussion of genius makes it possible to suppose that it might have provided the immediate stimulus for Blake's plate – perhaps awakening at the same time memories of other reading about the status of tutelary deities.

Later in his book Ogilvie comments on the attempts to represent evil geniuses such as Zoroaster:

I consider as one of the best proofs, that there is a principle of benevolence and rectitude in man, and that the good tendencies of his nature surpass their con-

[94] John Ogilvie, *The Theology of Plato* . . . (1793), pp. 90–1.

246

traries; that although his mind readily admits the idea of perfect excellence, it is invincibly repugnant to its opposite. Some latent spark of commiseration, some native propensity that is allied to virtue, are ingredients of every character whereof he exhibits a representation, or even forms a conception.[95]

This passage (with its use of the Blakean word 'contraries') is followed by a footnote in which he considers the example of Satan:

Some readers will find a striking evidence of the truth of this remark in the SATAN of Milton, as it is displayed in various points of view to our observance in his divine poem. Our great poet was sensible, that in order to interest his readers in the fate and actions of this personage it was necessary that the native malignity and pravity of the *Author of Evil* should be chequered with qualities that excite admiration. Hence, even in attempting to accomplish the ruin of mankind, unshaken fortitude, invincible courage, adherence to his ultimate purpose in circumstances the most hopeless and desperate, and even pity for the innocence which he is about to violate, are thrown with exquisite discernment into his character. In this various and interesting assemblage we find that attention is kept constantly awake, and that passions are involuntarily and powerfully excited, which, in the contemplation of a being *purely evil*, would have yielded to apathy or been absorbed in detestation.

Although the heroic nature of Satan had been commented upon by others, the psychological bent of Ogilvie's discussion is unusual: occurring as it does in a book which also stresses the theme of genius, we might well ask if it did not assist the train of thought that led Blake to identify Satan as a principle of energy rather than of evil, concluding with his famous comment: 'Note. The reason Milton wrote in fetters when he wrote of Angels & God, and at liberty when of Devils & Hell, is because he was a true Poet and of the Devils party without knowing it' (E35/K150).

Unfortunately, however, the chronological evidence discourages such conclusions. The *Marriage* is normally dated 1790–3; since Ogilvie's book did not appear until the last of those years, Blake could hardly have seen it, even in proof, before etching the plates in question. There are other possibilities, of course: he might have known Ogilvie, or read his work in manuscript; or Ogilvie might have seen the *Marriage* in manuscript; or we might yet discover some common source which was equally available to both men. In default of further evidence, however, it is safest to treat the

[95] *Ibid.*, p. 114.

parallels merely as coincidental, and as indications of a contemporary 'climate of thought'.

Another pair of possible parallels, raising equally tantalizing questions, is to be found in Sulivan's *View of Nature*, published in 1794. On page 347 of the last volume, Sulivan writes, of human wisdom, 'Can she change, let me ask her, that which is; or can she even dive into the essence of an emmet?' Five pages later, we find him commenting: 'it requires no mighty effort of genius to make out lame facts by conjecture . . . .'.

Despite the resemblance between the first passage quoted and the sentiments expressed in 'Thel's Motto':

> Does the Eagle know what is in the pit?
> Or wilt thou go ask the Mole:
> Can Wisdom be put in a silver rod?
> Or Love in a golden bowl? (E3/K127)

there can be no question of a direct influence, for *The Book of Thel* was already published by 1791. But the possibility remains that Blake at some point read the passage, recognized the likeness to 'Thel's Motto' and was prompted to write two further lines on the theme which appear in the later 'Auguries of Innocence' and which are surprisingly close to Sulivan's exact language:

> The Emmets Inch and Eagles Mile
> Make Lame Philosophy to smile (E483/K433)

At this point, we recognize, we are in the realm of attractive conjecture. In another instance, on the other hand, the resemblance between proposed source and Blake's writing seems far too close to be accidental. In his *Grounds of Criticism* (1704) John Dennis wrote,

And here I desire the Reader to observe, that Idea's in Meditation, are often very different from what Idea's of the same Objects are, in the course of common Conversation. As for Example, the Sun mention'd in ordinary Conversation, gives the Idea of a round flat shining Body, of about Two Foot Diameter. But the Sun occurring to us in Meditation, gives the Idea of a vast and glorious Body, and the top of all the visible Creation, and the brightest material Image of the Divinity.[96]

Here is it almost impossible to resist the sense that some memory of this

[96] John Dennis, *Grounds of Criticism* (1704), p. 17.

passage was working in Blake's mind when he wrote one of his best-known passages, the conclusion to 'A Vision of the Last Judgment':

What it will be Questiond When the Sun rises do you not see a round Disk of fire somewhat like a Guinea O no no I see an Innumerable company of the Heavenly host crying Holy Holy Holy is the Lord God Almighty I question not my Corporeal or Vegetative Eye any more than I would Question a Window concerning a Sight I look thro it & not with it.   (E555/K617)

If we suppose so, however, it is not, evidently, a question of influence through the language – or even through the intimate details – of Dennis's passage. Where Dennis speaks of a 'flat body of two feet in diameter' Blake speaks of a disk of fire 'somewhat like a Guinea' (thus aiming a shrewd blow at the money-worship of his age).[97] And there is a difference between the contemplative and detached mode of Dennis's 'Meditation', with its further suggestion of a 'bright image' for the Deity, and Blake's more energetic and immediate vision of the 'Innumerable company of the Heavenly host' in the body of the sun itself, directly perceived at sunrise. It is rather the *gestalt* of the passage from Dennis, the straightforward juxtaposition between flat dish and image of glory that seems to have survived into Blake's affirmation.

A THEME FROM ALCHEMY?

For our final examples we may turn to a source of possible influence which is more general still. This time, neither verbal nor visual resemblances are primarily in question, but a general set of ideas which might be thought to have influenced Blake's mind in a particular way, or if not that, to have offered it fuel for speculation.

The records of the alchemical tradition contain a vast and sprawling range of speculations, ranging across several centuries. Most people nowadays connect them with mistaken theories concerning matter which remained current until the establishment of a firm empirical tradition led to true knowledge of the physical world. Alchemists themselves are thought of either as fraudulent impostors like Ben Jonson's Subtle, or

---

[97] Cf. letter to Trusler, 23 August 1799 (on the world as a 'World of Imagination and Vision'): ' To the Eyes of a Miser a Guinea is more beautiful than the Sun' (E677/K793). Perhaps the associations of the guinea with the gold of Guinea, and so with African exploitation, should not be overlooked, either.

harmless cranks who hoped to discover magical keys to physical existence – the philosopher's stone that would turn all to gold, or the elixir that would give the secret of everlasting life.

The element which receives scant recognition is the appeal of alchemy to the imagination. It was not simply the appeal exercised by powerful romance. For what the alchemists were aiming to establish was the existence of a crucial physical correspondence between the nature of external matter and the nature of man. And whether or not the philosopher's stone or the elixir of life existed in external nature, they certainly corresponded to sensed potencies in human nature. The human imagination at least could turn all to gold, the life which sprang in every individual was at some deep level experienced as self-nourishing and self-regenerating.

Such considerations (which find some parallels in Jung's work)[98] lead one to wonder whether Blake did not at one time read certain alchemical texts in the hope of discovering clues, if not about the physical world at large, at least concerning man's enigmatic nature. How did it come about that the naturally imaginative and generous impulses of men and women became so demeaned and corrupted during their lifetime? Was there no hope of ever fulfilling the higher potentialities of human nature? These were questions that haunted Blake all his life.

They had a particular urgency for him in the 1780s, moreover, shortly before the appearance of his first prophetic books. From this point of view, therefore, the early manuscript poem 'Tiriel' plays a crucial part in the development. For although poetically an uneven and rather forbidding work, it is the work above all where Blake's human concerns reflect themselves in allegorical statements which lie very near the surface of his poetry.

The structure of the poem has been discussed by several critics. In my own account of the poem,[99] I argued that it was primarily intended as a new version of the loss of paradise in which it was the serpent (equated with the serpent of energy) that was expelled, leaving the beautiful Adam and Eve to grow old as the effete Har and Heva who live on in childhood innocence. Meanwhile the expelled energy, manifested in the despotic

---

[98] See, e.g., C. G. Jung *The Integration of the Personality* (London, 1940), chapter 5, and his *Psychology and Alchemy*. Jung's approach differs widely, of course, from Blake's.

[99] See my *Blake's Visionary Universe*, pp. 60–7, 336–42.

Tiriel, had gradually degenerated into tyranny, until, hated and despised by all his sons and daughters, he finally recognized the workings of his own hypocrisy and stretched himself out in death.

Other scholars have traced further elements. The story of Lear certainly seems to be relevant, as is also the story of Oedipus.[100] There must be a strong allusion to the actual tyrannies of Blake's time and the growing demand for political freedom.[101] The name 'Ijim' is derived from Swedenborg's allegorical commentaries on the Bible; that of Hela from northern mythologies, where she is described as the goddess of Death.[102] Such importation of proper names from other sources, unparalleled elsewhere in Blake, suggests that he had been reading voraciously in a variety of texts relating to the basic questions he was asking at the time.

This leads one on to ask whether that reading might not have included an engagement with alchemical texts. The thought is prompted by the fact that Tiriel's own name has alchemical connotations, 'Tiriel' being the name for the intelligence of mercury. This can hardly be accidental – though it may also be pointed out that Blake could have found the identification in nothing more recondite than the pages of the *Conjuror's Magazine*.[103]

It should also be noted that Blake on one occasion alludes to one of the greatest of alchemical writers, Paracelsus. His scathing comments on Swedenborg in *The Marriage of Heaven and Hell* include the observation that 'Any man of mechanical talents may from the writings of Paracelsus or Jacob Behmen, produce ten thousand volumes of equal value with Swedenborg's' (E42/K158).

Blake's interest in Paracelsus probably owes most to that philosopher's insistence on the importance of imagination, which in turn would assist a reading of alchemy for its inward, psychological insights. It is also worth pointing out, however, that Paracelsus's works are packed with references to mercury. The three great principles of the material universe, mercury, sulphur and salt, were, moreover, aligned by him with spirit, soul and body respectively.[104] Might not Blake also have explored the three

---

[100] Raine, *Tradition*, vol. I, pp. 40, 45–9.
[101] Erdman, *Prophet against Empire*, pp. 121–5.
[102] Raine, *Tradition*, vol. I, pp. 21–4; N. Frye, *Fearful Symmetry* (Princeton, 1947), p. 242.
[103] See the October 1791 number, and my *Blake's Visionary Universe*, p. 367.
[104] One might compare the definition of imagination in the *Chymicall Dictionary* appended to the

identifications, in the hope that they might throw light on the strange disintegration and corruption of human nature? In *A New Light of Alchemie*, which was published together with Paracelsus's *Of the Nature of Things*, Sendivogius included a dialogue between Mercury, the Alchemist and Nature, the upshot of which was that the physical alchemist was right in thinking mercury to be the key to things, but that by looking at it *in its physical form* he was looking at the wrong sort of mercury.[105] The possibility suggests itself that Blake, following such mysterious hints, asked himself whether a psychological point were not buried here – human nature, once it disintegrated into its component elements, showing its separate qualities as 'mercurial', 'sulphureous' and 'saline' by turns.

If this is so, it may throw light upon two of Tiriel's encounters during his dreary wandering through the wilderness surrounding the garden of Har and Heva. Ijim, who reviles him, has a noticeably fiery nature, while Zazel, the spirit of earth whom he encounters last, suggests an earth which is barren and alien – rather like salt itself. If the natures of Ijim and Zazel are not exhausted by such parallels, they are at least set in a suggestive frame of reference. In meeting them, Tiriel is perhaps encountering embodied elements of his own degradation, which will be completed when he ceases his endless raging at the end of the poem and lies 'outstretchd . . . in awful death'.

Such a use of basic alchemical elements as materials for psychological exploration might also throw light on the two other chief actors in the drama, Har and Heva. For these two fading beings have a vestigial royalty about them which is evident in Blake's visual portrayals of them, where they appear like a fading king and queen. In alchemy, equally, a king and queen figure importantly – namely, the Sol and Luna who must be

translation of Paracelsus's *Of the Nature of Things* (1650, p. Ddd2), '*Imaginatio* is a star in man, a celestiall and supercelestiall body', with Blake's Proverb of Hell: 'He whose face gives no light, shall never become a star'. Blake is not saying the same thing, of course, but he may have picked up a hint from the Paracelsians on the way. Paracelsus's further classification into salt, sulphur and mercury is implicit in another work to be found in the same volume, Sendivogius's *A New Light of Alchemie* (1650), esp. pp. 111–25. It may also conveniently be found in Crollius's *Philosophy Reformed and Improved* (1657), p. 33. There are other things in Crollius which mark his book as a possible source for Blake, such as his interest in the four elements in man (p. 26) (cf. *The Gates of Paradise*), his characterization of 'Imagination' as working in man 'like the Sun' (p. 71), and his use of the term 'twofold' both for earth and for heaven (p. 38). There is no clinching resemblance at any one point, however.

105 Sendivogius, *A New Light of Alchymie* (1650), pp. 59–74.

brought to marriage before the labours of the philosophers can be consummated. In some texts, this king and queen are represented as washing in the 'Bath of the Philosophers', which is described by Artephius as

the most pleasant, faire and cleere Fountaine, prepared onely for the *King* & *Queene*, whom it knoweth very well, and they know it; for it drawes them to it selfe, and they abide therein to wash themselves two or three dayes, that is, two or three *moneths*; and it maketh them young again, and faire . . . Let therefore the *spirit* of our living water, be with great and subtilty fixed with the *Sunne* and the *Moone* because they being turned into the nature of water, doe dye, and seeme like unto the dead; yet afterward being inspired from thence, they live, encrease and multiply like all other vegetable things . . .[106]

In Libavius's commentaries there is a representation of this fountain which shows the king and queen at its head, washed by the waters, while behind them is a scene described as 'a garden with a tree in it, bearing the apples of the Hesperides . . . In the middle a tree bears golden fruits, while golden stars surround crowns, to signify multiplication and increase, or else the fruit of projection.' In front of the king is a sun, in front of the queen a moon; down the steps are ranged a series of lions who represent a series of metals deriving from the leonine mercury, emblematized in the double-bodied lion at the foot from whose single head is spewed the 'mercury of the philosophers'. The whole design, in alchemical terms, represents the purification of gold and silver (the king and queen) for the purposes of the 'Great Work'.[107]

If we read 'Tiriel' against this frame of reference, we see that Har and Heva may represent a similar vegetative ideal in a state which has lost its dynamism. Their garden is no longer a paradise where energies sport freely but a more sleepy domain of fantasy, presided over not by the muse of inspiration but by Mnetha, priestess of memory. Their state is aptly depicted in Blake's two illustrations of them, the one showing them asleep in a beautiful bed ornamented with flowers, the other as awake, but steeping themselves in a stream which seems more like a river of oblivion

---

106 *Artephius his Secret Booke, Of the blessed Stone, called the Philosophers* (1624), p. 211. This quotation is taken from John Read's invaluable *Prelude to Chemistry* (London, 1936), p. 220, to which I am indebted for several examples.

107 Libavius, quoted by Read, *Chemistry*, p. 221. Read also reproduces (p. 220) the design in question, from Libavius, *Commentariorum Alchymiae* part II, bk iv, p. 56; in his *Alchymia* . . . (Frankfurt, 1606).

than a fountain of the philosophers.[108] Their 'Mercury', the expelled Tiriel, is not the winged messenger of the gods who might energize them back into realization of their lost paradise; he is more like the dull silvery fluid which nevertheless retains its capability of endless transformation into new forms.

So Har and Heva remain fixed in dreamlike state, while Tiriel is at once feared and elusive. Ijim, who is always trying to reduce him to stable form, finds him a veritable Proteus in his mercurial capability of metamorphosis:

> This is the hypocrite that sometimes roars a dreadful lion
> Then I have rent his limbs & left him rotting in the forest
> For birds to eat but I have scarce departed from the place
> But like a tyger he would come & so I rent him too
> Then like a river he would seek to drown me in his waves
> But soon I buffetted the torrent anon like to a cloud
> Fraught with the swords of lightning. but I bravd the vengeance too
> Then he would creep like a bright serpent till around my neck
> While I was Sleeping he would twine I squeezd his poisnous soul
> Then like a toad or like a newt. would whisper in my ears
> Or like a rock stood in my way. or like a poisnous shrub
> At last I caught him in the form of Tiriel blind & old
> And so Ill keep him
> (E278/K105)

To the various sources (from Homer, Ovid, Agrippa and Milton) which have convincingly been proposed for this passage, we may add the reflection, in another alchemical writing, that 'the *Mercury* of the Philosophers is shaddowed under the fierce and terrible names of Lyon, Dragon, Poyson &c. But this is not all, although it be Something.'[109]

The evidence for a larger alchemical strain in 'Tiriel' cannot be regarded as firmly conclusive; in particular, the absence of any *explicit* reference to sulphur or salt in the poem is an important lack. On the other hand, it is striking that all these various parallels should be found concentrated in a single poem of Blake's. There is nothing on this scale elsewhere in his work – though a few scattered references suggest that a pattern of interpretation based on these elements might still have been working in his mind for some years after. When the fiery dragon of revolutionary energy

---

[108] Blake, *Tiriel*, ed. with commentary by G. E. Bentley, Jr (Oxford, 1967), plates ii and viii.

[109] Elias Ashmole, *Theatrum Chemicum Britannicum* (1652), Prolegomena, p. iv. The other sources are listed and discussed by Kathleen Raine, *Tradition*, vol. I, pp. 62–5.

drives the white-haired priestly figure from the sky on an early plate of *America*, for instance, one notes his resemblance to the dragon-like figure who appears in an emblem of the Great Work in one alchemical text (figs. 18 and 19). And the sulphur and salt which are not mentioned explicitly in 'Tiriel' do make their appearance elsewhere. One of Blake's emblems for the fallen world of Urizen is that of an englobed earth surrounded by a salt ocean, on which a sulphur sun beats down. When the decline of Urizen is described, in the book named after him, he rages in 'whirlwinds of sulphurous smoke' and is first seen by Los as a 'surging sulphureous / Perturbed Immortal mad raging'. Gradually he obscures his prolific delight, 'hiding in surging / Sulphureous fluid his phantasies', until, under Los's efforts, the 'sulphureous foam' settles as 'a lake, bright, & shining clear'. By the end of the book, thirty cities remain, 'surrounded by salt floods', and it is finally recorded that 'the salt ocean rolled englob'd'.[110] In another work of the time Blake refers to a cosmic disaster in which Urizen called the stars around his feet:

18. *America*, Plate 6, copy P. Relief etching

[110] *The Book of Urizen* 4.47; 8.3; 10.14; 10.21; 28.9; 28.23.

19. Emblem from Michael Maier, *Tripus Aureus* (1618), p. 67

Then burst the center from its orb, and found a place beneath;
And Earth conglob'd, in narrow room, roll'd round its sulphur Sun.

(E57/K204)

Mercury, sulphur and salt might be said to correspond, respectively, to the fallen versions of Blake's threefold vision, twofold vision and single vision: the fallen light of threefold becomes the mercury of Tiriel (and so later of Urizen), the fallen energy of twofold becomes the destructive fire of sulphur, the fallen clay of single vision becomes the sterile salt of a dead sea. The two last elements also link on naturally to the usurping principle of Egyptian mythology, the Typhon who is pictured sometimes as the destructive sun that burns up the waters of the fertile Nile, sometimes as the devouring salt sea that finally swallows up its waters.[111]

And strangely enough, one discovers that in at least one of the alchemical writings the last-mentioned connection was explicitly made. In Michael Maier's *Atalanta Fugiens*, published in 1618, the 'Motto' to emblem 44 describes the killing of Osiris by Typhon; and the verse beneath has been translated as follows:

[111] See Plutarch's *De Iside et Osiride*, published with an English translation by S. Squire in 1744, and my *Coleridge the Visionary*, pp. 115–16.

Syria has Adonis, Greece has Dionysus,
Egypt has Osiris, who is nobody else but the Sun of Wisdom:
Isis is the sister, wife and mother of Osiris,
Whose limbs are dissected by Typhon, but which she joins together.
But the phallus was lost, spread over the waves,
For the Sulphur, which produced Sulphur, is missing.[112]

I have argued elsewhere that Blake, like others of his age, was attracted by the idea of a key to all mythologies, a lost concept of universal freedom, the fall from which he believed to be found recorded in many traditions such as those of the mythologists and visionaries, and which pivoted upon the sense of a fall from a productive dialectic between fourfold vision and threefold desire to a sterile contention between twofold energy and single-minded reason; from the Spirit walking in the Garden to the parched desert and rocky, watery shore; from the marriage between Osiris sun and Isis moon to the Typhonic world where a destructive sun beats down upon a salt sea. From the use he seems to have made of Paracelsus's themes, it may be argued that Blake found in that alchemist's emphasis on the three elements mentioned above another paradigm that fitted this pattern.

If so, it should also be emphasized that Blake never allowed himself to be fully enslaved to such influences, nor did he allow the pattern of interpretation which they suggested to settle into fixity. The existence of so many symbolic elements relatively near the surface of his narratives is not altogether beneficial to their final impact, indeed, and Blake was no doubt aware of this: the poem in which they came nearest to taking over the whole, 'Tiriel', is also one of the works which he left in manuscript. In successive works, Blake may be seen moving on from one possible organizing principle to another, while fragments from earlier processes occasionally rise up to prompt some timely but enigmatic image. So when, in *Europe*, the Angels of Albion fall and are buried beneath the ruins of their hall they are not totally destroyed, but 'as the stars rise from the salt lake they arise in pain'.[113] In the dark world of Ulro, similarly, 'Luvahs bulls each morning drag the sulphur Sun out of the Deep',[114] while, in *Jerusalem*,

---

[112] H. M. E. De Jong, *Michael Maier's 'Atalanta Fugiens': Sources of an Alchemist Book of Emblems* (Leiden, 1969), p. 273. The last two lines may be relevant to the status of Tharmas in *The Four Zoas* (see esp. iii.160–iv.43).
[113] *Europe* 9.13.   [114] *Milton* 21.20.

The Stars flee remote: the heaven is iron, the earth is sulphur,
And all the mountains & hills shrink up like a withering gourd

(*J* 66.81–2)

By now it is the decline of human visionary power that is paramount; former alchemical themes – if indeed they are present – are no longer acting in the same way. Yet one ought not to overlook them altogether. When, for example, Blake writes of Lot's wife that her being changed into a pillar of salt 'alludes to the Mortal Body being renderd a Permanent Statue but not Changed or Transformed into Another Identity while it retains its own Individuality'[115] or when he writes of the imprisoning power of sexual affection as

melting cadences that lure the Sleepers of Beulah down
The River Storge (which is Arnon) into the Dead Sea

(*M* 34.29–30)

do we not pick up some faint echo of a former set of organizing myths which owed something to the alchemists in its attempts to interpret the decline of human personality in terms of protean mercury, fiery sulphur and sterile salt?

From the foregoing discussions it will be evident that the identification of Blake's sources presents problems that are usually complex. In one or two cases, of course, other sources may later be discovered which (as actually seems to be the case with the *Comus* echo in Pope) offer a fuller explanation of Blake's usages. In the long run, however, as was said earlier, our critical intuitions have to be guided partly by our own sense of the controlling sensibility at the centre of Blake's enterprise, the organizing power which, while partly accepting and partly criticizing the creative productions of others, effects the transformations of them that are found in his own work. Although this sensibility sometimes seems bewilderingly diffuse and changeable, there are certain features that remain consistent. I also believe that Blake has left clues to its nature in some of his scattered sayings about himself, including what seems to be a curiously close and accurate self-diagram at one point, namely, the 'signature' appended to a pencil drawing for the illustration: 'When the morning stars sang together'

---

[115] 'A Vision of the Last Judgment', E546/K607.

(fig. 20). At the foot of this Blake wrote 'Done by' followed by a straight horizontal line; a hand; a sign resembling a letter B; an eye; and a circle. In *Blake Studies* Keynes writes 'This indicates Blake's belief that this drawing, the climax of a supreme effort, was created by the Poetic Genius in his own person' and goes on to quote from 'The Tyger': 'What immortal hand or eye, / Dare frame thy fearful symmetry?' He also quotes

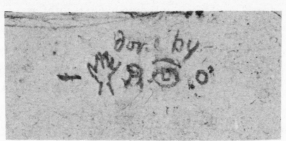

20. Blake's 'signature': detail from pencil sketch for *The Book of Job*, 'When the morning stars sang together'

Wicksteed's detailed interpretation, by which the straight line represents 'the simplest figure with no natural limit, i.e. immortality' and the circle represents 'symmetry', concluding: 'The inspired symmetry of this design and of the whole *Job* series could only have been carried through by the breath of God, that is, of the Poetic Genius, or Imagination.'[116]

The questionable point in this interpretation, as it seems to me, is Wicksteed's identification of immortality and symmetry as the two qualities represented by line and circle respectively. Symmetry, though obviously a feature of the circle, is not the quality most usually associated with it; nor is it immediately obvious that a straight line (even if it is 'the simplest figure with no natural limit') is a good emblem of immortality – for which, indeed, a circle would seem the more natural and traditional symbol. (We may compare the design of the serpent with the tail in its mouth, which Blake's friend Fuseli readily described as a 'Type of Eternity'.)[117] It should also be observed that the circle in the signature is not simple, but has two marks on either side which might suggest a sphere in motion.

[116] G. L. Keynes, *Blake Studies* (Oxford, 1971), pp. 188–9. The reading there 'simplest figure with natural limit' is, however (as Sir Geoffrey Keynes has agreed in private correspondence with me) due to a slip of transcription from the original version, which appeared in *Illustrations to the Book of Job by William Blake*, ed. L. Binyon and G. Keynes (N.Y., 1935), fascicle I, p. 19.

[117] Prospectus to *The Grave* (G. E. Bentley, *Blake Records* (Oxford, 1969), p. 170).

It is perhaps simpler – and certainly assists coherence – if one associates these figures more directly with the human parts that they flank. The line then belongs naturally with the hand, as indicating the graver or pencil which Blake uses and the line which his hand creates, while the circle belongs with the eye, as indicating the inward vision that he is always trying to express – a vision which may be symbolized by the shape of the sun – a circular form which yet contains infinite light and infinite energy. Read this way, the signature is less an assertion of triumph than an attempt to express in simplest terms the nature of Blake's enterprise – the central symbol standing for the central identity which tries to align his inward vision and eye with the expressive work of his hand. When the infinite vision which is seen 'through' his eye passes 'down the Nerves of my right arm'[118] to emerge into the bounding line of art, he knows that he is realizing himself as an artist. Although there is indeed a justified note of triumph in the affixing of such a signature to this particular design, then, it may be argued that the terms of the signature are better seen more simply as descriptive of the artistic process itself. We are back, in other words, with the coiling, spiralling, vertical, process which is rescued by the play of its own illuminated energy from any danger of returning into the dull barren round of the simple circle.[119]

I suggested earlier that the relationship between imagination and energy has come to be seen as crucial for our understanding of Blake. It helps to define that relationship further if we suppose that Blake himself found a ready focus for the duality in the activities, respectively, of eye and hand – indeed, the portraits suggest, to my eye at least, a figure in whom (naturally enough for an engraver) the central line of power runs along precisely that line. If I am right, anyone wishing to turn from Blake's transformation of his sources to the identity that was creating the transformation could do far worse than set up this signature of Blake's before him as a ready and simple touchstone.

And finally one might suggest that the very elusiveness of the central symbol, which looks like but is not quite a 'B', is congruent with our central theme. For between the illuminated eye of Blake's vision and the

[118] Milton 2.6.
[119] In an unpublished essay on Europe, Belinda Humfrey has drawn attention to the presence of a similar conception in the inner organization, both visual and verbal, of that book.

thrusting hand of his expressive art there is an area which hovers in ambiguity between a self-identification with general liberty and an assertion of rugged independence, sometimes expanding into impersonal and irradiating power, sometimes contracting into stubborn insistence upon its own individuality.[120] When Blake responds fully to the work of another writer or artist in his most characteristic way, therefore, first seizing on the 'illuminated' element in it and then creating his own highly individual version, we know that we are witnessing a manifestation of influence which, however necessary to the process, can never usurp the product, since that process is itself a reflection of Blake's originating artistic identity and its natural modes of expression. The inflow may be essential to the stream, but the stream itself will continue to flow free, for its ultimate springs are not to be found locked in the products of other men's minds.

[120] For further discussion of Blake's intellectual independence, studied in relation to Newton, Descartes and Burnet, see M. K. Nurmi, 'Negative Sources in Blake', *William Blake: Essays for S. Foster Damon*, ed. A. H. Rosenfeld (Providence, Rhode Island, 1969) pp. 303–18.

BLAKE INDEX

An asterisk indicates that the subject is illustrated on that page

'Abomination that maketh desolate, i.e. State Religion which is the Source of all Cruelty, The', 23
Adam, 169, 250
'Africa' (*Song of Los*), 216
Ahania, 243; *The Book of*, 127, 132 and n, 135n
Albion, 155–6, 167, 168, 169–72, 180–5, 186, 187, 189–93, 194, 195, 203; Angels of, 257; Daughters of, 182–4; Spectre of, 148, 153, 174, 175, 176, 178, 183, 192; (Spectre) Sons of, 184, 185
Albion rose, 76, 86*
'All Religions are One', 113, 139n
ambiguity, 15, 49, 60, 67, 76, 97, 118, 148, 150, 154, 163
America, 216, 217; Plate 6, 255*
Antichrist, 13, 14, 185, 191
antinomianism, 14n, 45–6, 51, 68, 84, 221
Apocalypse, 152, 155, 158, 160, 162, 163, 187, 188
apocalyptic images, 17–18, 59, 63, 68, 72, 104, 193
apple, image of, 77n
ark, *see* 'Moony Ark'
'Auguries of Innocence', 240, 248

Beast of Revelation, 11–14 and n, 20–1, 22, 60, 61, 218, 220, *see also* 'mark'
Beulah, 155, 171, 202; Daughters of, 172, 175, 189
Blake, Catherine, 71n, 161
Britannia, 170
Bromion, 214
Bunyan, John, *Pilgrim's Progress*, 83, 97 and n
butterflies, butterfly, image of, 72–3, 74, 76, 77n
Butts, Thomas, letter to, 117n, 145

caterpillar, image of, 72, 74
'charter'd', use of term, 6–10, 22, 57–9, 218
'Chimney Sweeper, The' (*Experience*), 16
'Chimney Sweeper, The' (*Innocence*), 34–48, 64
Christ (Jesus), 73, 77, 91, 103–4, 154, 160, 168, 169 and n, 172–3, 174, 180–94 *passim*
'Covering Cherub', 190–1
'Crystal Cabinet, The', 242
Cumberland, George, friend of Blake, 94n, 104; letter to, 112n

Dante, 147–8 and n, 157; *Divine Comedy*, 94, 206; *Inferno*, Blake's designs for Ugolino episode, 94–5, 203, 204–9, 211, 245

David, influence of, on Blake, 107
deathbed scenes, 105–8
Deism, 180, 182
Descriptive Catalogue, A, 127
divine Humanity, 146, 191
'Divine Image, The', 68
Divine Vision, 46, 154
Dove upon the stormy Sea, image of, 158–9, 235

'Earth's Answer' (*Experience*), 214
Eden, 77, 146, 156, 185, 193
elements, four, 72, 79–81
emanation, 3, 156, 157, 167, 244; of Satan, 148
Enitharmon, 153, 154, 161, 162, 173, 242
Eros, 81
Eternals, eternity, 109, 113–43, 144n, 146, 152, 172, 188, 194, 227
Europe, 163, 257 and n, 260n; frontispiece for, 96, 120, 121
Eve, 77, 98, 250
'Everlasting Gospel, The', 67–8, 238 and n, 239–40
Ezekiel, 12, 14, 164, 171, 186, 188–93

Father and sons, theme of, 203–11
female will, 156, 158
'Fire', 80
For children: The Gates of Paradise, *see* Gates of Paradise
Four Zoas, The, 13, 70, 143 and n, 154, 215n, 216n, 222n, 223n, 242nn, 243
'French Revolution, The', 242
Fuseli, Henry, Blake's defence of, 209; friendship with, 259

Gates of Paradise, The, 70–110, 229, 231, 252n; frontispiece, 74–6, 80
Plate *1*, 76–9; *2*, 230; *2–5*, 79–81; *3–5*, 230; *6*, 81–2; *7*, 72–3, 82; *8*, 82–6; *9*, 86–90; *10*, 90–1; *11*, 91–4; *12*, 94–6, 204*, 207, 209, 210; *13*, 105–8, 233*; *14*, 97–100, 233*; *15*, 100–4; *16*, 104–5
Genesis, Blake's ironical allusions to, 113, 114, 121, 134
'Genesis' fragment, 13n
genius, melancholy, 108
Golgonooza, 172, 177

Hand, 175, 177, 179, 194

Har, 250, 252–4
harvest and vintage, theme of, 158, 162
'Head of Pope', painting, 241
Heva, 250, 252–4
'Holy Thursday' (*Experience*), 16n, 52–6, 61, 62, 63, 67
'Holy Thursday' (*Innocence*), 47–8, 50 and n, 52–6 *passim*, 64, 234
'How to know Love from Deceit', 15
'Human Abstract, The', (*Experience*), 18, 22–3, 24, 64–7; illustrations to, 215n
human condition and hell, theme of, 20–2, 25–6, 27
'Human Image, The', 65
Hunt brothers, editors of *Examiner*, Blake's antipathy to, 176, 185

ideal type, 80
Ijim, 251, 252, 254
imagination, 29, 71, 72, 109, 113, 116, 143, 147, 152, 155, 163, 174, 180, 186, 191, 201–2, 260
'inlet', specific use of word, 223–5
'intellectual', specific use of word, 221–3
Isaiah, 191
Island in the Moon, An, 88, 112 and n, 234
Israel, Israelites, 174–9 *passim*, 188, 193

Jerusalem, 2, 3–4, 13, 14, 30, 46n, 77n, 121 and n, 127n, 146, 147, 149, 153, 154, 155, 216, 217, 222 and nn, 228–9, 257–8; frontispiece to, 181
  Plate *1*, 167; *3*, 167; *25*, 171; *27*, 194; *31*, 171; *32*, 178; *40*, 215n; *47*, 215n; *50*, 171; *51*, 181★, 182★; *52*, 180, 194; *55*, 173; *56*, 215n; *61*, 171, 172; *64*, 182; *69*, 184; *70*, 185; *77*, 185; *79*, 190; *84*, 14; *85*, 190; *86*, 190; *89*, 190; *91*, 173; *94*, 170; *99*, 203; final plate, 192
  Prefaces to, 164–95; 1st, 167–74, 194; 2nd, 174–80, 194; 3rd, 180–5, 194; 4th, 185–93, 194–5
Jesus, *see* Christ
Jews, 174, 175, 188
Job, Blake's illustrations for, 86, 259★

'Keys of the Gates, The', 77, 95, 97, 210
'King Edward the Third', 8, 15, 218

ladder, image of, 86–7, 89–90
Lamb of God, 171, 175
Lambeth: books, 163; period, 1, 2
Legends in a Small Book of Designs, 134 and n, 135
Letters: to Thomas Butts, 117n, 145; to G. Cumberland, 112n; to Dr Trusler, 166n, 249n
Leutha, 148, 156
life-cycle, 72, 108–10, 231
'Little Girl Found, The', 244
'Little Girl Lost, The', 244
Locke, John, Blake's attitude to, 93, 225, 226, 227
'London' (*Experience*), 2, 5–31, 56–64, 66, 67, 68, 143n, 218–21, 234
Los, 122, 128–36, 140, 147, 153, 154, 155–6, 161, 162, 163, 170–4, 175–89, 186, 187, 190, 191, 194, 228–9, 255; *Book of, The*, 131nn; Plate *4*, 237; 'Jealousy of, The', 214; *Song of, The*, 112 and n,

172, 190, 216, 217–18; Spectre of, 172
Luvah, 153, 183–4

'Mad Song', 86, 92
mandrake, image of, 77–9, 80, 91
'mark(s)', significance of word, 11–14, 20, 22, 57–8, 59–60, 62–3, 218–21
Marriage of Heaven and Hell, The, 26, 134n, 135n, 150, 164n, 203–4, 210, 223, 226, 245, 246, 251; prelude to, 217
'Mental Traveller, The', 77n, 187, 201, 244
Merlin, 179–80, 194
Milton, 2, 170, 188, 191, 235–6, 257n, 260; final plates of, considered, 3, 145–63
Milton, John, Blake's devotion to, 198, 200
'mind-forg'd manacles', 14–15, 61–2
'minute particulars', 228–9
moon, 86–90, 155, 159
'Moony Ark', 158–60, 235–6
Moses, First Book of, 114

Natural Religion, 157, 158, 180, 194; *see also* 'There is No . . .'
net, image of, 215
Newton, Sir Isaac, 75, 111, 185, 228
Notebook, 5, 6 and n, 15, 16, 17 and nn, 18, 19n, 64, 73n, 74n, 76, 87, 94 and n, 102 and n, 104n, 200, 204, 230n
'Nurse's Song' (*Innocence*), 68

ocean, image of, 90–1
Og, 176
old man, image of, 100–4
Ololon, 146, 151, 156–9, 161, 235
Oothoon, 161–2, 163, 214
Orc, Spectre of, 148, 157

Palamabron, 157
prophetic books, 1; illuminations to, 215; relation of language and content in, 145–63, 169, 173, 195
pseudo-symbolism, 27

Rahab, 156, 157, 158, 159, 180, 181, 182, 185, 194
rationalism, 157
Reuben, 175–80, 194
Reyolds, Sir Joshua, *Discourses*, Blake's annotations to, 111, 113 and n, 140n, 166 and n, 211n, 225nn
Rintrah, 157
Ripa, 83n, 93
Rousseau, Jean-Jacques, 111, 157, 227

St John, 173, 187, 190
'Samson', 92
Satan, 86, 98, 145, 146, 150–5, 157, 170, 174, 217, 239, 245, 247; Spectre of, 148, 152, 153
Saturn, 82, 83, 84, 93, 94 and n, 95–6, 108
Saviour, the, 169, 170, 173, 177, 178, 190, 191, 194
schematism, 79–80
Schofield, 182
self-annihilation, 151, 156, 158, 160, 163

self hood, 151, 153, 154

serpent, the, 84, 250

Shakespeare, William, Blake influenced by, 198, 218

shears, image of, 93–4

'Shepherd, The' (*Innocence*), 68

Six-fold Wonder, 158

Songs of Experience, 5, 16 and n, 17n, 20, 56, 68, 69, 214, 215 and n

Songs of Innocence, 32, 35, 46, 47, 50, 67, 68

Songs of Innocence and of Experience, 1, 24, 25, 32–69, 234

spectacles, image of, 91–3

Spectre, 148, 153, 154, 192, 244, 245; of Albion, 148, 153; of Milton, 148, 152, 153; of Orc, 148; of Satan, 148, 152, 153; of Urthona, 154; the Reasoning, 153

Starry Seven, 151, 152, 154

street-cries, 18, 19, 22

sunflower, image of, 78–9, 80

Swedenborg, Emmanuel, influence of, on Blake, 25–7; *Divine Love and Diveine Wisdom*, Blake's annotations of, 120 and n, 135n; *Heaven and Hell*, Blake's annotations of, 66 and n

Thel, The Book of, 248

'Thel's Motto', 248

'There is No Natural Religion', 113, 135nn, 138 and nn, 224, 225

'Tiriel', 250–4, 255, 236, 257

Tirzah, 104, 105

tradition, Blake's dependence on, 2, 81, 83, 196–202

traveller, image of, 72, 97–100, 103, 105, 187, 231, 233★, 238

Tree of the Knowledge of Good and Evil, 34, 67, 77

Trusler, Revd John, letter to, 249n

'Tyger, The', 69, 259

Ulro, 146, 149, 180, 257

Urizen, 96, 116, 145, 146, 147, 153, 156, 215n, 242, 243, 255, 256; Sons of, 184

Urizen, The Book of, 2, 215n, 242; and Locke's *Essay Concerning Human Understanding*, 111–44

Urthona, 154

Vala, 159, 175, 182, 184, 190

Vala, 241

Visions of the Daughters of Albion, 161, 162, 212, 215, 222n; frontispiece of, 213★

'Vision of the Last Judgment, A', 118, 142n–3n, 249, 258n

Void Outside of Existence, 158

Watson, Bishop, Blake's annotations to, 23, 56n, 168n

worm, image of, 71, 72, 75, 76, 77n, 104

Young, Edward, *Night Thoughts*, Blake's illustrations for, 77 and n, 78★, 86, 87, 237n

Zazel, 252

GENERAL INDEX

An asterisk indicates that the subject is illustrated on that page

Abel, Karl, 66n
'acedia', sin of, 83
Adamson, J. H., 119 and n
Agrippa, Cornelius, 254
Alchemy, 249–61
Alciati, 73
Apthorp, East, *Discourses on Prophecy*, 166 and n
Ariosto, *Orlando Furioso*, 87–8 and n
Artephius, 253 and n
Arwaker, 91 and n
Ashmole, Elias, 254n
Auden, W. H., 198 and n
Ayres, Philip, *Emblemata Amatoria*, 76 and n

Bacon, Sir Francis, 73n, 111, 185
Baker, J. A., 164n
Banks, Thomas, 106
Barclay, Robert, 49
Barlow, Joel, *Vision of Columbus*, 216
Bartolozzi, engraving after Cipriani, 211, 212*
Barton, Bernard, 34n
Bate, W. J., *The Burden of the Past and the English Poet*, 198
Bateson, F. W., 15 and n, 17 and n
Baxter, Andrew, *Enquiry into the Nature of the Human Soul*, 224 and n, 225, 239
Behmen, Jacob, *see* Böhme
Beattie, James, 'Triumph of Melancholy', 98
Beatty, B. G., 45n
Bede, 77
Beer, John, 4, 5 and n, 73n, 80 and n, 81 and n, 113n, 158 and n, 214n, 215n, 217n, 237n, 250n, 256n
Bell's Weekly Messenger, 208–9 and n
Bentley, G. E., 50n, 71n, 254n
Berkeley, George, *Principles of Human Knowledge*, 223 and n, 226–7 and nn
Bewick, T., 73n, 74, 101; engraving for *Emblems of Mortality*, 101*
Binyon, L., 259n
Bird, Edward, 71n
Blackstone, B., 97n
Blair, Robert, 71–2; *The Grave*, 97, 103, 104
Bloom, Harold, 12n, 17n, 111n, 116n, 151, 155, 158–9, 161, 185 and n, 193n, 235; *The Anxiety of Influence*, 198–9
Blunt, A., 82n, 203 and n

Bogen, Nancy, 15n
Böhme (Behmen), Jacob, 166 and n, 187, 188, 189, 200, 251
Bonasoni, Julio, 94n
Boswell, James, 207 and n
Boudard, J. B., 81n, 93
Bowles, William Lisle, 34, 35, 36, 40
Brewer, John, 42 and n, 43 and n
Burke, Edmund, *Letter to a Member of the National Assembly*, 61 and n; *Philosophical Enquiry into the Origin of our Ideas of the Sublime and Beautiful*, 165 and n, 225, 226 and n; *Reflections*, 8–9
Burton, Richard, 71n, 83, 88–9, 100; *Anatomy of Melancholy*, 89; 'Author's Abstract', 87
Bush, G., 27n
Butter, Peter, 3, 235–7

Caird, G. B., 187–8 and n
Carter, Elizabeth, 90 and n
Cassirer, Ernst, *An Essay on Man*, 191 and n
Chartered Companies, 7
Chastanier, Benedict, 27–8 and n, 29n, 30 and n
Chaucer, 3; *Canterbury Tales*, 188 and n; *Franklin's Tale*, 241 and n
chimney-sweeper, symbolism connected with, 42–3, 234
Chimney-Sweeper's Friend and Climbing Boy's Album, 34 and n, 36, 38
Cipriani, 211, 212, 214 (*see also* Bartolozzi)
Clark, J. M., 101n
Clarke, Samuel, 223n
Coleridge, Samuel, *Biographia*, 198; *Kubla Khan*, 198; 'Ode to Tranquillity', 244–5
Colie, Rosalie, 128n
Collins, William, 71 and n, 72; 'Ode on the Poetical Character', 198
Conjuror's Magazine, 251 and n
Cook, E. T., 206n
Cotton, Nathaniel, 93 and n; 'Death', 105 and n
Cowley, Abraham, 165 and n; *Davideis*, 165, 168
Cowper, William, 91
Crabbe, George, *The Village*, 52–3
Crollius, 252n
Cunningham, Allan, 71n
Curran, S., 165n

David, *Death of Socrates*, ~~107~~

Davies, R. T., 45n

De Gheyn, Jacob, 96 and n

De Sola Pinto, V., 237n

De Vos, Martin, 203

Dennis, John, *Grounds of Criticism*, 248–9, 248n

Digby, J. W., 74n, 90 and n

Dixon, John, 207n

Donne, John, 216 and n, 223n; 'Progress of the Soul', 77 and n

Doyne, V., 6n

Dryden, John, *Religio Laici,* 99; 'The Knight's Tale', 81–2

Dürer, Albrecht, 71n, 81n; *Melencolia I,* 83, 89–90, 95–6, 108

East India Company, 7 and n

Eaton, Daniel Isaac, 7n

education, 141

Eichrodt, W., 164 and n

Eliot, T. S., 121–2 and n, 196–9 and nn; 'Tradition and the Individual Talent', 196–9

emblem literature, tradition of, 70–110

Emblemes ou Devises Chrestiennes, 77 and n, 89

Erdman, David, 12n, 14n, 71n, 111n, 125n, 128n, 167n, 216 and n, 218n; *Prophet against Empire*, 15n, 16n, 17n, 52 and n, 58 and n, 61 and n, 67n, 86–7 and n, 176 and n, 216 and n, 251n; *The Notebook of William Blake*, 6–7 and nn, 73n, 74n, 94n, 102n, 104 and n, 230n

Estienne, H., 73n

Family Magazine, 47n

Ferguson, James, 4

Ficino, 96

Fink, Z. S., 99n

Fisch, Harold, 'Blake's Miltonic Moment', 187 and n

Foot, Jesse, 18n

Fowler, Alastair, 119 and n

Freud, William, 16n–17n

Freud, Sigmund, 66 and n

Fry, Elizabeth, 49

Frye, Northrop, 73n, 78 and n, 84–6 and n, 104 and n, 111n, 131n, 168–9 and n, 180

Füger, Heinrich, 106, 107

Fuseli, Henry, 208–9, 210, 211, 241, 259

George, M. Dorothy, 41 and n

Ghiberti, 104n

Gibbon, 3

Gillham, D. G., 16n

Gillray, 'The Slough of Despond', 86–7 and n, 89

Ginter, D. E., 7n

Glen, Heather, 1–2, 11n, 12n, 21n, 221, 234, 237

Goedeke, Karl, 111n

Goldsmith, Oliver, 'The Traveller', 97–8, 100

Goltzius, 96 and n

Gombrich, E. H., 73n

Gough, Richard, *Sepulchral Monuments of Great Britain*, 101

Grace, S. W. J., 88n

Grant, John E., 128n

Greene, E. J. H., 198n

Grierson, H. J. C., 216n

Hagstrum, Jean H., 82n

Hamilton, *Andromache Bewailing the Death of Hector*, 106

Hanway, Jonas, 35, 36n, 39, 46

Harding, D. W., 56n

Harvey, J. W., 166n

Hayley, William, 241

Heidegger, 192

Herbert, George, 'The Bunch of Grapes', 217 and n

Hermes Trismegistos, 26

Hervey, James, 71–2, 74n, 75 and n, 104 and n; 'Descant upon Creation', 103, 104n; *Theron and Aspasio*, 91 and n

Hesiod, *Theogony*, 86, 93, 95 and n

Hirsch, E. D., 16n

Holbein, *Dance of Death*, 101

Homer, 164, 254

Hopkins, Gerard Manley, 149 and n

Hugo, 91 and n

Hume, David, 32–3; *Treatise on Human Nature*, 225, 226 and n

Humfrey, Belinda, 260n

Hunt, Leigh, 176

Hunt brothers, editors of *Examiner*, 176, 185

Hurd, Richard, 165n

Hutchinson, Thomas, 116n

Hyle, 182

Imlay, Gilbert, 15n, 61

influence, concept of, 4, 196–261; from the alchemical tradition, 249–61; verbal: extensive, 237–49, intensive, 215–37; visual, 203–15

Jenyns, Soames, 65

Johnson, M. L., 74n, 91n, 94n

Johnson, Samuel, 6, 7n, 21, 32–3, 57, 61, 62, 76n, 79, 89, 245; *Preface to Shakespeare*, 33; *The Vanity of Human Wishes*, 92, 99, 231–2

Jonson, Ben, 249

Jung, C. G., 250 and n

Juvenal, 21

Kafka, Franz, 97

Kant, Immanuel, 198

Keats, John, 198

Kenney, E. J., 211n

Kent, Donald L., 18n

Keynes, G. L., 2, 71n, 73n–4n, 90 and n, 97n, 104, 111n; *Blake Studies*, 259 and n

Kiralis, Karl, 172 and n; 'A Guide to the Intellectual Symbolism of William Blake's Later Prophetic Writings', 175 and nn, 176 and n, 179–80nn; 'The Theme and Structure of William Blake's *Jersualem*', 193 and n

Kittel, Harald, 2–3, 225n

Klibansky, Raymond, 83 and n, 90n, 96n

Kmetz, Gail, 74n
Knight, Frida, 17n
Knowles, John, 208n, 241n

Laforgue, Jules, 198 and n
Lamb, Charles, 34
Langland, William, 3; *Piers Plowman*, 164
language, history of, 73
Lavater, John Caspar, 79, 238n
Leavis, F. R., 23n
Lewis, C. S., 165 and n, 166 and n
Libavius, 253 and n
Locke, 185; *Essay Concerning Human Understanding*, 2, 3, 93, 224 and n, 228 and n, 229; and Blake's *Book of Urizen*, 111–44
Logan, J. V., 73n
Longinus, 90, 92–3
Lowth, Robert, 165
Lutzelburger, Hanz, 101

Magna Carta, 8–10
Maier, Michael, *Atalanta Fugiens*, 256, 257 and n; *Tripus Aureus* 256
Malkin, Benjamin Heath, 50n
Margoliouth, H. M., 237n
Marston, John, 100
Maser, Edward A., 83n
Melancholy, emblems of, 70–110
Melanchthon, Philip, 90n
Mellor, Ann K., 'The Human Form Divine', 182 and n
Milton, John, 3, 26n, 71n–2n, 88, 94, 147, 198, 200, 254; *Areopagitica*, 79, 81n; *Comus*, 243, 258; *Il Penseroso*, 81, 90, 108; *Paradise Lost*, 81n, 86, 98, 118–19 and n, 122, 149, 150, 153, 168, 217 and nn, 235 and n, 242n; *Samson Agonistes*, 92
Mitchell, A., 7n
Mitchell W. J. T., 113–14 and n, 117 and n, 121n, 122–3 and n, 128n, 144n
Montgomery, James, 34n
Moore, D. K., 73n, 94n, 102n
Morning Post, 244
Morton, A. L., 45n
Moses, 84
Muggleton, L., 14n
Murry, J. Middleton, 173 and n, 198 and n

Nanavutty, 94n
Nature, 71
neoclassic stoic, 106
neoclassicism, 84, 92, 106–7
neoplatonism, 25n, 134, 222
'New Game of Human Life', 231, 232★
New Jerusalem Church, 26
New Jerusalem Journal, 29n
New-Jerusalem Magazine, 27, 28 and n, 29 and nn, 30–1 and nn
New Testament, Hebrews, 49, 75; Mark, 169; Revelation, 11–12, 13 and n, 14, 20–1, 59, 173, 218, 220
Newbery, E., 231n
Newton, Sir Isaac, 114

Nurmi, Martin, 50n, 112n

Odhner, C. T., 28n
Oedipus, 251
Ogilivie, John, *The Theology of Plato, compared with the Principles of Oriental and Grecian Philosophers*, 245–8 and nn
Old Testament, Daniel, 178; Deuteronomy, 176n; Exodus, 148, 173, 217; Ezekiel, 12, 60, 167n, 187; Genesis, 12, 13n, 90, 113, 114, 121, 134, 184; Isaiah, 182, 191; Job, 75–6, 182; Joshua, 176, 178; Lamentations, 60; Psalm 8, 75, 76
Ostriker, Alicia, 168 and n
Otto, Rudolf, 166n
Ovid, 254; *Metamorphoses*, 94n, 211n

Paine, Thomas, 6, 24; *Rights of Man*, 8, 9–10, 16, 58 and n
Painites, 24
Paley, Morton D., 13n, 23n, 80n, 86n, 92n, 187n, 201 and n, 223 and n
Panofsky, Erwin, 83 and n, 93 and n, 94n, 96, 108n
Paracelsus, 187, 200, 251–2 and nn, 257; *Of the Nature of Things*, 252 and n
Parisi, Frank, 2, 207, 230
Patch, Thomas, 104n
Peel, Sir Robert, 42
Petrarch, 96
Phillips, Michael, 13n, 23n, 80n, 86n, 92n, 109n, 182n; 'Blake's Early Poetry', 187 and n
Pierce, Frederick E., 116n
Plato, 107, 200; *Symposium*, 90
Platonism, 245
Platonists, 221
Plotinus, 221n, 222
Plutarch, 256n
Pope, Alexander, 3; 'Eloisa to Abelard', 241–2 and n, 243–4, 245, 258; *Essay on Man*, 80
Porter, Enid, 42n
Potts, J. F., 29n
Pound, Ezra, 199
Poussin, 'The Death of Germanicus', 106, 107
Price, Martin, 136 and n
Priestley, Joseph, *Disquisitions relating to Matter and Spirit*, 223 and nn, 224, 225

Quarles, Francis, *Emblems*, 71, 91 and n, 93, 94n, 99

Rainbach, H., 207n
Raine, Kathleen, 11, 25 and n, 26n, 27 and n, 28, 40 and n, 41, 104 and n, 111n; *Blake and Tradition*, 159, 221n, 223n, 224 and n, 226n, 234 and n, 251nn, 254n
Ramsey, Warren, 198n
Read, John, 253nn
Reynolds, Sir Joshua, painting of Ugolino, 207–8★, 209, 210, 225
Reynolds, S. W., 207n
Roach, *Beauties of the Poets*, 84
Roe, A. S., 204n, 208 and n

Rosa, Salvator, *Democritus Deep in Thought*, 83
Rose, E. J., 193 and n
Rosenblum, Robert, 106 and n
Rosenfeld, Alvin H., 112n, 187n
Roti, Grant C., 18n
Rudrum, Alan, 128n
Ruskin, John, 206–7

Sabri-Tabrizi, G. R., 29n
St John, 83, 173, 187, 190; *see also* New Testament, Revelation
Salviati, 'Saul', 82
Sampson, J., 73n
Saxl, Fritz, 83 and n
Schiller, Friedrich, 111 and n
Schorer, Mark, 112 and n
Sendivogius, *A New Light of Alchemie*, 252 and n
Shaftesbury, Anthony Ashley Cooper, third earl of, *Characteristics*, 230 and n
Shakespeare, William, 94, 147, 198, 218; *As You Like It*, 99–100 and n, 218–19; *Henry V*, 219 and n; *King Lear*, 186n; *Love's Labour's Lost*, 219 and n; *Much Ado about Nothing*, 219 and n; *Othello*, 219 and n; *Richard III*, 219 and n
Shelley, Percy Bysshe, *Prometheus Unbound*, 116 and n, 149, 151, 152
Shrimpton, Nick, 45n
Sickels, E. M., 71n
Simmons, Robert E., 128n
Smith, Eric, 165n
Smith, J. T., 71n
Smith, Stan, 12n–13n, 64n
Smithson, J. H., 27n
Southey, Robert, 26n, 27n
Spenser, Edmund, 'Hymn of Love', 80; *The Faerie Queene*, 164
Squire, S., 256n
Stedman, John Gabriel, 13n
Stevenson, W. H., 158 and n, 161 and n, 243n; 'Blake's Jerusalem', 187 and n
Sturt, John, engraving for frontispiece of Bible, 84, 85*
Sulivan, *View of Nature*, 248
Swedenborg, 3, 25–31, 40–1 and n, 42, 43, 60 and n, 136, 138, 234, 251; *True Christian Religion*, 29 and n
Swift, Jonathan, 2
Swinburne, A. C., 168 and n; *A Critical Essay*, 3

Tafel, J. F., 30n
Tatham, Frederick, 71n
Taylor, Jane and Ann, 50n
Taylor, Thomas, 221–2; *Concerning the Beautiful*, 222 and n, 229 and n

Thompson, E. P., 1, 2, 7n, 13n, 41n, 58 and n, 59 and n, 218, 220, 223n
Thompson, Stanbury, 13n
Tinker, C. B., 73n, 91n, 94n
Tolley, Michael, 238 and n
Toynbee, Paget, 94n
Trusler, Revd John, 249n; *The Progress of Man and Society*, 72–3; *The Way to be Rich and Respectable*, 72–3
Turner, Victor W., 42n
Tyndale, *The Dance of Machabree*, 101
Typhon, in Egyptian mythology, 256

Ugolino, 94–5, 203, 204–11, 245

Van Veen, Otto, 93; *Amorum Emblemata*, 94 and n; *Q. Horati Flacci Emblemata*, 83, 91–2, 102*
Vaughan, Thomas, 26n
Virgil, 11, 21, 164, 165
Voltaire, 111, 157

Wainscot, A. S., 27n
Wakefield, Priscilla, *Perambulations in London and its environs . . . in Letters. Designed for Young Persons*, 49–50; *Reflections on the Present Condition of the Female Sex; with suggestions for its Improvement*, 50–1 and nn
Wallis, John, 231n
Ware, Richard, Bible (1722), 85*
Warner, Janet, 84, 86n
Warton, Thomas, 71 and n, 72
Wedderburn, A., 206n
Wesley, Samuel, 84n
Whichcote, Benjamin, *Moral and Religious Aphorisms*, 237 and n, 238–40
Wicksteed, J., 181 and n, 259
Wilkite riots, 42
Williams, Raymond, 10n, 21n
Witke, Joanne, 193 and n
Wittreich, J. A., Jr, 165n
Wollstonecraft, Mary, 18
Wordsworth, William, 173; 'The Old Cumberland Beggar', 58; *The Prelude*, 21
Wynne, John, *Tales for Youth*, 73n, 74, 75*, 98*

Yates, Frances, 94n, 'Transformations of Dante's Ugolino', 206 and n, 207n, 208 and n, 209 and n
Yeats, W. B., 168 and n, 189, 198
Yolton, John W., 112n
Young, Edward, 3, 71–2; *Night Thoughts*, 75n, 77 and n, 78, 86, 87, 90 and n, 92, 97, 103, 237n

Zoroaster, 246